Dreams That Come True

Dreams That Come True

THEIR PSYCHIC AND TRANSFORMING POWERS

David Ryback, Ph.D.
with Letitia Sweitzer

THE AQUARIAN PRESS

This UK edition published 1989
First published in the USA by Doubleday, a division of
Bantam Doubleday Dell Publishing Group, Inc., 666 Fifth Avenue,
New York 10103, 1988

British Library Cataloguing in Publication Data

Ryback, David
Dreams that come true: their psychic and
transforming powers
1. Dreams. Interpretation. Parapsychological
aspects
I. Title II. Sweitzer, Letitia
135'.3

ISBN 0-85030-833-X

*The Aquarian Press is part of the Thorsons Publishing Group,
Wellingborough, Northamptonshire, NN8 2RQ, England.*

Printed in Great Britain by Biddles Limited, Guildford, Surrey

1   3   5   7   9   10   8   6   4   2

This book is dedicated to the young people in my life: David Surrency, Rhonda and Kenny Ryback, and Michael and J. J. Marx.

DAVID RYBACK

Acknowledgments

We would like to express our deep appreciation to all the contributors of dreams, both psychic and transforming, who are the heroes of this book. They opened up part of their lives to us, proving that dreams come true.

For their support and able assistance we thank Alix Kenagy, who brought us together; Bella Pomer, our literary agent, whose initiative and professionalism brought this book to its rightful place; and Casey Fuetsch, our supportive editor.

DAVID RYBACK and LETITIA SWEITZER

Special thanks to Fred Richards, Ronee Griffith, and Leslie Van Toole for their continuing personal support over the years I worked on making this dream book come true. I also want to express my deep appreciation to Stanley Kripper and the late Carl Rogers for their support in the early stages of this book project.

DAVID RYBACK

Special thanks to Kathryn Heath Gable for encouraging me to follow my dreams and to Virginia Stone Humphries and Holly Palmer Rhodes for keeping me clearly on the path.

LETITIA SWEITZER

Contents

"In dreams begins responsibility."

from an old play,
quoted by William Butler Yeats
in *Responsibilities* (1914)

Preface

When psychologist David Ryback first approached me with the idea of writing a book about psychic dreams, I confessed to him I was a skeptic. "That's all right," he said. "I was once a skeptic, too."

He explained how he had often amused himself by explaining away events that other people took for psychic phenomena. But psychic dreams, dreams that accurately foretold the future, he could not explain away. So he did an investigation to find out how many ordinary people actually had the psychic dream experience. The numbers of his subjects who wrote down accounts for him and the similarity of the dream patterns soon made him take the psychic dream experience seriously. Dr. Ryback invited me to take a look at the material.

He pulled out of his closet a huge dinosaur-green file box full of letters from psychic dreamers written to him after his investigation was publicized. A couple were typed on university letter heads; some were obviously written by people in the professions; most were handwritten on kitchen tables in towns across North America.

"If all these people have had dreams about unexpected future and distant events, if all these dreams have come true," said Dr. Ryback, "knowledge of the phenomena must change our whole concept of time and space." He started talking excitedly about future-time and holistic knowledge. I started reading the letters.

What I saw did not make me think of theoretical physics, theories of relativity, or futuristic time warps. What I saw primarily were people — frightened, happy, gregarious, reclusive, adolescent, elderly, puzzled, certain . . . And I fell in love with them.

I loved the confessions, made to a stranger, that they did not tell the people nearest them. I loved the innocence ("I had never dreamed about this old boyfriend before *because I was married*"), the irritation ("George says if I have to have psychic dreams why do they always have to be dreams of bad things that happen to him?"), and the sensitivity ("The dream was so vivid I told my best friend, but I left out the part of it that would have hurt her feelings"). I loved the domestic details of the dreamers' lives. While Dr. Ryback's attention was caught by the dreams of death that came true (because death is irrefutable to the scientist), mine was caught by the insignificant — a dream of an agate that was found in the snow or a dream about an avocado stone. For death haunts us all, but who dreams of an agate or an avocado stone?

And so my skepticism was melted by the earthy realness of these people as Dr. Ryback's had given way to the numbers.

While attending, in preparation for writing this book, a class on symbolic dream meaning taught by Dr. Ryback, I noted that some dreams reported by the participants came true in a symbolic, if not in a literal, way. It seemed that this kind of dream should be a part of our book too. Dr. Ryback did not agree at first because he wanted to keep the purely predictive dream that comes true in literal detail uncontaminated by subjective symbolism. He did not want to weaken the evidence of psychic dreams by anything so speculative as the meaning of symbols. I certainly understood this argument.

Then something happened that made me even more determined. A Belgian woman my family had met on a tram in Brussels and whom we had come to know as a friend was visiting us here in Atlanta for three weeks. Over the weeks she told me, a little bit at a time, about her life. As the story unfolded, I learned that in childhood she had been mistreated by her father, had chosen a husband who also mistreated her, and had generally accepted her punishment as deserved. Though suffering resulted from her mother's early death and the two invasions of Nazis who burned her family's farm and conscripted her brother, the suffering of her psyche came mostly from a lack of self-esteem originating in her father's rejection.

Towards the end of her visit, ever seeking material for the book, I asked her if she had ever had a dream that had influenced her life in an important way. "Oh, oui, le rêve le plus important de ma vie," she said, and recounted a dream whose significance I understood immediately from my study of Dr. Ryback's method of dream analysis. It was a clear symbolic drama depicting, in forceful disguise, her rejection and her unsuccessful defense: the quintessential symbolic dream.

Then, to my surprise, my friend related that the morning after the dream the drama began to play itself out, not symbolically but literally, until the entire dream came true. I was then completely convinced that there was an important overlap between the psychic and the symbolic. One validated the other. I found in the green leviathan file other examples of overlap between psychic and symbolic, and these along with my Belgian friend's dream became Chapter Eight of *Dreams That Come True*.

Although many of the interviews in this book were ones I carried out using both my journalistic skills and the method of dream analysis Dr. Ryback taught me, the body of the book is written in the first person because this is Dr. Ryback's story. It was he who had the idea that psychic dreams might be so frequent among ordinary people that their reality could not be denied, even among the scientific community; it was he who speculated how this reality could be explained in scientific terms; it was he who had faith for ten years that this idea and this data had the makings of a book uniquely concerned with the whole range of dream experience, including psychic revelation. I finally pulled together his ideas along with insights from the letters and my interviews into a theme: that you — believers or skeptics still — can all benefit from dreams that come true if you listen to them and respond, setting your foot on the positive path.

LETITIA SWEITZER
December 1988

Introduction

Dreaming is a universal mental phenomenon not only among human beings but also throughout the various mammalian species. Scientific research has discovered that dreaming is more essential to normal brain functioning than sleep itself. In studies conducted both on people and on cats, when both have been wakened from dreaming but allowed to sleep undisturbed during dreamless sleep, they become irritable and disoriented. When they are finally allowed to dream freely, both species catch up on their dreams by excessive dreaming, returning finally to their normal dispositions.

We dream much more than most of us admit. As much as one-third of our sleep time may be spent dreaming. Yet most of us remember little if any of our dreams. Why is that so?

Psychologically, our mind is divided into a tripartite system — *id*, *ego*, and *superego* — described originally by Freud. The *id* comprises our unconscious, a vast store of impressions and long-term memory reaching back to our childhood which, by definition, is unavailable to our conscious mind. Dreams form in the id and, for the most part, remain there. The *ego* is our conscious mind and defines our self-concept and its relationship to the rest of the world. We develop the ego at about the time we acquire language skills, roughly at the age of two. The *superego* is most easily described as our conscience which we acquire from our same-sexed parent, according to Freudians, roughly by the age of puberty.

Now, the reason we don't remember most of our dreams is because of the functional relationship among these three parts of the mind. The function of the superego is to keep material which is morally incompatible with the self-concept out of reach.

It acts as a censor and passes judgment on any dream material which is not congruent with the ego. Sometimes we remember a dream just as we awaken, but moments later the dream vanishes from our memory. Only vague images may remain, and even these ephemeral traces soon vanish. The superego is doing its job.

So any dream we may remember is soon lost unless we write it down quickly or relate it to someone. It may appear unreasonable that the person to whom we tell our dream will much more easily remember it than we do. However, this makes perfect sense: the superego is censoring the id; the person hearing our dream, on the other hand, has no emotional investment in the morality or ego-compatibility of the dream — his superego is not involved. He will have no problem remembering our dream, the substance of which we shall soon forget.

There is great variation among individuals in this regard. Some individuals swear that they *never* dream; others report lengthy dreams in vivid detail night after adventurous night. Most of us fall, however, in the middle of this range.

Although the importance of dreams was recognized in biblical times, the interest in their significance has changed greatly over the past few decades. Freud's influence, and that of Jung, have had much to do with the way we interpret our dreams. Psychoanalysis and its variations which preceded current modes of psychotherapy found dreams "the royal road to the unconscious", as Freud expressed it. over the past decade or so, certain modes of psychotherapy have come to rely more and more on dream analysis, such as Jungian dream work and Gestalt therapy.

Certainly there is disagreement among dream scientists. Some argue that dreams are nothing more than random firing of neuronal networks just as sets of muscles might twitch while we sleep. But even if we entertain such a limited view of dreams, it stands to reason that in such random activity, whatever unresolved emotional conflicts remain when we retire at night will find free reign without any structure to limit expression. That does explain why dreams are as chaotic and free-form as they seem at a perceptual level. At an emotional level, however, we find an elegant structure that transcends the surrealistic illogic of the dream. Drawing on Jung's conceptualizations, I have realized that each dream asks a deeply meaningful question, answers that question, and often goes on to suggest to the dreamer how to resolve the dilemma expressed in the dream.'

In addition, through the medium of dreams a whole other area of awareness has been discovered: future knowledge. In my work with dreams over the years I could not find any rational explanation for the fact that some people reported having dreams that predicted future events. Prior to my research, there was no scientific survey of the frequency of reports of such dreams among ordinary people.

I determined to plough ahead into this "unrespectable" area of research, at least to satisfy my own curiosity about how common the phenomenon was, if not to confront the scientific community with evidence of psychic dreams that had been previously swept under the rug. Unless hundreds upon hundreds of the individuals were lying to me or to themselves, here was a body of evidence that could no longer be ignored. Because psychic dreams follow several discernible patterns, these hundreds of individuals would have had to conspire from disparate parts of the continent to concoct dreams congruent with the patterns. Such a conspiracy would be even more fantastic and incredible than the premise of psychic dreams itself. Any way you look at it, this is monumental evidence of a phenomenon that must shake the scientific community.

Ironically, I initially met great resistance to publication of my research on psychic dreams. The conventional scientific journals understandably found the material too unscientific, and the psychically-oriented journals did not appreciate my skeptical approach to the subject. My scientific inquiry into an area associated with occultism and mysticism found itself in a no-man's-land. Fortunately, however, the book you now hold demonstrates that there are still publishers prepared to advance the boundaries of human credibility.

Dreams That Come True contains several unique qualities. First, it looks at a provocative and heretofore unproven subject from a perspective of initial skepticism. As a social scientist with over thirty publications to my credit, I was educated with the assumption of causality. Every event, I understood, has a preceding and causally linked event and only through functional laws can we understand the workings of the world, including human behavior and even the inner sanctum of the mind. Yet here was the phenomenon of psychic dreams which could not be explained in any conventionally scientific sense. All my training told me that psychic dreams were nonsense. Yet the data I obtained through a scientifically valid survey contradicted my assumptions. I could hardly believe the results myself so I could certainly appreciate the dismay of my scientific colleagues that I could even research such a topic. I remember meeting my dissertation professor years after I had graduated from his tutelage. When I told him of my area of research, his look of puzzlement and condescension said, "Where did I go wrong with you, Ryback?"

A second unique quality of *Dreams That Come True* is that the book goes beyond the study of psychic dreams to explore those dreams that fall in the grey area between psychic and ordinary symbolic dreams. Would that everything would fall into discrete piles! Nature is not so, certainly not the nature of the mind. The book goes on to help the reader discover what his own symbolic dreams offer. So whether the reader's interest is in psychic phenomena or in ordinary dreams, this book will have something pertinent to say.

For dreamers everywhere, I hope you will find this book reassuring, instructive, and entertaining.

Happy dreaming!

DAVID RYBACK
December 1988

ONE

The Discovery

I'll never forget the day I opened the letter from Jim T. containing a most poignant message. I have read it over many times, and each time I feel overwhelmed with the same complex emotion, a mixture of sadness and a kind of closeness, which comes from the straightforward eloquence with which he shared his grief. The writer, a former Marine and a teacher with a master's degree in education, introduced himself to me, explaining that he had read in the news of my research on dreams. He was not given to hallucinations or wild imaginings, but he added, "I have a strange story to tell."

One night as we were sleeping I was awakened by my wife, Allison, who was crying in her sleep—I could tell she was frightened and unable to wake up. She was having a nightmare, and I knew from her cries and restlessness it was a bad one. I shook her and tried to comfort her, telling her she was having an awful dream—it didn't really sink in. She kept crying and I held her in my arms to let her know she was only dreaming.

When I managed to waken her she said, "It was awful . . . it was just awful." She kept crying and telling me how real and awful it was. I could barely get her to tell me the dream.

Finally, she said, "It was a train—a train was coming and it ran me down." I can't remember her exact words, but I do remember she had been killed in the dream by a train.

She immediately got up to check on our four-year-old daughter, Tessa —I have a ten-year-old boy, but I don't believe she went to his bed. But she did go to Tessa's bed to see if Tessa was all right. In the dream she had run in front of the train to try to save Tessa who had gone onto the tracks.

Allison was extremely shaken. I comforted her for some time during the night. She couldn't return to sleep. But I remember telling her that if I saw a child on the railroad track, I would not try to retrieve the child in the normal way if a train were coming with great speed, but I would run as hard as I could, grab the child in a football tackle and let my forward speed carry me and the child clear of the tracks. It was a long time before we got to sleep again.

David, I cannot tell you for sure when this dream occurred before the accident, but I would say not more than two weeks.

On January 5, 1976, while waiting to see some friend off to New York after the Christmas holidays, Allison and Tessa were at the train station in De Land, Florida.

Tessa saw the train porter pushing a baggage cart, and a thermos bottle fell off the cart between the tracks—Tessa rushed to retrieve it—Allison saw the train coming too late and rushed to save Tessa.

They both were killed on impact—they died instantly I think—I wasn't there, thank God. . . .

Jim T.'s letter, although more moving than most, is typical in many ways of letters I have received in the fifteen years I have been exploring psychic dreams. It describes an exceptionally vivid dream about a life-and-death event, and there is a hint of positive value to the precognition. The bereaved husband and father explains, "Somehow [the dream experience] makes me feel close to Allison and Tessa, because something I don't understand forewarned her. We were very close."

Within the universal experience of dreaming, there lies one uniquely extraordinary realm—*psychic* dreams, dreams that come true. Allison's dream is one example.

Was Allison's dream of her own and her daughter's death really a precognitive psychic dream, a dream that looked into the future? The skeptics may say, no, it was just a remarkable coincidence.

Picture yourself saying to Jim T., "I'm sorry about your wife and child. And that dream—what a coincidence!" If I were Jim, living with the memory of holding my wife shaking in my arms, and someone said that to me, I'd be furious.

Putting my emotions aside, however, I have to consider objectively the question, "Could Allison's dream have been a coincidence?" And, knowing what I know about chance, I have to answer, yes. The word *coincidence* means two or more things that occur together by chance, and anything can happen by chance. Even this tragedy could have been the one-in-a-million event that happened to occur shortly after a bad dream. I understand this reasoning well because on the subject of psychic dreams I was once a skeptic myself.

I had never had a psychic dream. In fact, I rarely remembered my dreams at all. Nevertheless, I was interested in dreams because, as a clinical psychologist, I used the interpretation of symbolic dreams to help patients in psychotherapy understand their conflicts.

In my years as a student of psychology, I had studied dream analysis from Freud to the most modern theorists, and as a clinical psychologist, I have combined, adapted, and streamlined traditional methods of dream analysis for use with patients. I have also taught this method of analyzing symbolic dreams to ordinary dreamers just as you will see it formally presented later in this book. While using symbolic dreams in therapy, I have known those electric moments when I suggest to a patient his own dream symbol and in response he articulates a new idea, an insight he'd never had before. His eyes widen as he hears himself proclaim the new self-awareness out loud and relief flows visibly over him. To guide a patient through the distorted dramas of emotion I have relied heavily on intuition. However, I have never considered myself psychic, mystic, or anything but scientific. I certainly did not deal in psychic dreams; I didn't even believe in them—I was, I'd convinced myself, a twentieth-century scientist.

Then one day, while on a cruise, I suddenly found myself in an intellectual dilemma. That summer I had embarked on a transatlantic voyage as a reward for a year of particularly hard work and as a breather before I took up new duties as an assistant professor of psychology. I chose the leisurely ocean crossing to clear my soul of the pressures of my ordinary schedule, but leisure, I found, did not suit me.

The ship sliced through the miles of ocean, day by day. Genoa and the beckoning European cities would be all the brochures had promised, but the empty days till landing could not be filled for me by three-course breakfasts, midmorning Danish pastries and coffee, sun on the deck, five-course lunches, midafternoon snacks, cocktails . . . I was trapped at sea.

I began pacing the decks, looking for conversation to fill the hours. I found conversation—and something startling.

I had joined a group of fellow travelers who were in the midst of telling extraordinary things that had happened to them. One young man told of a dream he'd had about a death in his family. He awoke from the dream startled because of the content and the unusual vividness of the dream. He could not go back to sleep for several hours. In the morning someone called to tell him that the family member whose death he had dreamed about had, in fact, died suddenly. The person had not been sick and her death was a shock to the family. The dream account was striking enough, but what startled me more was that several others in the group responded to the young man's story with accounts of their own dreams that came true—dreams of deaths, injuries, and one pleasant happening that seemed highly unpredictable.

The dream accounts followed a pattern: The dreamers spoke matter-of-factly, not straining to convince anyone of anything. The dreams they recounted had been exceptionally vivid, portrayed serious events, and concerned people emotionally close to the dreamers. The events in the dreams were rare or were unlikely to occur at that particular time. They actually did occur, however, at the time of the dream or soon after.

I, who often took delight in pointing out, at least to myself, the scientific explanation for what others called psychic phenomena, could not explain these. "Oh, yes, but you see . . ." I started to say and found there was nothing I *could* say.

Sure, I'd heard of psychic dreams, the stuff of legends, like how Abraham Lincoln had dreamed he would be killed. And I'd heard of the dreams of the ubiquitous "friend of a friend of mine" that later came true. But I had never paid any attention to such secondhand stories.

Yet here in front of me were people whose veracity I could judge for myself—sensible, credible people, businessmen and professionals. Each person told his tale matter-of-factly and answered questions that naturally arose from the listeners.

I went back to my stateroom puzzled. I had explained away scientifically all sorts of things that other people thought were psychic experiences, but these dream happenings I could not explain.

Did psychic dreams really exist?

The only explanation I had for the dreams I heard on board the ship was that these were coincidences, random occurrences. All of us, that is, hundreds of millions of people, dream every night, I figured. Out of those dreams, thousands must concern death, for example. Thousands of people actually die every day, so it stands to reason that some of those deaths must occur in families where someone in the family, by chance, has had a death dream shortly before. And so it could be for all the events in dreams.

But if dreams come true only when they randomly collide with rare events in the vastness of time and space, how was it that so many of these dreamers were on my ship?

What if the odds of dreaming about a person's death and then having that person die in an accident soon thereafter were one in a million and what if this coincidence actually occurred to one person in one thousand? Would it not suggest that some force other than chance was at work?

With this thought in mind I planned my next research project: I would find out how many people in the general population actually have apparently psychic dreams, both precognitive (those that predict future events) and telepathic (those that communicate events happening at the same time as the dream but which are outside of the dreamer's range of knowledge). I figured the numbers would be few, but it didn't matter—I was curious enough to pursue this piece of research anyway. There was a chance that something exciting would turn up. In spite of my skepticism I found I could hardly wait to get started on this project.

Upon my return, I reviewed past research on psychic dreams and found that although many studies had been done on small numbers of subjects chosen for their interest in psychic dreams, no one had done a study using large numbers of randomly selected, ordinary people as subjects.

To prove or disprove to myself that psychic dreams existed, I first had to find out how often this phenomenon occurred in the general population. The larger the number of people who report such dreams, the less confidently the dreams can be explained by chance alone. Also, the more the details of the dreams coincide with the details of the actual events, the less plausibly such concurrence can be explained as random.

As an assistant professor of psychology, I administered a questionnaire to four hundred thirty-three undergraduate students to determine how many had experienced dreams about actual future events or simultaneous distant events outside the range of their knowledge. The questionnaire also explored the parameters of the psychic dream experience. The subjects reported the period of time between the dreams and the events they foretold, their emotional closeness to the people in the dreams, and their feelings about the psychic dream experience. I also asked each subject for a written account of one such dream and the event that followed.

Two hundred ninety subjects, 66.9 percent of those who answered the questionnaire, reported psychic dreams. I was stunned. The two hundred ninety people felt they had experienced, at least once, a phenomenon that is considered by many scientists and laymen to be impossible.

In truth, many of the accounts of dreams that reportedly came true were felt to be psychic by the dreamers but were not convincing to me. Some of the dreams of misfortune, for instance, expressed ongoing anxiety about a dangerous situation. A woman, for example, had been worrying about her elderly husband, who was working on the roof. She dreamed he would slip while working up there, and the next day he did. The real event in such a case could have been anticipated by applying common sense to the facts.

Other dreams were so unspecific or the events with which they corresponded were so commonplace that I could not consider them psychic dreams. An example of such a dream is this one: "My dog, Racer, had been missing a few days, and I thought he was gone for good. One night I dreamed that Racer was scratching on my back-door screen. The next day he was home again."

This is a typical account of the kind of dream I rejected as evidence of psychic dreams. Lost dogs frequently come back. If there were unusual details in the dream that corresponded with the details of the dog's return, it would be a different matter. This is not to say that I categorically deny the possibility that the subject in the study had a psychic dream. Perhaps the dream did arise from psychic precognition. I only say that the commonness of the event and the lack of corresponding specific detail preclude the experience from being used as evidence of the existence of psychic dreams.

I had to think in terms of criteria: the amount of detail in the dream, the degree to which the specifics matched the event, the unlikelihood of the event occurring in the way it did, how soon after the dream the event occurred, etc. I wanted very much to avoid calling a dream psychic based on something so subjective as feelings, either mine or the dreamer's.

Even after imposing stringent criteria, I found that dreams come true not for one out a thousand people, not for one out of one hundred people, but, at the very least, for one out of twelve. I discovered that out of the two hundred ninety reports, thirty-eight dreams recorded by thirty-eight dreamers, or 8.8 percent of my subjects, could not be explained as ordinary happenings.

Is 8.8 percent—one psychic dreamer out of every twelve people—more than can be explained by chance? Yes, when you consider the odds. What are the chances, for example, that you would dream of being in a bank holdup and the next day find yourself looking at the bank robbers' guns? One subject in my research project described a short but detailed dream in which he found himself in a bank, opening a checking account. Two armed robbers came in. The dreamer was standing near a desk to one side of the room, and the robbers were at the teller's cage. In the dream one of the robbers put a gun in the subject's mouth. This subject described to me how vivid the dream was and how the dramatic clarity of the dream impressed him so much that he felt compelled to tell a friend about it in the morning.

Later that day, while the subject was in the bank, opening a checking account, two robbers rushed in and held up the bank. The subject was standing to one side and the robbers confronted the tellers with guns. The robbers took exactly the same positions as in his dream and his view of them was exactly as his dream view. Although the robbers threatened the customers with their weapons, neither robber, the dreamer conceded, actually put a gun in his mouth.

This dream meets all of my criteria for a psychic dream. First, there is detail reported for both the dream and the event—two men, guns, the dreamer's position to one side of the bank, the robbers' position at the teller's cage, and the holdup itself. The number of men, the guns, the positions of the dreamer and the robbers, and the act itself correspond. There is one discrepancy. The fact that one robber did not put a gun in the subject's mouth in the real event may take away a point from this dream as a psychic phenomenon, but the subject's noting the discrepancy makes the dream more convincing. The detail of difference offered by the dreamer demonstrates that he is not, consciously or unconsciously, exaggerating the details of the dream to better fit the event. The discrepancy probably is a representation of the dreamer's feeling of extreme threat.

The main strength of the dream is the unlikelihood of the event occurring at all and the even greater unlikelihood of the event occurring the very day after the dream. Bank robbery is relatively rare. The chances of being in a bank during the few heart-stopping minutes it is being robbed are rarer still. The odds against being in a bank during a robbery the night after dreaming of a bank robbery are astronomical.

Another point made by this subject seems to be a signal of the psychic dream. The dreamer found the dream so vivid that he felt compelled to tell someone about it. Psychic dreamers often are aware of a special quality or strangeness about the dream, and, for that reason, they find someone to tell. The person to whom the dream is communicated before it comes true can give valuable corroboration.

This bank robbery dream, like more than half the psychic dreams in my study, was precognitive. It depicted an event that would occur in the future, which no one but the robbers could have known about. The following dream is also a detailed, precognitive description of an event that no one could have known about at the time of the dream. Every detail accurately predicted makes the dream more convincing as a true psychic dream, one that could not have been dreamed in such accurate detail by chance alone.

In April my husband and I were looking for a new apartment. One night I dreamed I was a passenger in a red Volkswagen with a blond-haired girl driving. Her baby was strapped into a car seat in the back seat.

We were coming off a side street onto a busy street. I was familiar with the busy street but not the side street. There were four lanes of traffic and we were trying to go to a gas station on the other side. We were checking for the traffic to break as we inched out. We were hit on the driver's side by a car. The girl started screaming, "Get my baby," over and over. Before checking my own condition I got out of the car and into the back seat with the baby, where I collapsed, unable to move because of pain in my back and right side. Blood started dripping from my face.

That night I told my husband about the dream. He claimed it "was just a nightmare," and passed it off, remarking, "We don't even know anyone with a red Volkswagen."

I also told my mother and she didn't want me ever to get into a red Volkswagen—with anyone.

I forgot about the dream as we continued looking for another place to live. In June we moved to a duplex on a side street off of the busy street in my dream. Our neighbors living in the other half of the house owned a red Volkswagen; the girl was blond, and they had a baby. We became friends in a matter of days.

When we went out during heavy traffic times, we always went one block over to the traffic light. One day my neighbor and I forgot and went out our side street to get the oil in her VW changed. As we eased out into traffic, we were hit, and everything happened just as I dreamed. Only after I had got into the back seat and collapsed, however, did I realize it had all been predicted in my dream. The pain in my side was a badly bruised kidney, and the blood dripping from my face was from chipping the bone in my nose on the dashboard.

In the emergency room later my husband said, "You dreamed this and I didn't pay any attention to it."

My mother, who was traveling with my father to Canada, told me later that she suddenly began to have pains in her right side and back, and her sinuses hurt so her eyes began to swell. She attributed the problems to a change in water and climate, but she had an almost uncontrollable urge to call me. Later that evening when she did call and heard what happened she had to hang up and regain her composure. Then she called again. . . .

Dreams with this much detail and such a high degree of accuracy are rare but not as unusual as you might think. The Michigan woman who sent me the following robbery dream could have filled out the entire police report from the list of missing items in her dream.

I had just moved from the state of Washington in March. When we left, I merely took what we could in the back of our pickup and left everything else locked in the house. I hoped once in a while my parents could go over and check on things.

One Saturday night toward the end of August I dreamed very vividly of my home in Washington. It was as if I was floating through a broken window and then proceeding through every room of the house observing a complete mess. I remember making a mental note of items missing from their usual places.

I awoke the next morning remarking to my husband, "I never want to go back to our house in Washington because it has been robbed and whoever did it left it a complete mess." My husband gave me that usual "You're-really-going-mad-this-time" grin. I then gave him a complete list of items I dreamed were taken during the robbery.

Well, two weeks later, I made a believer of him. I received a frantic call from my mother who had gone to my house in Washington. She said the police were on their way because my house was a mess and she was sure some items had been stolen. I then told her of the broken window off my daughter's room and exactly what items to look for that were stolen. My mother was appalled because my detail was exact.

Sometimes it was not the overwhelming import or the wealth of accurate detail of a dream that impressed me but rather one odd, almost surrealistic detail it seems a person would never dream in a million years by chance. Here's one of my favorites:

Close friends of ours were moving from Los Angeles to northern California. They were having a party to say good-bye to all their friends. The night before the party, I had a dream in which I saw a strange dark object all by itself. It was not a human heart or a large dark plum but something like these. I had never seen anything like it before so I told my husband about it the next morning.

At the party, the children of the family that was moving had decided to give each person something to remember them by. Some guests received plants, old library cards, etc. The oldest daughter came through the door holding out the next gift, something in a glass jar. I immediately recognized it. I reached for my husband and told him that the object in the glass was the strange thing that I had dreamed of the night before. I said I was sure she was going to give it to me. She did. It turned out to be an avocado pit in a glass of water that had not started to sprout yet. They said it could become a lovely plant with proper care. It was the first time I had ever seen one.

In another dream that centered around a single striking image, a woman dreamed she was carrying her nephew wrapped in an animal skin. She could tell by his limpness that he was dead, and she awoke grief-stricken. Soon after the dream, her nephew was hospitalized for what was described as flu. It was not considered serious at first, but his condition worsened. When the dreamer visited the child and saw him lying on a *sheepskin* pad, she knew he was going to die. She had never heard of using a sheepskin to make sick patients more comfortable, she said, but the animal skin in the dream was the same as the one her nephew lay on. That was the last time she saw her nephew before his death soon after.

In the case of the avocado pit dream and the sheepskin dream, I accepted the dream as psychic not because of the quantity of accurately predicted detail (both dreams were one-image dreams) but because of the oddness of the signif-icant detail and the certainty the dreamers expressed when they recognized the dream object in real life.

My colleague, Letitia Sweitzer, who helped put together my material for publication, was not a clear believer when she first joined me. Part of her believed my findings and part of her didn't, she said, but she expected to give me the necessary editorial assistance in any case. She told me she wanted to interview some additional dreamers in our vicin-ity so she could learn more about the part psychic dreams played in their lives. I told her finding them locally "would be like finding a needle in a haystack."

Ms. Sweitzer challenged me on this: "Don't you believe your own research?" she asked. "If one in twelve people in the general population has had a clear-cut psychic dream, I should only have to ask twelve people before I find one psychic dreamer to interview." Although not quite statisti-cally true, we agreed the point was well taken. I pleaded guilty to having reverted to previous skeptical notions about the reality of psychic dreams and said no more.

Ms. Sweitzer set about asking people if they had had psychic dreams. Although, in her search for interviewees, her method of choosing people was not what would be considered scientifically random, it was to a certain extent an informal test of my research conclusions.

Ms. Sweitzer left my office after my needle-in-a-haystack remark and went to pick up her child at school. While there, she asked another mother if she had ever had a psychic dream. Not even the hint of a psychic dream, the woman replied.

Ms. Sweitzer then stopped on the way home at a dress shop to buy a dress. She asked the clerk at the cash register if she had ever had a psychic dream. The clerk said, "Yes, all the time." When asked to tell one, the clerk could not relate a specific example.

Ms. Sweitzer then went to visit a close friend. The friend to whom she posed the same question recounted three apparently psychic dreams, one that foretold a fatal injury to a close relative, one that revealed to her a friend's secret good fortune, and one that imparted useful and otherwise unknown information on solving a problem.

The writer did not know it then, but the pattern set by these first three haphazardly chosen "subjects" was one to be repeated over and over throughout her search. Out of every three people she encountered, one would say "no" when questioned about psychic dream experience; one would say "yes" but, when pressed, offer nothing specific. A third would relate a credible psychic dream.

Surprised by having found a psychic dreamer in her first three tries, Ms. Sweitzer felt she had "cheated" by going to her good friend, whom, she knew in advance, paid a good deal of attention to dreams. To make up for this, she next decided to approach the person she thought the least likely in the world to have had a psychic dream—her mother-in-law. Since this conservative lady was religious in a traditional sense and perhaps unsympathetic to the "occult," Ms.

Sweitzer did not even want to ask straight-out if her mother-in-law had experienced a psychic dream. She asked instead, "Do you believe in psychic dreams?"

The older woman answered, "Yes."

"Why?" Ms. Sweitzer asked.

"Because I had one" was the astonishing answer.

She went on to relate a dream in which her sister-in-law's brother was killed in a jeep accident. She found the dream "strange" because she rarely remembered dreams of any kind. Word came that same week that the brother, one day away from being sent home from military service in the Philippines, had been killed in a jeep accident.

Impressed by the ease with which she had discovered these first two psychic dreamers, Ms. Sweitzer tried to remember to ask "The Question" in every gathering in which she found herself, whenever she could work it into the conversation.

One evening she went to a party of about thirty people at a friend's house. She talked at some length to about ten people, and among them three asked her about her work. She told them about her writing project and popped the question. One said she'd never had a psychic dream; one said yes, she was sure she had, but couldn't think of one. A third told her she dreamed that an out-of-town friend she had not talked to lately had twins, one in good health, one with defects that would make its survival unlikely. A few weeks later the twins were born. One soon died. There was the pattern again: Two out of three people say they have had psychic dreams; one out of three relates an impressive one.

A few days later Ms. Sweitzer and I went into a neighboring office to photocopy our book proposal. In the office were two women and a man. Ms. Sweitzer, pursuing her "experiment," asked if any of them had had a psychic dream. The man said no. One woman immediately said yes, but when asked for an example, said, "I don't believe I can think of one right now." The other woman told about a precognitive dream of a death in a family. Then, after a pause, she added, "Oh, I almost forgot! I did have another one." She then related a detailed, meaningful psychic dream.

At this point Ms. Sweitzer pointed out to me that her small, ongoing survey was running one psychic dreamer out of three, more than I found in my formal research. She also observed that two out of three people *said* they had psychic dreams, exactly the percentage that replied in the affirmative in my study, and that one of those, also like many in my study, could give no specific examples and had to be discounted. Her experience demonstrates what is an essential element in scientific research: Findings in a sufficiently large sample of randomly selected subjects should prove true when applied to the general population.

The fact that Ms. Sweitzer encountered and continues to encounter a psychic dreamer in every group of three people instead of one in twelve as I expected may have several explanations. First, her sample may still be too small a number from which to judge. Second, the people she encounters are of all ages. The college undergraduates in my study were mostly young and had fewer years to experience such a dream. In addition, the writer's friendly person-to-person conversation may have elicited more ready response and evoked more almost-forgotten experiences than the cold demand of my questionnaire.

In any case, from a scientific point of view, I am not ready to expand my claims beyond one person out of twelve being a psychic dreamer. I am, however, open to the considerable possibility that psychic dreaming is more common than is provable.

"Proof" is elusive and skeptics will remain skeptics. I think of an acquaintance who recently made polite inquiries about my work. After listening patiently to a synopsis of my thesis, my findings, my four hundred letters and interviews, and finally my book, the woman announced firmly, "That is a bunch of hooey!"

Then, in almost the same breath, she added, "A good friend of mine told me she dreamed her father-in-law died, and. . . ."

I pursued the lead. This is what the dreamer told me:

One night I dreamed my father-in-law died. No one seemed unhappy. In fact, my mother-in-law was even giving a party. I was sure he was dead, and I couldn't understand why nobody seemed to care.

I woke up in the morning feeling anxious and insisted that my husband call his family, who lived in another state. He wouldn't call, said it was silly.

That evening his father called because, he said, he was afraid we would think he was dead. My husband turned white. The UPI wire service, his father explained, had sent his obituary out all over the country. The erroneous death notice had even run that morning in the New York Times. *My father-in-law was afraid that we would hear about it. My husband was so freaked out, he never told his father about the dream.*

The explanation for the error was that my father-in-law, a prominent physician, had the same name as another doctor who actually had died. The wire service made a mistake.

"Wasn't that a coincidence?" exclaimed the skeptical lady who helped me find this dreamer.

Death comes only once in a lifetime. Having your obituary run in the New York *Times* while you are still alive is far less likely than death itself. When your sleeping daughter-in-law and the wire services make the same mistake on the same night, can this be a "coincidence"? As you meet more and more of the psychic dreamers, I invite you to judge for yourself.

TWO

Meet the Psychic Dreamers

When the results of my survey were publicized in *Psychology Today* and other publications across the country, letters flooded my office by the hundreds. Writers from Houston, Coral Gables, and Ottawa; from Michigan, California, and Vermont; from Laurel, Mississippi, from Two Buttes, Colorado, from Willowdale, Ontario, and from Dix Hills, New York, recounted their dreams that came true. Word of my study got around Atlanta, and people called me up to tell me their experiences. I gave workshops on dreams, where I met people who had been drawn to the subject because of their own dreams. I met people at dinner parties, in my office building, and at the symphony, who asked me what I was working on, and, when I told them, said, "Oh, psychic dreams. I've had several. One in particular . . ."

Who were these people who had seen in their dreams unusual events that were at that very moment taking place hundreds of miles away or would take place the next week? They were very ordinary people just like you and me. Many of them were students from places as varied geographically as Hunter College in New York City, to Regis College in Denver, and Trinity University in San Antonio, Texas. Many of the dreamers were housewives and mothers; many of them were office workers. A few were psychologists, clergymen, and teachers. Some were soldiers, nurses, factory workers, computer programmers, and farmers. One was a former stripper now trying to make it as a screenwriter, and one was a gold prospector who had retired because of his health.

People have asked me if these dreamers had special characteristics. Were they, for example, people of deep religious faith? My findings show that some were religious, but others were not. Most simply did not mention their religious beliefs. Not one of the hundreds of dreamers who contacted me said he or she had seen or heard God in a dream. Although God did not appear in any of the dreams, several dreamers who saw people or future events in a dream said they believed God had sent the dream to help them. It may also work the other way. One man who took stock in his dreams was inhibited in discussing them by his religious wife. The man, himself religious, remarked, "My wife thinks if it's not Baptist, it's from the devil."

In addition, very few of these people indicated they considered themselves mystics. Few of them had been studying dreams prior to their first psychic experience, and only one or two of them mentioned karma or terms of "new age" interest. Nearly a quarter of the dreamers with whom I have been in contact did cite psychic episodes they had experienced other than dreams.

"How come people who have psychic dreams are always ones who already believe in psychic phenomena?" demanded one critic. The premise is not necessarily true. Remember that the people who wrote me had already had a mind-boggling experience, sometimes several, in which a dream did come true. After that, they believed. There is no indication that the dreams came to *a priori* believers. More than a few prefaced their dream accounts with the words, "I have never believed in psychic dreams, but . . ." Many others seem to have had no opinion on the phenomenon at all before it occurred. By far, most of the dreamers seemed just as surprised and puzzled as I was to have dreams that played themselves out in real life.

About half the dreamers who wrote me described "the only psychic dream I've ever had." The other half said they had many such experiences of varying significance. Dozens of people used the same words: "I could write a book of my psychic dreams, but I'll only tell you a few." The largest number of psychic dream accounts I received from any one person was eleven.

It seems obvious that if a nonbeliever had, for whatever reason, one clearly precognitive dream, it could make a believer of him. One skeptic, however, argued with me. "I dreamed my partner died last night. If it comes true today, I will not consider the dream psychic because the death of my partner, who is just forty-seven, is always a possibility." It is my guess that the dream about the partner was a symbolic dream representing some kind of inner conflict of the dreamer. I'll bet, however, that if this man woke from an exceptionally vivid dream with a very strange feeling of the reality of his partner's death and soon after got news of his untimely demise, his tune would change. Not only would he believe he had had a psychic dream, but the experience would lead him to notice and examine other dreams as possible realities. It was clear that my subjects who had more than one experience with psychic dreams began to recognize those that were possibly telepathic or precognitive, to remember them, and to act on the content. In the sense that verifying psychic dreams requires paying attention to dreams and remembering them, people who pay attention to dreams and remember them seem to have more psychic dreams than people who deny their existence.

But whether her premise was correct or not, the critic who posed the question about why psychic dreams came especially to believers in psychic phenomena may have a point. It is a generally accepted fact that people act in such a way as to confirm their beliefs. This is especially true in the area of psychological aspects of behavior and especially in the unconscious area.

People who do not accept the existence of psychic process will unconsciously avoid its effects. In a book entitled *ESP and Personality Patterns,* Gertrude R. Schmeidler and R. A. McConnell point out that individuals who believe in ESP tend to score above chance in card-guessing experiments while those who don't tend to score below chance expectation. Both groups respond in accordance with their beliefs. Or so it seems.

An absence of psychic ability would result in chance scores. In order to score below chance, it is first necessary to know enough to score above chance and then deny that response. Mean scores either significantly above or significantly below chance would necessitate psychic ability. So the disbelievers cited by Schmeidler and McConnell intended, consciously or unconsciously, to deny their psychic ability by scoring below chance but ended up proving their psychic ability to the statistically sophisticated researcher. In other words, they blocked out or refused to respond to their psychic knowledge. In the same way, people who do not believe in psychic dreams may forget them or block them out.

Very young children usually have not heard of the psychic dream phenomenon to believe or disbelieve before-

hand. In fact children encounter so many new and unex-
plained experiences in life that they do not have a good
criterion by which to judge some as extraordinary. One
writer said, "As a child, I dreamed many times about events
that came true and thought nothing of it. It was only later
when I discovered other people didn't do this, that I began
to think of precognitive dreams as something special."

The youngest writer who shared a psychic dream with me
was a fourteen-year-old girl. Although the people who
wrote were of all ages—the earliest event described occurred
in 1909—many of them recalled that their first psychic
dream occurred when they were very young; more than one
mentioned the age of five. One person said she had not
realized that everyone did not have dreams that came true
until she went to school and discussed them with her classmates. When they regarded her dream experiences as
strange, she stopped talking about them.

Thus the reaction of others may be a potent reason why
some people don't dream psychic dreams or are unwilling to
recount these psychic experiences.

Many psychic dreamers speak of mothers or grandmothers who were known to have dreams that came true. This
phenomenon may suggest that psychic ability is inherited.
Or it may be that people who have heard of their relatives'
dreams, permit themselves to observe, remember, and relate
similar experiences themselves. Their relatives' admission to
such an experience validates their own. On the other hand,
lack of acceptance of psychic dreams in a family inhibits
members, especially young people, from discussing them.
Youngsters, fearful of family disapproval, may even learn to
block memories of such dreams when they do occur.

Dana, an Atlanta woman who has had many psychic
dreams herself, told me accounts that shed light on psychic
dreaming in families. One March her six-year-old son had a
nightmare from which he woke up screaming and sweating.
It took him a long time to quiet down. He finally told his

mother that he had dreamed of an automobile accident in which he was badly hurt. Dana comforted him as best she could. He'd had dreams that came true before so she could not promise him that this one would not. She pointed out, however, that some of his dreams did not come true and probably this one wouldn't.

In June, Dana's parents gave her a blue Chevrolet. The boy looked at the car quietly with a blank face.

"Don't you like it," Dana asked him.

"It's the car in my dream," he said apprehensively.

In late September the boy had the same nightmare with the same feelings of terror.

On October 5 Dana's four-year-old daughter had a screaming fit as they set out to drive up a certain hill on their usual route to town.

"Don't go there! Don't go there! There is a hole in the road," the child screamed. She wouldn't stop screaming so the mother drove eight miles out of her way to avoid the hill this one time.

The next day they were on the way to town in the blue Chevy. On the crest of the same hill they had avoided the day before, the little girl did something disruptive in the back seat and Dana turned her head to see. At that moment she lost control of the car, ran off the road, and struck an unseen culvert abutment, in effect a "hole in the road." Dana lost her teeth in the crash, and the son who had dreamed went headfirst through the windshield, cracking his skull open so his brain was exposed. After difficult surgery and months of treatment, he recovered from the devastating accident.

This boy afterward had other dreams which he could not help but take seriously, including one by which the family may have succeeded in avoiding another tragedy. Happily, not all his bad dreams came true. As he grew older, he talked about the dreams less and less. Once when he was in Army boot camp during the war in Vietnam, he made a rare call to his mother. "I know you are worried," he said, "and I wanted you to know that I am not going to Nam. I'm going to be stationed stateside."

"How do you know?" his mother asked.

"I just know," he said.

"But what makes you think you won't be sent over," she persisted.

He never would tell her how he knew, but he was sure. Dana was equally sure that soldiers in basic training do not know such things until they get their orders after boot camp. She was convinced her son had had a dream he wouldn't tell but in which he believed. True to his prediction, he spent his service time at Fort Riley, Kansas.

A few years later, she asked him, "Do you still have psychic dreams?"

He nodded his head and refused to elaborate. "He has clung desperately to the rational," says Dana. "He's afraid people will hear about it. He's afraid if he tells me, I'll tell other people—and you see, he's right." She laughed. Dana thinks boys are particularly sensitive to the opinion of others (which they share) that psychic dreaming is not rational behavior and, as a result, they not only don't tell psychic experiences but may block them in such a way that they are not aware of dreaming themselves.

In Dana's family, however, it was the boys who dreamed the most accurately precognitive dreams. Her sister's son was about fourteen when he dreamed of an accident at a nearby intersection in which a car hit a power pole, the pole snapped and fell on the car, and in a spray of sparks everything burned. The driver, a man, was killed, and the woman passenger with the unusual name Cleo, whom the dreamer had never heard of before, was injured. As firemen worked to control the flames, ambulance attendants pulled the man's body from the fire and laid it on the sidewalk. The boy woke up and called everyone in the house together to tell them in detail of the accident he thought was real. They all bundled up and went down the street to find nothing—no accident, no ambulance, no injured people. He went back to sleep. One hour later everyone was awakened by a commotion. The accident had occurred, the power pole snapped, the sparks ignited the car. Then the ambulance and firemen came, and the man was stretched out dead on the sidewalk. The woman who was injured was named Cleo. Everyone else was very excited; Dana's nephew went sleepily back to bed. It seemed he'd had his excitement earlier.

These two male cousins, who had these and other precognitive dreams when they were young, still dream, they admit, but they don't discuss their dreams. Their mothers each have psychic dreams and are not uncomfortable talking about them. Dana, a psychotherapist, thinks that precognition is an instinctive talent we are born with rather than one that is learned. She thinks boys, more steeped in the tradition of believing only what science can explain, unlearn or block the skill more than women.

The idea of blocking or denying was also suggested or expressed several times by dreamers who wrote me. One said, "I used to dream a lot. After that *one,* I rarely remember my dreams anymore." Another said, "I think I block them now." Several said, after particularly unnerving psychic experiences, they *tried not to remember* their dreams.

One woman said that her psychic experiences came during periods of stress, and another said she dreamed psychic dreams when she was especially tired. One explanation is that, in times of stress, disquieting matters are more likely to be strong enough to break through the barrier of sleep into the waking mind. Another explanation was suggested by a dreamer who said that when she was very tired she was less able to defend her rational, conscious mind against instinctive images usually relegated to the realms of impossibility.

Nine out of ten of the dream accounts I received were from women. Perhaps women are, as is often observed, more in touch with their intuitive side. Perhaps women are more willing than men to admit to dream experiences whose existence is not validated by science. Many women wrote that their husbands laughed at their dreams or said, "Don't tell me about your dreams." One woman said, "My husband is the scientific type, so he doesn't believe in any of this."

When a man is about to experience a disaster, it often seems, he doesn't have a precognitive dream. He leaves that to a woman in his life—in the following case, his ex-wife.

I had retired early. I dreamed the telephone rang and I answered it. It was my ex-husband. He was highly distraught, seemingly close to tears. It seemed he and the woman he left me for had not married but lived together. He said he had given her everything. Diamond, mink stole, the works. (Our bank account had been depleted.) He said he had left work early, had driven up to the home they shared, and parked. Before he could get out of the car, he glanced to the house and saw her and a man coming down a long walkway from the house to the street. They were carrying suitcases, which they deposited in the trunk of the car. She had left him.

Now I remind you that this is only skimming the top of the barrel as far as this dream conversation is concerned.

What happened next would have made me doubt my own senses aside from the fact that I had told my next-door neighbor and my mother the dream. Only in more detail than I have related here.

Within the week I again went to bed early. The phone rang and I arose to answer it. I immediately knew it was my dream. Sure enough, it was my ex-husband. He was terribly upset, so upset that at one point I thought he would cry. He began by telling me in detail what had happened—just exactly what happened in the dream I told you. I heard him out until he reached the point where he parked and glanced at the house. I said, "So you saw her and a man coming down a long walkway with suitcases which they stowed in the trunk of the car."

He said, "You've had another dream."

I could go on and on.

Maybe wife number one had the psychic dream instead of the man because *she* was due some satisfaction. The men, however, who *have* had psychic dreams often begin by assuring me that they had never been interested in ESP or other psychic phenomena. One said, "I don't believe in psychic dreams, but I did have this one dream . . . ," and he went on to tell me a hair-raiser.

One factor that may explain the many more-numerous dream accounts sent to me from women is simply this: Women write more letters than men. In my captive research group, in fact, one out of three of the psychic dreamers were men, considerably more than wrote spontaneously. I wonder how many men have had dreams that came true but never thought of picking up a pen to communicate them.

Many dreamers who wrote expressed relief that I took the subject seriously. "At last I can tell someone," wrote a middle-aged woman. "You're the first person I have told," said a student. Another dreamer, a professor at Ball State University, said, "I rarely if ever discuss these with anyone since past experience has taught me skepticism on the part of other people is enough to make them think one is strange to have dreams like this, much less keep a detailed record of them."

Others are not quite sure even I will believe them. They offer touching little assurances of their credibility. "We own our home, at least almost," wrote a woman from Cleveland, "and I think we would be considered an average household." "I got the highest grade in my class in chemistry and people consider me intelligent," explained another. "I have a friend who is a lawyer and another who is high up in the bank," one offers as proof of his stability by association. One dreamer sent me a character reference from his employer. Many told me the people I could contact who could verify hearing their account of the dream before the event took place.

One reason I pursued my research so long and ultimately

published this book has to do with the sincere entreaties from those who shared their psychic dreams with me. Typically, these people were neither proud nor smug about their psychic dreams. Many, instead, were confused and fearful. Some who told their dreams to family or friends have been ridiculed. When their prophetic dreams of unhappy events came true, their families and friends no longer sneered—they then feared hearing any more about such dreams. Those whose dreams accurately predicted death or accident often felt guilty. Those who dreamed even harmless dreams suffered from being called weird or from the fear that they would be thought ridiculous. They had no one to assure them that they are, after all, normal people. Unaware that nearly ten percent of the population has experienced dreams that come true, these individuals may feel unnecessarily alienated.

After sharing three pages of precognitive dreams with me, Ms. W. P. of Oshkosh, Wisconsin, ends her letter with these words: "I don't know why this happens to me. If you could explain it, I'd be so grateful, and perhaps these dreams would not frighten me so much anymore."

Because of this and many similar requests, I have tried to offer the individuals who have taken the risk of sharing their dreams the hope of finding some answers and some validation of their psychic experiences.

As for me, I was moved to be able to share in a small but intimate way, through letters and interviews, the important events in the lives of ordinary people, the births and deaths, the marriages and breaking up of relationships, the job successes and disappointments. At the same time, I was delighted with the glimpses into the more trivial events, the domestic scenes I rarely find in books, the unexpected words, thoughts, and acts of people I probably would not have met in any other way.

THREE

Dreams Out of Time

PRECOGNITIVE DREAMS

ONE WAY says the traffic sign on the cover of the February 1987 *Discover* magazine, but the arrow is pointing in both directions. The contradictory sign dramatizes what the respected magazine of science and technology considers a theoretical dilemma:

In the universes of both Newton and Einstein, time flows backward into the past as readily as it does forward into the future. Which means we should all have memories of the future. That we don't—and that physicists can't find a single arrow of time that points in any direction but ahead—is one of the most profound and vexing mysteries in nature.

Begging *Discover*'s pardon, the precognitive dream is a dramatic example of the future-memory scientists consider theoretically possible.

Tony Rothman, Ph.D., author of *Frontiers of Modern Physics* and *Discover*'s provocative cover story, goes on to cite examples gleaned by Oxford physicist Roger Penrose from scientific disciplines ranging from quantum mechanics to thermodynamics showing instances where processes should be reversible and time should be irrelevant but are not perceived to be. In speaking of subjective time, Rothman quotes *Alice in Wonderland*'s White Queen, "It's a poor sort of memory that only works backward."

He then dismisses the idea of bidirectional memory, saying, "Perhaps clairvoyants would claim that dual ability, but for the rest of us, when memory works at all, it's sadly—or mercifully—limited to events that have already taken place."

Rothman speaks of clairvoyants as if they were a separate and dubious species. I protest! My research has demonstrated that one out of twelve of us garden-variety people has had a dream that literally came true, and these may be the elusive events in which perception agrees with the theoretical possibility of future-memory.

The following dream, for example, was sent to me by a woman now living in Brisbane, California.

My first experience came as a child of perhaps fourteen years old. My parents and I lived in a very secluded, wooded area of Delaware, with one and a half miles to walk to the nearest trolley. It was not often I was able to go "downtown." One night I dreamed I was on a trolley going down Delaware Avenue, passing Wilmington High School, when I saw a bright yellow open-top roadster skim by between the trolley tracks barely missing an oncoming trolley.

I had never seen this type of auto; so the following day, I asked my mother if she had ever heard of a car of that description. She hadn't, for my father had only had the sedan-touring type of car.

I had occasion to use the trolley car shortly after. I sat watching the scenery from the window. Suddenly, a bright yellow open-top car dashed by the trolley between the tracks barely missing an oncoming trolley. It so happened, we were on Delaware Avenue, passing Wilmington High School. I never forgot it.

Argue if you will that this teenager may have seen a yellow roadster somewhere or a picture of one that she forgot or failed to notice consciously. Still the car appearing between the trolley tracks in front of Wilmington High School would make the rarest of coincidences. The startling episode cannot be dismissed as *déjà vu* (a common phenomenon in which one feels during an experience that he has already had that same experience some time in the past) because the dreamer specifically remembers seeking information about the car after the dream but before the actual event occurred. This dream is a simple and benign example of the precognitive dream.

When the yellow car sped down the trolley tracks, its image, the images surrounding the happening, and the girl's emotion of surprise all made an impression on her brain, an electrochemical impression, for the method of transmission of thought as well as its storage is an electrochemical process. At the time of the event, the electrochemical patterns of the images and impressions of this event became available as memory—not only past-memory but possibly future-memory. The pattern coming forward may have gone backward in time to a point before the event actually occurred. For in the electrochemical processes of physiology, as in other fields of scientifically described reality, for every activity there is a reflection in time. In *The Tao of Physics* physicist Fritjof Capra writes of molecular activity: "For every process there is an equivalent process with the direction of time reversed and particles replaced by antiparticles . . . all particle interactions seem to show a basic symmetry with regard to the direction of time."

Time seems reversible in every area of science except the psychological one, our perception of life. Man's particular makeup is such that he can only function seeing time as going forward, for that is the basis of the most important of learned behavior: cause and effect. Without the one-way time arrow, man would be lost. For this reason, it is possible that he learns to ignore future-memory—information about the future reflected back. Children like the girl on the trolley have not yet learned to disregard future-memory so completely. Sometimes, in the unguarded moments of sleep, adults, too, allow a strong reverberation from the future to slip by into the consciousness, where, for once, they regard it as almost real.

Also, like the girl who was surprised by the open-top roadster, young people dream of things that are novel and that, in their inexperience, they don't understand. The following dream remembered from girlhood was the oldest dream memory anyone told me.

One cold winter in 1909 a teenaged girl dreamed she saw a beautiful young woman with long floating hair running across a meadow toward her. In a flowing white gown and with bare feet, the vision looked like "an angel without wings."

When the girl told her mother about the beautiful dream of the bare-footed lady, the mother objected that it was too cold for anyone to go without shoes.

Three days later while waiting for a streetcar with her mother, the girl looked up and said, "Here comes my dream! She's real." A young woman with long hair, flowing white gown, and no shoes was running toward them. She asked the young girl and her mother if they could give her shelter. They took her in.

Later, the dreamer's mother learned the "angel" was a disoriented patient who had wandered away from the Norristown State Hospital. Future-memory of her appearance had impressed the sleeping girl, who had no idea who the angel was.

The following precognitive dream sent to me by Tracy, a college student in Charleston, South Carolina, includes a not-uncommon element—the insistent repetition of a dream theme before the event it depicts. In this case, future-memory of the event was jogged three times. The details of the dreams are not exactly like the event (as is often the case with past-memory as well), but I expect you will consider them close enough.

Tracy had three dreams in two months, not identical in every way but obviously presenting the same frightening event. At the time of the first dream Tracy was looking for another student to share her apartment. She was working the late shift at an all-night restaurant. In her dream someone rushed into the restaurant calling out for her, saying her apartment was on fire. She went straight home, where she found her apartment building engulfed in flames while people stood outside watching it burn. Tracy says she thought the dream was strange, but she was not particularly frightened. The dream did not haunt her.

The second dream came after Tracy had found an apartment mate, Cynthia. The second dream also began with Tracy at the restaurant. This time it was Cynthia who came to tell her their apartment was on fire. The two of them went back to the burning building together. Tracy, of course, found it even more strange that the dream had occurred a second time, but still she was not frightened.

In the third dream Tracy was again at her job. Someone, not Cynthia, came to tell her the apartment was on fire. This time, when Tracy rushed home she found only her apartment—the middle one of nine—in flames. She ran through the crowd calling out for Cynthia but could not find her. She was anxious when she awoke.

A couple weeks later Tracy had some car trouble and left her car in her hometown to be repaired. When her mother called on a Monday to say the car was ready, Tracy explained that she would have to wait till the weekend before she could get home to pick it up. On Tuesday she began to feel very nervous. By Wednesday she felt inexplicably panicky. She persuaded a friend to take her to the bus to go home for her car, but she knew it was not her car she was concerned about. She had an irrational but overwhelming desire to get out of her apartment.

At home, she remembers, she told her mother several times, "I hope my roommate is all right." Her mother, puzzled, finally said, "Can't your roommate take care of herself?"

When Tracy got back to Charleston, she was severely agitated. Neighbors stared at her when she got out of the car. The building seemed strangely dark, and it smelled as if someone had burned something in the kitchen. She went in and checked the pot on the stove. When she lifted the lid, the smell of old food made her nauseated.

Tracy wondered where Cynthia was. As she went up the stairs in the late-afternoon light, the hallway seemed darker than usual, the walls seemed black, and she wondered if her emotional condition was casting a gloom over all her perceptions. She went into her apartment mate's room. All Cynthia's belongings were gone; the room was empty. Tracy went to her own room. When she got to the doorway, she was overcome with a sickening horror. The bed was a heap of charred wood. Where the head had been there was a hole burned right through the wall. The tiles of the floor were bubbled from heat. Beer bottles were scattered around the room. Tracy screamed and ran down the stairs.

The manager at the rental office explained that Cynthia, drinking and smoking in bed, had set the mattress on fire. Her boyfriend had found her body.

The dreams all fell together suddenly as a series of foretellings. Why hadn't she realized their meaning, Tracy asked herself. Why hadn't she seen the dreams as a warning?

Could she have saved Cynthia? Or was it fate and no one could have saved her friend? Were the warnings meant for Tracy alone so that she, at least, would not die there in the fire?

The questions this dreamer asked about the purpose of the precognitive dream are ones none of us can answer yet, but the intense urgency of the dreams and the horror of their aftermath make us sure there is *some meaning* to these warnings. Less and less can we believe in mere chance.

Such precognitive dreams depict events that had not actually happened at the time of the dream but would occur later. They look into the future, not just in a vague way, but in substance and detail. They evoke again questions philosophers have tangled with before. If time can run backward as well as forward in our minds, is the future already written? If so, where and by whom? The answers to these questions will radically change our whole concept of time, sequence, and the meaning of life, opening up new dimensions and expanded worlds.

Ancient Greeks had extensive knowledge of the sky and the way that the heavenly bodies moved. They knew an astronomer could predict the position of the stars tomorrow just as accurately whether he knew their positions a hundred years from now or if he knew their positions today. The movement of the heavens could be rolled back and forth in time like a home movie without disturbing anything. The lives of men, they believed, were ultimately linked with the immutable voyages of the stars. The Greek idea of destiny certainly indicated a fate written out.

In the famed Greek myth about Oedipus, for example, an oracle from Apollo foretold to King Laius of Thebes that his son would kill his father. When Laius' son was born, the king, in an effort to thwart the prediction, left the baby to die on a mountainside. A kindhearted peasant found the baby and took him to King Polybus of Corinth, who named him Oedipus. As a young man, not knowing his true identity, Oedipus sought out the oracle of Apollo at Delphi, where he was told that he would not only kill his father but marry his mother. Thinking his father was Polybus and wanting to avoid this fate, Oedipus left Corinth and returned to Thebes, the kingdom of his birth. After a complicated series of events, he killed his father unknowingly and married his mother. Upon discovering many years later what he had done, Oedipus blinded himself in despair. The Greek myth, though the inspiration for Freud's theory about boys and their mothers, demonstrates more clearly the Greek belief that what will be will be: You can't trick fate. We can speculate that if the king had only let matters be and kept the boy at home, the murder and incestuous marriage never would have taken place. It seems the very prediction itself caused the tragedy.

While humans, by agonizing over decisions and making heroic efforts to achieve, daily demonstrate their belief that they can somewhat control their future, there lingers in the human psyche the inhibiting notion that all their efforts make no difference: that destiny is indelibly written.

In the accounts I have collected I have found a range of dream experiences that support the theory of the predetermined future as well as experiences that suggest quite the opposite. Let us see which are more convincing.

The first dream in this book in which the mother dreamed of her own and her child's death in front of a train is a most poignant example of a dreamer who did not change her plans in order to avoid the tragedy foreseen in the dream. It seems that if the mother had simply refused to go to the train station in another town and let her guests find another way home, the accident could not possibly have happened, at least not in the way the dream clearly foretold. The theory of future-memory, however, suggests that, if the mother had not gone with her daughter to the train station and had thereby escaped death, the nightmare would never have come to her. The dream was a function of the future reality; changing the future would have changed the dream as well.

In other examples of precognitive dreams of tragedy, the dreamer did beg the dream victim to change his plans. When the dreamer failed to dissuade the person, the tragedy did occur. For example, a woman in Texas dreamed that her twenty-three-year-old son drowned. When he told her the next day that he was going with some friends to a lake about thirty miles away, she pleaded with him to stay home. He had his mind set, however, and went off to spend the day at the lake. A few hours later he suffered hypothermia in a cold area of the lake and drowned. The misfortune occurred after the dreamer was *unable* to change the circumstances.

The big question remains: If the dreamer *succeeds* in changing the circumstances seen in the dream, can he thereby change the outcome? The answer is maybe.

Let's look at another real-life attempt to change a fate foreseen in a dream. The following account only illustrates how difficult it would be to prove or disprove that a psychic dream can be changed by the forewarned dreamer.

Brad, a high school student, dreamed he and two friends had an accident in a car coming home from a party they "were not supposed to go to." The dream worried Brad to the extent that he refused to accompany his friends. The next evening, on the way home from the party, the two friends' car broke down and they ran over a mailbox and went into a ditch. Brad concluded the dream "kept me from getting injured." He felt "relieved and amazed."

My definition of a psychic dream requires that the dream come substantially true. The fact that the main character of the dream was not in the accident rules Brad's dream out of my psychic dream data by my own definition. In the same way, any other dream would be ruled out if some action by the dreamer prevented it from taking place in reality.

What if Brad had gone to the party? Would the accident still have occurred? Who knows for sure? Was it actually a psychic dream? There's no way to tell. If I could prove it were a psychic dream, I could prove that the events predicted can be changed by the action of the dreamer. I can't prove it was a psychic dream, however, because the only way I know to prove that a dream is psychic is to observe that it comes true. Brad's dream was, at least, productive since it kept him from injury.

In another letter, a young man dreamed that he was driving rapidly along a certain road, put on his brakes approaching a turn and went into a skid. His car ran off the road and was heavily damaged. Not long after the dream, he was actually driving along that road at a pretty fast rate. As he approached the turn, he remembered the dream and slowed down considerably so that he did not need to brake. Going slowly he noticed a dark place on the road and, curious because of the dream, got out to examine it. The dark place turned out to be an oil spill. "If I had put on my brakes right there before the curve, I surely would have skidded off the road," the young man wrote. He considers the dream a psychic warning. I must reject it as a psychic dream by definition because the accident never happened. The only thing that really occurred was his discovery of some oil on a road. Again, however, I consider the dream productive because it may have caused the dreamer to drive more safely.

I received two letters from a young mother in Galveston, Texas, that give further insight into the question of changing the outcome of a psychic dream. The young woman said she'd had several dreams come true and therefore examines each realistic dream for its precognitive possibility. Here is her first letter:

I have had this dream three times this year. I see everything so clear, catching details, colors. My two-year-old, Kenny, is traveling ahead of us in my stepfather and mother's truck. We are following in our car. My grandfather is in the truck bed with the guard down because of some crated item that is being moved. Our dog is also riding in the truck bed.

The crated object starts to slide. My grandfather yells to my stepfather, who is driving the truck. My grandfather is pulling on the crate and slipping. I see our dog sliding, too. All of a sudden the truck is braking. We almost run into the back of the truck. My husband, who is driving our car, starts braking, too. Then I see a blur start to fall from the truck. At first I think it is the dog, but then I see Kenny going slowly out the window on the driver's side. We are still braking but can't stop and neither can the truck. I yell, "It's Kenny. Stop the car! Stop the car!" I see him hit the pavement. I see his head hit, then his body hit. As we pull the car to a turn, I see a car run over him before I can reach him.

It scares me so. I haven't told anyone this dream. I just hope that is all it is.

About a month later I received the following letter from the same woman who had this frightening dream several more times and feared even more that it was precognitive. She had attempted to keep the tragedy from happening.

First of all, I gave away the outfit Kenny wore in my dream because I didn't want him to be able to wear it again.

When I tried to figure out how the accident might occur I couldn't understand why we would be following my stepfather and mother's truck in our car. Later I found out why.

We had ordered a glass shower door for our new home. We needed my stepfather's truck to haul the door home. He said he would drive my husband, Stephen, to Penney's to get it. Stephen wanted me to come along, too.

The situation was starting to fall into place. Already there were three in the truck and that is the limit, when my mom says that Kenny hasn't had a chance to ride in the truck for a while and he wants to go, so she will take him in the truck, too. I told her we couldn't all five ride in the truck so Stephen and I would have to follow them in our car. When I heard myself saying that, I got scared.

The dream was starting to take hold. I reasoned with my mom that Kenny could go another time when we weren't hauling something and that he might get in the way of the guys. Since Stephen wanted me to go along, I asked her to please stay at our house with Kenny so we wouldn't be crowded.

When we got to Penney's and picked up the crated shower door and I saw the guys slide it in the truck bed, I really did breathe a sigh of relief that Kenny was at home. This was the object I'd seen earlier in my dreams even before I thought about ordering a shower door.

I hope this put an end to the dream. I hope it is possible for such dreams to be foiled. At least I haven't had the dream since.

Notice that at no time did the young mother consider telling the dream to explain her desire to keep the child home. Such a strain it is to hide one's belief in dreams that come true—a burden, alas, one can only tell a stranger.

What do you think? Was this mother's dream a psychic dream whose outcome was changed? Or was it a productive dream that suggested caution? You can judge as well as I.

You may remember Dana from the last chapter, whose sister, son, and nephew all have had psychic dreams. Her young son had dreamed of a horrible accident in a certain car and had been grievously injured in just such an accident. When Dana remarried and moved to another city with her children and new husband, her son had another dream about an auto accident. Naturally, the whole family took the dream seriously.

The boy described a frightening dream in which three women—his mother and two others he didn't know—were in a car. One of the strangers was driving, and her car was involved in a collision in which Dana was killed. The family talked about the dream, agreed the accident was possible but not inevitable, and tried not to let it worry them.

Soon afterward, at church Dana introduced her son to Barbara, a new parishoner. The boy did not respond even when Dana joggled his elbow to try to shake some politeness out of him. Afterward, Dana remonstrated with him.

"Why didn't you even say hello?" she asked. "I don't ask for much; just a smile would have sufficed."

"That's the woman," the boy said glumly, "the woman who was driving the car in the dream."

Dana grimly acknowledged the sign of a psychic dream coming true: One unforeseeable element had just been made known as real. She made some inquiries and came back relieved. Barbara did not know how to drive and did not have a car; therefore, the dream could not come true.

Shortly thereafter, the church newsletter announced a six-week course on an important women's issue being offered in a city about thirty miles away. Only three people signed up: Dana; the woman named Barbara; and a third woman whom Dana's son had not yet met.

As the time for the course drew near, Dana heard that Barbara's husband had given her a new car for her birthday, along with professional driver-training lessons. She got her license in short order. Immediately, she approached Dana and said that since she had bummed rides for so long from everyone else, she would like to start doing her share by driving the three of them to the course.

Dana immediately recognized that Barbara's new car and driver's license were the previously missing keys to her son's dream coming true. With them the dream could easily come true, indeed, seemed set up to become reality.

Dana told her husband the latest development and confessed to being apprehensive. "No way," Dana's husband declared. "No way I'm going to let you ride with her." At the risk of insulting the woman, Dana declined the ride, offering the dream as an explanation. To be doubly sure, Dana's husband himself drove Dana to the course in the neighboring city once a week for six weeks.

Nothing at all happened to the new driver or her passenger. So, once again, nothing is proved. Indications are, however, that deliberately avoiding the dream circumstances averted disaster.

Dana's sister, Ella, also had a dream of a disaster, which she feels she negated by changing her actions. She dreamed she was camping with her family near a river, as they frequently did. She dreamed that she and her son, then four years old, went down to the river to wash out some clothes. At the riverbank, she realized she had forgotten the soap, and so she went back for it. On the way, out of the corner of her eye, she caught sight of her son's arm flinging a rock into the water. She turned back just in time to see her son lose his balance and fall into the water. He was swept along in the river before she could reach him, and he drowned. She awoke very upset.

On their next camping trip, Ella and her young son went down to the river to wash as usual. She discovered she had come without her soap. She turned back to get it, and as she did, she saw out of the corner of her eye that familiar flinging of her son's arm lofting a rock into the water. Instead of going on for the soap, she instantly spun around and reached out for her son, who teetered in the follow-through of his throw. She grabbed him just before he fell and gave him a long, long hug.

These dream experiences suggest that although the future may be written, the script can be revised. Or part of the future is written and the rest depends on the dreamer's response.

How does this fit into the theory that says the directionality of time is irrelevant? It has been observed that while every micro-process is reversible and therefore scientifically independent of the direction of time, the big picture, the macro-process, does not seem to actually be reversible. This is explained by many scientists as an increase in random disorder, known as entropy. Entropy is a measure of the amount of energy unavailable to work during a natural process; it is therefore unaccounted for when the work process is reversed. Random heat loss during chemical reactions, for example, prevent the reaction from being exactly reversed.

Some scientists think that entropy, which always increases and never decreases, is what gives time its directionality. Others think that entropy is not true randomness but the result of missing information and that if we truly knew all the principles and had all the data, entropy would be seen to disappear and all processes would be reversible.

The relationship between the scientific model of psychic dreams as future-memory and the real experiences of dreamers like Dana remind me of a fish pond. If you picture the facts of a certain event as a handful of rocks thrown into a pond, you can imagine the concentric circles of waves spreading out from the point on the pond's surface where each rock entered the water. As the waves from one rock interfere with the waves of the next rock and the next, the configuration of waves becomes very complex. Yet the pattern at any point in time could be caught photographically, for example, and a scientist with the aid of a computer could tell not only what the pattern was a few seconds before but how many rocks were thrown in, at what angle, and how big they were. He could also tell what the pattern would look like in the future. A prediction of the future configuration is as available as a reconstruction of the past. What the scientist could not predict was that a fish would flop in the middle of the pond and change the configuration altogether. The dreamer who objects to the pattern depicted in a precognitive dream can apparently disrupt the pattern. He does not know exactly what form the disruption will take because in leaping he has little more precision than the fish.

The changes I have recounted in the working out of psychic dreams do not seem in any way to be random occurrences. The changes are willful acts of the dreamer, dependent on the dreamer's perception of cause and effect: "If I change this circumstance, I will change this result." Apparently, these willful acts are inserted into the pattern altering the actual event.

When you think about one willful act of a precognitive

dreamer changing the future you have to wonder why these particular people dreamed these particular events. Why do they not know the whole future and rewrite everything as they wish? There certainly is a huge degree of selectivity in future-memory. But remember that there is a huge degree of selectivity in past-memory, too. We remember those things that had a highly emotional impact on our lives. We also remember a surprising number of inconsequential things, about which we say, "I don't know why I've always remembered that." Theoretically, memories of *all* past experiences are stored in our brains. Innumerable events can be jogged from memory by a related stimulus; others can be reached only by hypnosis and similar imperfectly understood processes. The same may be true of future-memory. Certainly, precognitive dreams are highly selective, in much the same way as memories of the past. They are usually of events that will have a highly emotional impact on our lives, and a few are about seemingly inconsequential things. Perhaps future-memory, too, can be jogged by the right stimulus and in states of low arousal such as hypnosis, meditation, and sleep—the dream state, in particular.

Investigating another parallel between past-memory and future-memory, Jeremy Orme, a physicist at Middlewood Hospital, Sheffield, England, recorded the frequency of precognitive experiences as a function of the time span between the psychic experience and the actual event. He found that precognitive experiences dropped off the farther they were from the actual event. In other words, people are more likely to predict events in the *near* future. This finding suggests that precognition operates in much the same way as ordinary memory. Both diminish with time—past-memory recedes with forward time and the holographic reflection, future-memory, drops off with backward time.

Because of its emotional impact on our lives, the life event least often lost in future-memory, as in past-memory, is the death of a loved one. This event is therefore the most common subject of precognitive dreams.

A young woman from Louisiana, for example, wrote me that she dreamed her sister would be killed in a white car in a head-on collision. She told her parents the dream. Three days later the sister was actually killed in a white car not her own. Because the sister, in her twenties, was not likely to die and because she was not usually in that white car at all, the odds against this dream of death coming true by chance so soon after the dream are astronomical. This dream seems to be a clear, straightforward example of future-memory in some detail.

Some death dreams, by contrast, are little more than a presentiment of loss with little factual detail—like this experience, described by a woman from Birmingham, Alabama.

Some time between 10 P.M. and daylight I dreamed I was sad and grief-stricken because my husband had left me. I awoke crying, tears on my cheeks. My husband left for work the next morning as usual. Within a few hours, I was notified of his death. He had fallen from a smokestack and was killed instantly.

Besides death, there were many other events that dreamers "remembered" from the future. There were dozens of accounts, for example, of car accident dreams. This one from a young man in Reseda, California, stands out because of an eerie detail:

The setting of the dream was at night on a highway somewhere. I saw a car that had just been in an accident. The windshield was smashed in, and it was badly wrecked. All around there were flashing lights. I saw no people in this dream. But one thing stood out—the car was not running, and everything was quiet except for the eight-track tape player. In the dream, I could hear the tape by the group Black Sabbath playing the title song, "Sabbath Bloody Sabbath."

Then some time later, some friends and I were out late at night up on a road called Mulholland Drive. It is mostly paved, but there are some dirt parts. We had problems with the brakes of my car; it got out of control, and it ended up rolling over on its top. We all got out of the car OK. The car was upside-down, the engine was off, the windshield was smashed— and one other thing. In my tape deck the song "Sabbath Bloody Sabbath" was playing. I totally freaked out. . . .

In that case the dreamer had one vivid, totally accurate scene complete with music, flashback to him from the future. In the next case, a sister foresaw some family difficulty in a dream.

One night I dreamed my brother was sitting at the kitchen table telling my father that he was going to get married because the girl was in trouble. At that time he wasn't even going with anyone. In the dream I saw the girl and a baby with curly black hair. It was a boy. About three months later he met this girl and she did get in trouble. They got married and she had this baby boy with black curly hair.

A woman from Wheat Ridge, Colorado, writes:

A high school sweetheart whom I almost married has remained a close friend. During one of his periodic phone calls, I asked him how he felt since he had a heart attack in one of my dreams two nights earlier. He listened patiently as I told him that he had complained of severe pain where the ribs come together in the chest. Laughingly, he told me his health had never been better. Two months later, he told me I must never tell him of another dream in which he was the star. The afternoon of our earlier conversation he had a heart attack and the worst pain was where his ribs came together.

The unfortunate victim's request to be told no more such dreams indicates he thought the telling of the dream caused the heart attack to happen. I have a healthy respect for the power of suggestion, and if the man had blanched at the recounting of the dream and had seemed to take it seriously, I could believe the dream account aggravated a preexisting heart condition. Since the man laughed the dream off, I find it unlikely that hearing the dream was a contributing factor. The case for the power of suggestion may be stronger, however, in the following dream from a young graduate student.

I was sleeping in Bob's arms when I dreamed that he met a beautiful woman and left me. I saw her—a blonde, almost albino, but with eyes so dark blue they seemed black. She was youthful and had long blond, almost white hair, very pale skin. In the dream I knew that she had taken Bob away from me. I woke up very upset. I was shaking and my heart rate was very high. . . .

Later, at an open house at our co-op, there was a young woman named Peggy whom neither Bob nor I had ever seen before. She exactly fit the description. Bob was very attracted to her immediately. Bob and I were still physically making love as late as January. However, he would that spring decide to become Peggy's roommate. He is still very much in love with her at this time, though Bob and I are always still able to "say hello."

That dream may have set up a perceptible alienation of the dreamer from Bob and thus contributed to the dream becoming a reality. Equally likely, the dream prepared her for the eventual realization that Bob was not completely satisfied with her. In either case—the power of suggestion or the unconscious knowledge of the fragility of Bob's affection—the detailed knowledge of the unusual coloring of the girl that supplanted the dreamer in Bob's affection seems more than coincidental.

Another woman was prepared for the loss of her husband by this recurring dream.

My husband had been my childhood sweetheart. We'd had our ups and downs and weren't really close, but there was no mention of divorce and I really thought we'd always be together . . . I would dream that my husband left me for another person . . . I knew what she looked like, how she walked, talked, and even that she came from a farm town. I knew he loved her and they were happy.

After he'd moved out of the house, I heard he was dating and I decided to pay him a visit at work. No one had told me who she was or what she looked like. The minute I walked in and saw this girl behind the desk, I knew she was the one. I'd seen her two years before in my dreams, even though we couldn't have met because at that time, I learned, she lived several states away. I knew there wasn't anything I could do to stop him, so I accepted the fact that he wasn't coming home.

P.S. He married her last year.

Note that in the two "loss of lover" dreams recounted above, the relationships that took the men away turned out to be enduring love relationships rather than quick flings. The dreams were a means of breaking the news of inevitable loss gently to the hurt partners. There is a certain peace in the wife's remark, "I knew there wasn't anything I could do to stop him, so I *accepted* the fact that he wasn't coming home."

I am reminded of the familiar prayer: "Lord, grant me serenity to accept the things I cannot change, courage to change the things I can, and *wisdom* to know the difference." Such wisdom is sometimes the stuff of dreams.

As we have seen before, dreams of bad news often have a redeeming value. Some dreams, in fact, are happy ones from beginning to end, like this "hot tip" that came to a woman in California:

One time my husband and I were preparing to go to Las Vegas. About three days before we were to leave, I had a dream showing me winning $250 for a nickel at the Mint in downtown Las Vegas. I told all my friends I was going to win $250 and they just thought I was being funny. When we arrived at the Desert Inn on the Strip, the friends with us kept fooling around and I kept begging them to go downtown to the Mint so I could win my money. They finally gave in and off we went. With my fourth nickel, I won $250.

This woman "usually" dreams winning roulette numbers, and once, in a dream, she read the name of a horse and the payoff on the mutual board. She had never heard of the horse but checked the paper and found it was going to run back east at Aqueduct. The horse won and paid exactly what she dreamed. (Incidentally, psychic information of this sort comes spontaneously rather than from the will of the dreamer. To my knowledge, no one has ever become rich by willfully and consistently evoking it.)

Happy dreamers dreamed of auditioning for a play and getting the part, of winning a photography contest, of finding a dream house, of marrying a wonderful man named Richard. Ironically, such a dream of a fortunate event can rarely be offered as strong evidence of the reality of psychic dreams because when the dreamer seeks to fulfill good dreams, the events become more probable. An occasional happy dream, however, seems convincing as a scene from future-memory.

The following happy dream, for example, recurred about twenty times to a young mother in Czechoslovakia. It took over eight years and the crossing of thousands of miles for Maria to learn that dreams can come true.

In her country at that time there was a great scarcity of housing. Young married couples often had to live with parents or relatives. When Maria got married, she and her young husband felt lucky to get a room to themselves, even without running water or heat. Within two years, she had two babies. She longed for a kitchen and bathroom, but there was no hope of finding larger quarters.

Only in her dreams did she see such luxury. In a recurrent dream she saw herself stepping out of an elevator into a long hallway, carpeted wall to wall with a red plush carpet, fit for the entrance of a queen. She walked in awe down the halls past dark doors with numbers on them. Tiny lamp-lights sparkled beside each door. What an elegant hotel, she thought.

In real life only elegant hotels had such long carpeted halls with numbered doors. But in the dream she had the very pleasant feeling that certain friends lived in a comfortable apartment behind one of these doors. She had only to knock and there they would be. How laughable! These friends actually lived in two damp rooms down the street.

When she woke, she told her husband she had been in her hotel again.

Then, in 1968, as radio bulletins blurted out the news of invading Russian troops, Maria and her family hurriedly packed their bags and fled the country. After many anxious days and uncomfortable nights as refugees, they settled in Canada. Maria and her family found lodging in an old duplex in Ottawa. They knew no one except a few Czechs, and they missed their old friends (the ones in the dream) who had decided to stay and make the best of life under Russian domination.

After a few years, when Maria had a job and her husband a better position, they decided to look for a nice apartment. A building superintendent gave them their first look at the inside of a high-rise apartment house. When Maria stepped out of the elevator, she was overwhelmed. There was her dream—a long hallway with wine-red carpet, dark doors with numbers on them, little lights twinkling beside the doors. "This is it," she told her husband. "This is my dream."

Two months later, their friends astonished them by arriving in Ottawa. As soon as they could afford it, of course, they too moved into the dream "hotel," and to see them Maria had only to knock on the door.

Only one small thing detracts from the joyousness of Maria's tale: She finds it sometimes "frightening" to walk down the halls knowing that this is the place she dreamed of for eight years.

If Maria were the only one who had a psychic dream, she might well be troubled to know why she was so different. But she has experienced a world that scientists cannot fathom but that openminded people dare to explore. I hope she will stop being afraid, accept her dream, and enjoy those red carpets and sparkling lights.

FOUR

Dreams Out of Place

SIMULTANEOUS DREAMS

Along with time-defying dreams, I discovered an equal number of dreams that brushed aside distance to bring the dreamers face to face with dramas hundreds of miles away, and mind to mind with loved ones, strangers, and, yes, even animals. I call these dreams about events taking place at the same time as the dream but in another place *simultaneous* dreams.

A simple example placed the dreamer at the actual scene of her grandmother's death. In the dream, a young woman recalled, she saw her grandmother lying very pale in her bed at home. The young woman, living hundreds of miles away from the grandmother's home in Tennessee, could hear the older woman's breathing grow fainter. She was struck by the peacefulness of the scene and thought she saw her grandmother smile before she actually died. This dreamer woke up immediately and looked at the clock, which showed the time to be a little after 5 A.M. When, later that morning, she received news of her grandmother's passing, she asked the time of death. The death occurred at or near the time of the dream.

The dreamer saw a scene going on in another place at that very time (or as close as can be determined later) which she could not have known by ordinary means. She seems to have been psychically transported to another place to witness a scene. How could this be?

I have considered the possibility that the processes of precognitive and simultaneous dreams were one and the same. When future-memory provides images for a dream *before* an event, it is precognition; when future-memory comes into play *at the time of* the event, it is the same process. It would be no startling coincidence for future-memory to be turned on at the exact time of the occurrence because the memory includes information about when the incident happened. I call this phenomenon simultaneous-memory, the midpoint between future-memory and past-memory.

The theory of future-memory might explain the dream of the grandmother's peaceful death. In the young woman's dream she had future-memory of the knowledge that her grandmother had died as well as an accounting of the peacefulness of her death by someone who was present.

The trouble with my theory was that the content of most simultaneous dreams was not presented from the point of view of someone *receiving the news* about a distant event but from the point of view of the dreamer observing or experiencing the dream event *directly*. In many cases the dreamer was aware of details that would not reasonably have been divulged upon receiving the news and that the dreamer could verify only by asking specifically for verification from someone who was there. The vantage point of the dreamer *present* at the event makes me question the future-memory theory as a model for most simultaneous dreams.

I looked then at telepathy. *Telepathy* is a word formed from the Greek prefix *tele-*, meaning "distant" or "transmitted across distance" (as in *telephone, television)*, and *-pathy*, a Greek suffix, meaning "feeling" or "suffering" (as in *empathy* and *sympathy)*. *Telepathy* is the word most commonly used to describe the phenomenon in which thoughts and images travel across distance. Even Sigmund Freud, author of the most respected tome on dream interpretation, suggested the possibility of a stage of man's development prior to attaining linguistic abilities when he was able to communicate with his fellowmen through some sort of telepathic brain-to-brain process in the absence of language. As language developed, mused Freud, this telepathic ability was overridden by speech. But this ability may be the means by which telepathic processes take place.

Several investigators have tried to devise a model of brain function that would accommodate telepathy. Stanford University neuroscientist and brain surgeon Karl Pribram explains the function of the brain by postulating micropotential fields. Very small fields of electrical force are generated within the brain by hundreds of thousands of neuron-synapse-neuron connections in a conglomerate configuration. These tiny electrical fields end up in tiny areas on the cerebral cortex, the outer layer of the brain where thought, judgment, and recognition take place. Not only are the electronic forces microscopic, but the electrical currents are of extremely low magnitude and last for only minute fractions of seconds.

Sir John Carew Eccles, winner of a Nobel prize in physiology, says, "The modules of the cerebral cortex . . . are . . . ensembles of neurons. The module has to some degree a collective life of its own with as many as ten thousand neurons of diverse types and with a functional arrangement of feed-forward and feedback excitation and inhibition. . . . Each module may be likened to a radio transmitter-receiver unit."

This conceptualization of modules in the brain, which Eccles compares to radio transmitter-receiver units, is not just speculation. Stanford University scientist B. Bridgeman, among others, has been able to simulate the precise operation of such modules on a computer. Electrical currents along the synaptic connections among hundreds of neurons fire in a symphonic pattern, according to Karl Pribram.

If we accept the brain as functioning on the frequency modality, like a radio (or television, as well), we can see how it could account for mental telepathy.

Still, systems sophisticated enough to detect the slightest hint of a radio wave in farthest space have not been able to trace the telepathic energy paths that should, according to my data, be criss-crossing the country nightly.

Another theory involves what Karl Pribram calls the "holographic" model, in which all thoughts, acts, and images in the world—the big picture—are out there like a complex pattern of overlapping ripples in a pond where stones have been thrown and fish have flopped. Each of us has a small piece of this pattern in our minds. Just as a computer can re-create from one wedge of the ripple pattern the entire pattern and from that determine which size pebbles have fallen where in the pond, so our minds can analyze from the information we have what is going on in the rest of the pattern. The holographic model is just a high-tech version of what famed psychiatrist Carl Jung referred to as the collective unconscious, in which all of us are tapped into the reservoir of all human experience near and far, past and future. Whereas Jung's theory deals with an innate characteristic of the psyche, Pribram's model deals with the external world.

Is it then possible that in psychic dreams, space is as irrelevant as time, a psychological concept rather than a physical barrier? *Discover*'s article uses the term "space-time" to reflect the relativity of time and space theorized by Einstein in his theory of relativity. Neither time nor space, in the final analysis, has a definite scale; each is relative to the other.

Marilyn Ferguson, author of *The Aquarian Conspiracy,* and *The Brain Revolution,* goes one step further: "If these events occur in a dimension transcending time and space, there is no need for energy to travel from here to there. As one researcher put it, 'There isn't any *there.*'"

Another way to look at it is offered by Pribram: "Time and space are collapsed in the frequency domain. Therefore the ordinary boundaries of space and time, locations in space and in time become suspended and must be "read out" when transformations into the object/image domain are effected." Simply put, time and space are irrelevant as separate entities in the abstract level of scientific formulation.

Indeed, just as time was suspended in precognitive dreams, space seems to be eliminated in the simultaneous dreams in which dreamers have described to me the unique vantage point from which they viewed the dream event. The distance-defying vantage point of the dreamer is demonstrated in all types of simultaneous dreams, which I have divided for discussion into *observer, participant, vicarious, visitation,* and *shared* dreams.

The dream about a grandmother's peaceful death was an *observer* dream. Another example concerns a woman who, sleeping at a friend's one night, dreamed her trailer was being robbed. She saw the men back in the bedroom. She heard someone yell, "Put the TV down." In her dream she knew the thieves would be caught. When she went home, she found her TV taken off its table and abandoned on the bed. The police did catch the people who had broken in, just as her dream assured her.

In a series of *observer* dreams, another woman became graphically aware of a severe illness in the family of her sister with whom she was not in close contact.

In dreams spanning eight days I constantly see my brother-in-law dying. He is bald, terribly thin and white, and seems to be in a coma or deeply asleep. I can feel grief and anger swirling around in these dreams, but mostly it's just him lying there in bed. I have this same dream so often that I begin to dread falling asleep and begin to suffer great fatigue. I do not call my sister despite the extreme clarity of these dreams, figuring that it will frighten her. The dreams end on the eighth day.

Five days after the last dream, my sister called me to report that her husband has a brain tumor, had received radiation treatments, gone bald, and had begun to die. He slipped into a deep stupor but did not die. After eight days he suddenly regained consciousness and showed signs of recovery. Then I told her my dreams. The dates coincided.

In this dream, like many *observer* dreams, we see telepathically transferred emotion as well as factual detail. The "grief and anger swirling," which, though they could be the emotions of the dreamer, seem more like emotions of the patient or of his wife.

The following child's dream seems to be an *observer* experience, also, because the child, as children often do, reported the dream as a reality, a fact, rather than as an event in a dream.

When I was five years old, living in Arizona, I awoke one night crying. I told my mother a horse had gotten out of the stable and had been hit by a truck. It was lying in the middle of the street bleeding. She said it was a nightmare.

The next day we drove down by the stable where my father spoke to the owner. A horse had gotten out of the stable at night, the owner said, and was struck by a truck and died.

One of the most striking experiences of this type I have heard was described to me by a woman who, in her dream, was an observer of an airplane piloted by a man she didn't even know.

While I was a junior in high school, I became exceptionally close to a girl my own age who had just moved from Salt Lake City, Utah, to Lau,

Hawaii, where I was living. She was staying with an aunt while her parents remained in Utah. One morning I had a very vivid dream concerning her father.

In the dream he was piloting a small plane when it lost altitude and crashed into a low, even hill. The pilot died. I can still see the glass of the plane windows breaking just before he blacked out.

The entire incident seemed at the time very strange because I had never discussed her father with my friend—in fact, I was not sure he was living or still married to her mother—and because I almost never remember dreams; I basically considered myself "dreamless." The dream was exceptionally vivid and, for some reason, exceptionally emotion-producing.

When I awoke in the morning, the most important thing was to share this dream with my friend. I was unable to contact her until 10 A.M. I excitedly told her I had something important to tell her and asked if her father had ever piloted a plane. She told me she had just learned an hour before that her father had been killed when a small chartered plane had crashed into the side of a small hill.

Later facts indicated that my dream occurred within a half hour to one hour of the actual incident. Her father was officially listed as a crew member but not the pilot of the flight. Only those who saw the plane take off and I myself knew he was actually piloting the plane. This was a significant fact that was not settled until months later in an insurance court battle.

The reason the death of a man she had never seen had enough emotional importance to break through the barrier of rational scrutiny into this young woman's consciousness may be revealed in her comment,

I was a very lonely, introverted person, extremely dependent emotionally on my relationship with this friend. Her father's death had significant impact on my life in that the friend had to leave Hawaii immediately because of it. I was left emotionally bankrupt, and subsequently got involved in a chain of events that still deeply influence my life.

In contrast to *observer* dreams in which the dreamer is not seen and does not himself take part in the dream, in *participant* dreams the dreamer is one of the characters. This automatically introduces an apparent error into the literal truth of the dream because the dreamer, home in bed, cannot (according to conventional thinking) actually be in the dream scene at the same time. Yet this "error" does not, in my opinion, negate the credibility of the dream.

In a *participant* simultaneous dream from my original dream study, the subject arrived home from work to discover a crowd of people around the house—policemen, neighbors, and his own family. When the dreamer discovered that a man had been murdered in his house by a gunshot to the head, he asked to see who it was, but the police had covered the body and would not show it to him. In the dream, he concluded that the dead man was his brother since his brother was the only member of the immediate family who was absent. In reality, at the time of the dream, this brother was out of town visiting a cousin.

The next morning, after the dream, the family received a call delivering the news that the cousin whom the brother had been visiting was dead—shot through the head by his wife the night before. Needless to say, the dreamer was horrified by the event itself. In addition, the dreamer expressed an uncomfortable sense of responsibility for the murder because he had dreamed about it at or close to the time it was actually going on. This sense of unwarranted guilt reappeared in many accounts of psychic dreams about tragic events. (It is my desire to reassure such dreamers that psychic dreams are simultaneous or precognitive awareness of events, not causes, and that, as dreamers of psychic dreams, they are in good and plentiful company.)

The distinction between *observer* and *participant* dreams is not always clear. Several dreamers mentioned floating over the scene they were observing, putting themselves both in and out of the dream. One dreamer said, "I was both an

observer outside the dream *and* a participant in the dream."
The sensations of seeing oneself in a dream and observing
the dream through one's own eyes are apparently distinctive
perceptions.

Another distinctive dream perception forms a category of
its own: the *vicarious* dream. The vicarious dreamer feels he *is*
another being and experiences events in the other's life
physically and emotionally as if he were in the another's
skin.

Deborah K., from a town in Pennsylvania, wrote about
feeling the tragic experience of someone she loved:

*On March 24 I was in bed at Butler Memorial Hospital. I was given
sleeping medication around 10:30. I was still watching TV, "David
Frost's World Book of Records." I apparently fell asleep some time during
the program. The last I looked at my watch it was 1:45.*

*At exactly 2:10 the next morning I awoke, sat straight up, as though
something had hit me. I sat for a moment stunned and disoriented, trying
to recall what had wakened me so suddenly.*

*In the dream, I just remember an impact, sudden, violent, and can only
describe it as hitting a brick wall. At the same instant as the impact it
seemed as if I had put my head through a plate-glass window followed by
a great amount of red, thick liquid as though I had red paint thrown
directly at my face. This was followed by a loud scream, which I can't say
was either male or female. The scream was "Deborah!" Then I woke up.*

*After thinking about the dream, I lay down and fell asleep immedi-
ately. I usually cannot get back to sleep once disturbed. That morning I
was awakened by a nurse around 8:45 A.M., announcing visitors. It was
my husband and son. They had come to tell me my brother had been
killed in an automobile accident.*

*My brother, Peter, age thirty, was killed that morning in a violent
head-on collision involving two other cars. One car had hit him head-on,
killing two elderly persons, and another car hit him at the same time from
behind, injuring a girl. Peter had gone through the front windshield on
front impact and come back through when hit from behind. He was
pronounced dead at Kittanning Memorial Hospital, nineteen miles from*

where I was, at 2:15 A.M. *March 25, only four minutes after I had awakened from my dream.*

I have never understood why any of this took place. It is still very painful for me to recall. My brother and I were only thirteen months apart in age and very close to each other.

It is clear that Deborah experienced vicariously the death of her brother, as if it were happening to her. She was not an observer of the crash from the outside but from her brother's point of view. She did not feel *her* sorrow at losing her brother, but *his* sudden sensation. Identifying with the victim is a very common, meaningful pattern that is repeated often in dreams. A dreamer who is close to someone feels with that person.

In the following *vicarious* dream a young woman in Jackson, Mississippi, experienced what, the next day, happened to her mother.

One Thursday night I had the following dream:

I had been in a work-related accident (that was not part of the dream) and had lost most of my left hand. After treatment, I now had popsicle-stick metal fingers attached with string and they now worked as normal fingers. I had regained complete use of these fingers. I was not upset but kept telling people that they just didn't look the same—that was my greatest concern.

Because the dream was so unusual, I related it to my co-workers the next day, Friday. On Sunday afternoon my mother, who lives eight hundred miles away, called me to tell me she had gotten her left hand caught in a machine in a health spa on Friday evening. Her hand had been restored with a skin graft and she would regain complete use, but "it would never quite look the same." Those were her words.

I thought this experience too odd to be coincidental, as did the people to whom I related it.

Why the dreamer substitutes herself for the star of the drama is uncertain.

The most unexpected *vicarious* dream sent to me was, once again, a child's dream remembered.

I felt myself to be a rabbit and was running literally for my life. Something was chasing me and I knew I would die but was running to the end. The dream was short, but I vividly remember the feeling of being a rabbit—the strong legs, the soft fur. As I was running, the only thing I remember seeing in the darkness was a white picket fence as it flashed by.

Upon awakening, I was shaking, sweating, and breathing heavily, as if I had been running. I stayed awake quite a while pondering the dream and marveling at the amazing feeling of myself as a rabbit. I also remember questioning the dual feelings of fear and, at the same time, the exhilaration of running so fast.

The following morning, my father warned us not to look in the basement window gutter because something had killed and partially eaten a large white rabbit. It was not till later that day I noted the miniature white picket fences around our flower garden in direct line with the basement window.

With a sort of primeval instinct, this child, like the one who dreamed of the dying horse, demonstrated a special empathy with a creature in trouble. The fact that children have more than their share of psychic dreams and the fact that this child empathized with an animal tend to confirm Freud's theory that the skill comes from a prelingual past and fades with the long use of language.

In most *vicarious* dream situations, the dreamer and the real person share close emotional bonds, which seem to be the basis of the highly selective communication. The following dream from a woman in Pepperell, Massachusetts, is all the more puzzling because the dreamer did not even know the person whose place she took in a dream.

I have never been psychic, but at one point in my life I had a dream that was most disturbingly realistic. About thirteen years ago, my husband was in the army, stationed at Fort Wainwright, Alaska, and we had an apartment in Fairbanks.

I dreamed one night I was another girl, that I was skating in a roller rink several miles from where we lived. There was a calmness there until a man suddenly went berserk, shooting the people with a shotgun, mutilating and killing them. I ran in panic to the ladies room, bolting myself in a booth. All the while the noise and screams went on outside. In the dream I was in a state of absolute terror. I heard the door open and the man came in.

I awakened then and told my husband of the strange feeling I had regarding this dream. I cannot emphasize enough that when you have a dream like this, the feeling of realism is overpowering.

My husband said it was very strange and he could not imagine why I would dream such a thing. Shrugging it off, he turned on the radio to hear that two or three people had been killed and several severely injured under the very circumstances I had just dreamed. What was really strange was that a girl had locked herself in a restroom booth, thereby saving herself, just before the police arrived.

I found out later, when I read the newspaper accounts, that I did not know the girl involved and that conditions were identical with those in my dream. The only connection with us was that the man, a soldier my husband had never met, was also stationed at Fort Wainwright.

I think the girl and I must have had something quite similar in our personalities for me to pick up her thoughts. I was very happy she was all right.

In this case, there was no explanation for the transposition, if that's what it was, between the frightened girl and the dreamer. This was one of the few dreams in which I cannot see or at least speculate on a meaning or a value to the connectedness between the dreamer and the dream subject. If only the dreamer had responded by contacting the girl and seeking out the connection, she might have learned something important about the selective nature of the psychic dream experience.

In all the above—*observer, participant,* and *vicarious* dreams— the perception of the dreamer is that he or she is going psychically *to* the scene of the dream event.

The following dream, one of the strangest I have ever received, especially supports the idea of the dreamer in some psychic form actually visiting, even appearing at the scene of the dream. A nurse in Central Islip, New York, wrote:

I was a per-diem-relief R.N. two days a week at a local hospital, and the dream involved one of the units where I sometimes worked. As the dream opens, I am standing in the darkened hallway of this unit. A patient's call light is on over the door, and I move down the hall to answer it. I pass the lighted area of the nurses' station, and no one is there—which I think is unusual.

I enter the room and an elderly man tells me he has spilled his urinal in the bed. I recognize this man from "real" work. "No problem," I tell him, "I'll change your bed."

My eyes search the room, and on the shelf in the closet is a stack of linens. I am surprised at my lack of strength, for it takes extended effort to bring the sheets down and change the bed, but somehow I manage it. I want to rub his back but find I can't open his bedside cabinet for the lotion.

I ask him if there is anything else he needs before I go, and he requests pain medication. I feel for the narcotics keys in my pocket and realize one of the other nurses has them, so I tell him he'll have to go to the nurses' station and tell one of the nurses.

I have just enough strength to gather up the soiled linen and tote it to the laundry basket in the hall.

I woke up and went to the bathroom. It was about 4 A.M., and I felt as though I had been worked over with a rubber hose. In the morning, totally exhausted, I told my husband about the dream and remarked how funny the sleeping mind is. My waking mind laughed about telling the patient to go to the nurses' station for his pain medication because this man was a double amputee (above the knee) and couldn't go anywhere.

A week later I was working a unit adjacent to the one in the dream and was a little late getting off. As I walked through the unit that was in my dream, one of the night nurses stopped me to tell me of a complaint from Mr. X, the patient in Room 254. She assured me that, while Mr.

X thought me very gentle and kind in general, he was in a rage because I had told him he had to go to the nurses' station for his pain medication after I had changed his bed.

I asked the nurse what night that was supposed to have happened. Then I told her I hadn't worked that night, and besides I knew the patient —he was an amputee, and of course I would not have told him that. I fled!

Now, Dr. Ryback, did that patient dream with me the same dream at the same time? Or was I a ghost who was able to change his bed?

How I wish I could check somehow to see if the bed had really been changed! The fact that the patient saw and heard the nurse make the unreasonable request that he go down the hall demonstrates that the dreamer had come psychically from her domain into his. The only other explanation is that the patient had the same dream, so vivid that he thought it was real.

Just as memory may work both forward and backward, so may psychic travel. In *visitation* dreams, the dreamer is not transported to the scene of an event nor into the mind of another person. Instead, the image of another person is transported to the mind of the dreamer and seems to be in the bedroom of the dreamer, delivering a message that is later found to be a thought or intention of that person at the same time far away. The following *visitation* dream brought the dreamer a deep dark secret to keep. The dream came to a fourteen-year-old whose sister had run away against the family's wishes to marry a man out-of-state.

Two weeks later I dreamed I was lying in bed. All of a sudden the room was full of light. I looked around and my sister was sitting at our desk writing something. The room was full of boxes and suitcases. I jumped up, ran to the door to get my parents, but the door wouldn't open. I tried to yell, but I couldn't. My sister stood up, held my hands, and said, "Don't tell anyone I was here. I've got to go now, but I'll be back. I'll be home soon." She backed away and vanished; all the boxes were gone, too; the room was the same as it had always been. Then I woke up.

I couldn't bring myself to tell Mom and Dad about the dream because in the dream my sister said not to tell anyone she was here. But ever since that dream, I knew she would come home.

About two weeks later, she came home. We're all glad she's home and we thank God she's safe.

While the dreamer in one place in her account called what she saw a dream, she also said elsewhere in the letter that it did not seem to be a dream but something she really saw. This comment accompanies most *visitation* experiences including visits from the dead.

Another whole category of dreams I call *shared* dreams, *simultaneous* in the sense that two or more people had the dream at the same time. A woman who has had a large number of striking psychic dreams of all types described her experience of *shared* dreams:

My friend Linda's dreams sometimes enter my dreams and wake me up. She occasionally has nightmares that show up in my dreams. I am able to identify them as things that Linda is dreaming about. It's sort of a joke between us now, as I've often been tempted to interrupt her dreams so I can sleep peacefully. Alas, she has no telephone or I would.

Another example of a shared dream occurred in the family of a friend of mine. Norma, who was eighteen years old, dreamed that a younger girl was pregnant. The small dark-haired girl in the dream was someone close, someone too young to be pregnant, but Norma couldn't identify her. She told her mother about the dream, and her mother said she had had the very same dream and was not able to identify the pregnant girl either. Norma told her best girl-friend about the dream; the friend said she had dreamed the same thing and wondered who the dream was about. Within a week, Norma's sister came to her asking if she could keep a secret. She thought she was pregnant, she confessed, and needed help. Norma took her sister to a Planned Parenthood Center, where the pregnancy was confirmed. "She was only fourteen," says Norma, "and the thought of her getting pregnant never crossed our minds." The dream was shared by three people on the same night, perhaps the same time when the young girl was first agonizing over her predicament. Whether or not the dream was simultaneous with some thought process in the pregnant girl's mind, the dream was certainly psychically shared.

So many people have told me their experiences with *shared* dreams that I have to think it's a fairly common experience. When you consider that a *shared* dream goes unrecognized unless the dreamer happens to check with the person with whom he has shared a dream, there have probably been many more such dreams than anyone knows about. A dreamer is more likely to discover that a dream has been shared if it actually comes true and the dreamer is therefore especially motivated to tell it.

Some *shared* dreams retold to me were indeed *precognitive;* others were *simultaneous* with a distant event; still others, apart from being *shared,* were not psychic at all.

In one *shared precognitive* dream a woman dreamed her husband, who was actually a pilot, was taking off but having trouble getting up over some power lines. When she told him the next morning, he confided that he'd had the same dream. The next week his plane failed to gain sufficient altitude on takeoff and crashed.

A *shared simultaneous* dream from a woman in Baltic, South Dakota, reads:

When my eldest brother was in the service during World War II, I dreamed that another brother and I stood beside a hospital bed in Europe. My eldest brother lay there. His leg and back had been hurt. I wrote to my mother to tell her of my dream. I received a letter back from her, saying she had had the same dream, that she had been there beside my brother's bed the same night.

When my brother came home from the service, we were all home. When he got out of the car and walked up the sidewalk, he was limping. He had been in a jeep accident and injured his back and leg. He had not written his mother during the several weeks he was in the hospital because he thought she would be so upset.

That *shared simultaneous* dream was an *observer* dream in which both dreamers seemed to be transported psychically to the place where the injured brother lay. If each dreamer had had a future-memory of seeing the injured soldier walk up the sidewalk and explain why he was limping, we might expect that each dreamer would have dreamed the future event differently—perhaps one would have seen the jeep accident itself and another seen him being taken to the hospital. The fact that they both had the same dream makes me think the dreamers, summoned telepathically to the bedside of the soldier, who was perhaps thinking about them, observed the same hospital scene. Another possibility is that only one woman had an *observer* dream and the other picked it up telepathically.

In some ways, the phenomenon of *shared* dreams is more interesting when the dream was neither precognitive nor simultaneous with an actual event because it seems to require communication between the minds rather than psychic travel or future-memory of information they both eventually had. Here is such a dream. It especially interests me because the dreamers were two friends, one of them married to a professor of geophysics at Georgia Institute of Technology, Robert G. Roper, Ph.D. I was curious to know what reaction such a scientist would have to the events he observed directly.

Bob Roper awoke one night to hear his wife, Claire, saying to him, "You've got to stop Margaret. She can't leave now. It's ridiculous for her to come all the way from Australia just for a two-day visit. Please get her to stay!"

"You're having a dream," Bob told his wife. "Margaret isn't here."

In the morning Claire explained that she had dreamed her girlhood friend had made the thirty-hour plane trip from her home in Australia all the way to Atlanta, Georgia, to see them, and, after staying only two days, had decided to leave.

Claire wrote her friend a letter telling her about the dream and put the letter in the mail, expecting the letter to arrive in about a week. In five days a letter arrived in the Ropers' postbox, having crossed Claire's in the mail.

"Dear Claire," the letter from Australia began. "I had the strangest dream I wanted to tell you about. I dreamed I had come to visit you all the way over there in Atlanta and after two days decided to come home. Isn't that ridiculous to go all that way just for two days? I don't know why I dreamed that. . . ."

Dr. Roper knows it happened. He knows something like what we call telepathy had occurred. Dr. Roper is both a religious man and a scientist. I wondered which discipline he would draw on to explain the happening.

"I believe God performs miracles," he said, "but I don't believe he breaks His laws of nature when He does. I couldn't be a scientist if I thought that the principles I'm working on so hard today might change tomorrow. If there is divine intervention, it does not brush aside scientific principles—we just haven't discovered the principles yet."

I agree with the professor.

FIVE

The Potential for Good

As I reread letters and recall my conversations with psychic dreamers, my eyes widen at the candid details of complicated love affairs; they fill with tears over the mothers who dreamed of losing their children and did; they light up when a dreamer says he reached out to someone he dreamed about and it made a difference. *Made a difference.* Isn't that what it's all about?

Making a difference is not only a function of the dream but of the response. We cannot very well control the content of the dream, but we can determine our response. Dreams, I have discovered, can become meaningful and beneficial for those who accept the dreams and make of them a positive experience either through their actions or their attitudes.

Dreams are more likely to be frightening or discouraging to those who just wait in fear, embarrassment, or silent puzzlement till fate plays itself out. Let me be clear: I do not blame those who do not react. How can anyone be expected to respond to a strangely intense event that comes in the middle of the night and whose origin and significance is not understood? I do notice, however, that those who accept the dreams as natural, who share them with someone, explore them, take them seriously, and respond appropriately find— if not a joyful ending—a certain peace. In the case of some dreams that were shared with me, responding was unavoidable; in other cases, responding took extraordinary courage.

Here is a dream so insistent that the dreamer could hardly do anything but react, and the action itself took the horror out of the psychic dream. A woman named Wynona from a town in central Florida wrote:

I have a younger brother who races stock cars. I dreamed of seeing him working on the car—I saw him disconnect a small narrow rod that had a strong curled-up spring on each end. After he had fixed or done whatever he was doing to the car, he forgot to rehook that rod and spring. Since I know nothing about the mechanical workings of a car, I didn't know what he had left undone. I dreamed he climbed in through the window of the car, cranked it up and started to test-drive it. I started yelling, trying to make myself heard over the loud noise of the engine. I can remember yelling and yelling, but this is all of the dream.

Early the next morning my brother called. He said that a very strange and terrifying thing had happened during the night. He had dreamed that I woke him up yelling something, but that he couldn't understand what I was saying. My sister-in-law had apparently wakened while my brother was dreaming, and she woke my brother up and told him to please get out of bed because she had just seen my face directly over the bed and that something was terribly wrong. They both got out of bed and turned on all the lights and looked through the house to make sure that I hadn't come in during the night—and when they couldn't find me, they sat up till daylight to call me, afraid to go back to bed.

I told him about the dream, and he said that he had no idea what I could be describing, but that he would check the car over and would call me back. He called within the hour and said that even though he had not been working on the car, the cable that connects the brake pedal was broken and if he had test-driven the car in that condition, he would surely have been wrecked.

There was no way Wynona could have ignored a dream that roused her family all the way across town. The dream was impressive; the communication across several miles was certainly telepathic. The dream is not, however, proof of precognition because the brother did not roar off for a test drive in the unsafe car as he did in the dream. The value of the dream to Wynona, nevertheless, was that it possibly saved her brother's life.

The following positive response to a dream took more courage. Not only did the woman, a registered nurse, have to have confidence in her conviction but she had to assert herself in face of an uncooperative employer. In 1933, the nurse was on a case in a private home when she had a "feeling" her mother was ill. Her charges, five-year-old twins, had scarlet fever but were "doing nicely." She told the twins' mother, her employer, she wanted to go home to see her own mother. The employer objected. Later the employer told the nurse that she had called to check on her mother and found she had nothing serious, "just a cold." That night the nurse had a dream.

That night I dreamed I was walking along a dark dirt road and suddenly daylight shone on something on the road. I picked it up. It was my mother's black Sunday shoe. As I turned it around, I saw it was open in the back, the kind of shoe they put on you when you're dead. The dream disappeared.

In the morning I packed my suitcase and after breakfast told my em-

ployer, "I had a bad dream and I must go home. Your children are doing nicely."

When I got home to New Jersey, Mother was in bed and so happy to see me. The doctor came. He said if I had not come that day, he was going to Philadelphia to get me. He had been calling my employer to send me home, he said.

Three days after I got there, Mother said all her [deceased] sisters and brothers were waiting for her, and she went to sleep and never woke up.

As in most families, it was very, very important to both the dying mother and her children to be together during the last hours. The nurse felt that without the dream she would have been denied this last visit, which gave her a feeling of peace that sustained her in the months after her mother's death.

A few dreamers, like the nurse, recognized positive effects of their dreams. Many did not. Those who were fearful, horrified, or feeling guilty, I want to comfort. Those who were passive or merely curious about their dream experience make me want to take them by the shoulders and say, "Wake up. Don't you see, you've missed an opportunity to take a positive step in your life!"

About half the psychic dreamers in my research say they have had more than one psychic dream. These people generally learn from their first experience to consider the possibility that each dream may come true. The first psychic dream, however, takes the dreamer by surprise. Sometimes the dream seems interesting, but the dreamer barely notices it until it comes true. Then the dreamer is shocked. For others, the dream itself is so strange or vivid that the dreamer knows right away it carries special significance and looks for or fears the predicted event. In such a case, the dreamer may feel helpless in the face of fate; the resulting anxiety is intensified if the dreamer is afraid to deal with the dream because of what other people will think. When the actual predicted experience is traumatic, the dreamer may try to forget or to block out dreams after that.

Those who accept psychic dreams as real, normal phenomena, however, are more likely to feel that the information gives them an advantage in dealing with an event that is going to happen anyway. Not surprisingly, these people also are more likely to remember and benefit from additional dreams.

Recognizing and achieving benefit from psychic dreams is a skill that can be learned, just as primitive people recognize subtle messages in nature missed by their more urbanized brothers and sisters. The native American Indian, for example, did not avoid the opportunity to read footprints just because he saw the footprint of a bear and was frightened; he was grateful that he found the footprint and could prepare to deal with the bear.

In any case, the possibility that one can change the outcome of a warning dream makes the following account of a missed opportunity disturbing.

While her daughter-in-law was pregnant, Betty S. dreamed about a baby wrapped in a blue blanket. Everywhere there was darkness, except for magnificent celestial colors at the top of a long flight of stairs, the stairway to heaven. There at the top was the baby.

When I awoke I was very scared. I knew that something was going to happen to my daughter-in-law's baby. I wanted to go to her doctor and tell him to double-check her and make sure everything was okay. I didn't because I was afraid the doctor would think I was kooky.

The following week Betty's daughter-in-law went to the hospital and her baby boy was born dead.

My heart goes out to Betty because I know what it feels like to want to do something about something worrisome but not feel able to because of the judgment of others. It is agonizing to sit passively because you fear those voices saying, "Oh, don't be ridiculous!" and "Calm down, you're such a worrywart." At the very least, I want to reassure Betty that she is not "kooky." As a psychic dreamer, she is not strange and she is not alone.

In addition, I wish I could have encouraged Betty to go to her daughter-in-law's doctor and urge him to check the mother and baby one more time very thoroughly. Maybe he would have listened to the baby's heart again and heard some signs of weakening, or maybe he would have done more extensive tests and discovered some signs of distress. Then he could have done a Caesarean section and perhaps saved the baby's life. On the other hand, maybe a more extensive checkup would not have revealed any information that would have saved the baby's life. Still, wouldn't Betty feel better now, knowing she had done everything she could? As it is, she remembers, "I wanted to go to her doctor and tell him . . . but I didn't because I was afraid. . . ."

A woman from the Southwest did go to the doctor, but it took two very different dreams to get her there. One night she dreamed she had a mastectomy and was happy about it. The next day Happy Rockefeller announced to the press that she would be undergoing a mastectomy. The dreamer supposed that her happy feeling about the mastectomy related to the nickname of this public personality.

When the dream was presented in a pleasant way, the woman took no action. Later, however, she got another chance to get the message, this time more frightening:

I later dreamed that a surgeon (wearing surgical mask and cap and gown—light green) told me, "You must have surgery soon or you will die." The voice was a woman's. . . .

I should add that my husband had a series of dreams in which he feared he was "losing me" at the same time I was having my mastectomy dreams. . . . This series of dreams alerted me to the fact that I should have mammography.

As a result of the mammography, I was sent directly to the hospital for emergency surgery. The surgeon was a woman, Dr. Amalica Katsigeanis.

The large tumor removed via radical mastectomy was malignant . . .
Dr. Katsigeanis said that had I waited much longer, the cancer cells
would have spilled over into my glandular system, imperiling my life
. . . I was indeed happy that the mastectomy saved my life.

The dream of the surgery thus came true, and the dreamer
benefited from the dream message. It was advantageous
only because she took the message seriously and made an
appropriate, positive response.

In many cases, however, no response is appropriate at the
time of the dream except for paying attention and preparing
to act. Carole, the young woman who had the following
dream experience, did just that.

I dream of a street in the city where I live. I am hovering above it,
floating around so that I can see what's happening to everyone. Below me,
I can see myself just walking along on my way to lunch. I can also see a
man with a black coat, big horn-rimmed glasses, and a battered, falling-
apart brown briefcase. He suddenly seems very sick with bad chest pain
and nausea. He can't breathe and he feels great fear. I know because in
the dream I also am feeling the pain, nausea, shortness of breath, and
fear. It is very vivid and real. He falls down on the pavement, and I am
suddenly no longer above it but in my own body on the way to lunch. I
realize he's having a heart attack and run over to him.

The same day on her way to lunch Carole saw the man in
the dream become ill and fall in the same way. She ran over
to him immediately. "It was an eerie feeling, to say the least,
to *know* what was wrong with him." Her instant understanding of the situation enabled her to make a quick decision to
call the rescue squad and tell them the man was having a
heart attack. "I must have sounded very authoritative," she
says. He was taken very quickly to the hospital, where the
heart attack was confirmed and treatment was successful.

The details of a dream well-remembered triggered a life-
saving response from one of the few men who wrote me, a

professor at Brooklyn College of the City University of New York.

First, let me say that I don't put much stock in ESP or similar paranormal experiences. But I did have a vivid dream once, which about six months later was reenacted in toto.

I dreamed I was driving my station wagon uphill on a four-lane divided highway. Around a bend at the top, a car and two-wheel trailer came into view, coming downhill rather swiftly. Suddenly, the inside wheel on the trailer came off with a shower of sparks as the axle dragged along the road. The loose wheel came rolling at a frightening rate diagonally across the road toward my own speeding car. At that point, I woke up. It had seemed terribly real, but the locale was not known to me. Nothing else about the dream seemed important or memorable either. But I didn't know how the dream "came out."

Nearly a half-year later, as I was driving uphill toward "Honey in the Rock," a summer outdoor pageant in West Virginia, I was suddenly aware that this was the exact moment my dream had begun and that at that instant a car and trailer would come around the bend at the top of the hill. I said so to my fellow traveler, who was puzzled why I seemed so urgent about it. He was surprised when the car came into view as I predicted. I then said that the wheel would come off and might hit us. At that moment it did, with great force and many sparks. I speeded up as much as I could, pushing the car ahead. The flying wheel just missed the rear of my car as it rolled off the highway down the grade below.

If I hadn't dreamed this and recognized the moment at once, that wheel might well have wrecked my car—and us. Ordinarily, I'd say a dream as a warning is nonsense, but in this case I believe that's what happened. I have no logical explanation for it.

This dreamer seems to have averted disaster by taking a detailed dream seriously and preparing to respond. The details of many psychic dreams, however, are not specific enough for us to know what event might actually happen. The dreamer of the next dream, nevertheless, understood the import clearly enough.

In September my husband and I were on a camping trip in Tennessee. I dreamed that my husband and I were upon a hillside. I thought we were standing in fresh bull-dozed dirt. I looked down the hill and coming up the hill were some of the members of our church. I thought they were wading in yellow mud up to their ankles. They came up to where we were standing, and one of the brothers from the church asked us to sing a song we sang in church or at least say if we remembered the name of a song. We could not remember the name of any song that we sing.

The next morning when I got out of bed I told my husband something was wrong at home, something that concerned the whole church. So we got ready and came home.

When we got to the church, we discovered that one of our dearest friends had died. Her body was at the church. She had been dead for nine days when they found her. We sang over the casket.

The members of the church had been worried about us, they said, worried that we would not be at the funeral. None of them knew how to get in touch with us, where we were five hundred miles away.

One of the ladies came up to me and asked, "How did you find out? Who told you?"

The woman's conviction about the meaning of the dream was sufficient to prompt a response the couple was glad to have made. Maybe you or I would require a more specific message, but for people with such commitment to their church community, this visit by church members sufficed.

Dana, the psychic dreamer you have met several times before, has often been given the opportunity that all parents wish they could have. She dreams about her children's secret problems. The dreams alert her to trouble and allow her the time to react constructively. She can first blow off steam privately, if necessary, before she approaches the child in trouble, and then plan the most positive course of action. Dana usually brings up the problem gently in conversation and tries to guide the child to make a responsible decision.

In one such dream, Dana saw her nine-year-old daughter very upset because she owed some money she could not pay back. Dana could not imagine how this could be, but when she asked the child if she was in any kind of trouble involving money, her daughter quickly broke down and told her mother her plight. It seems on school mornings she had been choosing to spend her lunch money on treats from the snack machine at school instead of saving it for lunch. She had planned to skip lunch, but by the time noon rolled around, she was very hungry. She had repeatedly borrowed lunch money from the school office and now was being asked to repay it. Naturally, she was reluctant to confess all this to her mother.

"How much money are we talking about?" asked Dana.

"Seven dollars," answered the tearful child.

Dana helped her daughter work out a way satisfactory to everyone, whereby she would do extra chores to earn the money to repay the school.

Dana considers the whole episode was a learning experience in responsibility for her daughter. She knows that children sometimes resolve such dilemmas in less healthy ways, like stealing money, for example. Dana is grateful the dream gave her the chance to teach her child that facing up to problems doesn't have to hurt as much as she might fear.

Dana had a dream about her son that did not have such an immediate reward but was very helpful for Dana. In the dream she discovered her high-school-age son smoking in his bedroom. And in the dream she hit the ceiling because she was terribly opposed to the addictive habit that in the long run can ruin health. She yelled her disappointment, screamed her anger. When she woke up, she felt she had gotten some of her negative emotion out of her system. She knew a loud voice and angry words would be counterproductive, so she planned the calm positive approach she would use.

When she finally asked her son if he had been smoking, he said (knowing by now that Mama had uncanny ways of knowing the truth), "Well . . . I tried a cigarette once." She pressed him a little, and he confessed to having "experimented" several times. They had a long talk about why young people feel the need to experiment with things they know are harmful. He indicated obliquely that what he needed was some "instant sophistication," as Dana expresses it. Later, through alert observation, Dana realized that her son was a regular smoker and there was nothing she could do about it. In a few years, however, he became more committed to fitness and gave up smoking.

Although she did not succeed in persuading her son to stop smoking, Dana knows that venting her anger as she first was inclined to do could have turned his habit into a power struggle that she would lose. If she had not had the dream, she would someday have walked in on the smoking scene and blown her top. She feels the dream gave her the opportunity to prepare a better way to deal with the problem. Perhaps her calm approach was one factor in the young man's decision to kick his habit.

Dana also dreamed about her other daughter, who was in college at the time. In the dream Dana saw the young woman running across a field naked. There was a man chasing her. Finally, she tripped and fell to the ground. Dana awoke quite upset. She considered what the dream could mean, considered how a sexual involvement might affect her daughter, who at the time was recovering with difficulty from an unfortunate relationship. Dana sorted out her feelings, planned her approach, and called her daughter.

"What's going on in your love life?" she asked. "I have the feeling that you're having some problem having to do with sex."

The young woman confessed that she was having a rapidly escalating relationship with a new boyfriend, that she was considering getting the pill and becoming actively sexual with him. Dana led her to think about the emotional risks at this time. The daughter expressed some hesitation she herself had felt. Her mother served as support for this hesitation, which she could not have got elsewhere, certainly not from the young man. Dana left her to make her own decision. The daughter decided not to become sexually involved.

If these stories sound like fairy tales, remember that Dana herself is a psychotherapist. She is experienced in dealing with such problems. All she needs is the information, which her children naturally did not readily provide her, and some time to get over her hotblooded parental reaction. The dreams gave her both.

Asked how her children felt about her tattle-tale dreaming, she answered, "They used to say it was spooky and to joke about it among themselves. I don't think the knowledge that I would get wind of their doings ever kept them from trying things though. They were all pretty independent kids."

Not all Dana's dreams were psychic. The understanding of that fact kept her from rushing into anything. She *considered* what she would do *if* the dreams were true. She always started her conversations in an *exploratory* way.

People like Dana, who pay attention to the content of their dreams and consider what they would do *if* the dream were true, have time to prepare for the possible reality. A precognitive dream of death, for example, can give the dreamer a chance to repair or develop a relationship before it's too late. The dream serves as a stimulus for communication but, being less than a real-life death sentence, allows the dreamer to do so in relative serenity. It also lessens the shock of the eventual death and offers the dreamer the peace of not having left certain things unsaid.

About ten days after my granddaughter announced her engagement in June, I dreamed that my son's plane crashed on his way to the wedding to be held August 2.

About ten days later, I again dreamed that this plane crashed and that it was traveling from Los Angeles, not where he lived. I dreamed that, when I heard the news, I ran to check the newspaper and an article about it was there. This awakened me in a state of shock.

I told a close woman friend about these dreams. She advised me to tell my son. I was not too close to my busy son. I never mentioned it to him or anyone else, but I had a feeling of foreboding.

On the Sunday before August 1, I talked with my son by phone and found myself saying many things to him that I wanted him to know and assured him of my love. My son, a trial lawyer, was so busy that I was always brief and to the point in all our conversation except this one.

Unknown to me, he left for Los Angeles later and returned on his way to the wedding.

On August 1, my son's plane disintegrated a little past Mobile, Alabama. He was a Navy-trained pilot from World War II and had flown in many storms, but the FAA said the cause was bad weather and crosswinds.

The news of the crash did not shock me.

How sad that this son gave his mother the impression he was too busy to listen to her conversation. How fortunate that the dream gave her the justification to take a few minutes of his time to express her affection and tell him other important things.

I think the dreamer's friend was right; she should have told her son about the dream. It sounds as if he could have profited from looking at the possibility of his mortality himself. Maybe it was time he slowed down and looked at what was important in life. Maybe he could have flown out of his way to avoid the thunderstorm, taken the trip earlier or later, or taken a commercial airline. If not, he could at least have picked up the phone and said a few important things to his wife and to his daughter on the eve of her wedding. Maybe he would have responded to his mother in a way that would have made her feel he was not too busy for her.

Even when no action can be taken to save oneself from tragedy, a psychic dream can have a beneficial effect. In the following case, a forewarning of the death of a son contained a message that has eased a nearly unbearable loss for Marcia C. of Huntingdon, Pennsylvania.

In my dream my husband and I went to a viewing at a local funeral home. The room was so filled with people that we waited for a long time before viewing the body. When we reached the casket, my son, David, lay there. He was talking to everyone, shaking hands and was his happy self. We sat on chairs beside him and talked with him, and shortly after we went home. There were no tears and it was not seemingly an unhappy occasion. In, perhaps, a few nights or a week later, I had the same dream. I mentioned it to a friend—my husband does not want to listen to my recounting of dreams. I thought no more of it then.

On the morning of December 21, 1975, a state policeman came to the home and informed us of our son, David's, tragic death. He was walking or jogging along the road, was struck by a car and was instantly killed. Later, when life became bearable, I pondered the dream. Was there any meaning?

I feel, surely, that it may have been a warning, not recognized as such, but also a message that David's existence would not end at the casket but goes on just so sweetly and happily as before. Thank you for listening.

Nothing can take away Marcia's loss, but it seemed that her psychic dream later brought her some comfort. The positive value of the psychic message that her son would die validated the entire dream and gave credence to the second message that her son is now in a happy state somewhere.

Taking a dream message seriously paid off in a different way for a twenty-one-year-old student:

My first psychic dream occurred more than five years ago. I dreamed I was reading the third page of my biology regent. There was a diagram in the dream and several questions connected with the diagram. The following morning I woke up early and flipped through my biology text until I found the diagram. I then studied it intensely. Later that morning when I took the regent, I turned to page three and sure enough the material on the exam coincided with my dream!!

Over and over, dreamers who took their dreams seriously, and thought out what they should do if their dreams contained truth, profited from the dreams or at least softened the impact of their fate. This is the message I found in the hundreds of letters and conversations with psychic dreamers: When a vivid dream calls attention to a possibility, the dreamer is given an opportunity to consider that possibility before it happens and to respond positively.

When that dreamer is you, will you be ready to maximize the opportunity?

SIX

Psychic Dreams and You

"But what about me?" you say. "I don't have psychic dreams. . . . And what if I did have a psychic dream? I'd want to be one of those people who accepts it and *responds positively*, like those you've been talking about. But how would I *know* it's a psychic dream?"

These are good questions, for which I have a good answer. The positive response works equally well for psychic dreams *and* for nonpsychic dreams. The appropriate response to a dream is usually the same whether or not the dream actually comes true.

There are several steps to take when you wake up remembering an impressive dream:

1. Write it down or record it as soon as possible after waking.
2. Consider the possibility of your dream coming true.
3. Prepare yourself mentally for the realization of the dream.
4. Take preventive measures if the dream event is unpleasant.
5. Do what you think should be done before the dream comes true.
6. Plan what you will do during and after the dream event to minimize its negative impact or maximize its positive impact.
7. Tell someone your dream.

Let us apply these steps to a typical death dream. Suppose you, as an adult, dream of your father's death. *Write it down* with all the details so you will remember it well. *Considering the possibility* of the death is frightening and sad. Accepting the reality of death, however, is a step toward maturity. Whether or not your dream proves psychic, maybe now is as good a time as any to begin to accept this eventual reality.

Once you have looked at the possibility that the dream might, could, and will come true, you spontaneously take the next step: You *prepare yourself* for it. Most of the dreamers who have told me about death dreams that came true, expressed a feeling of greater peace and less shock than they would have felt without the dream preparation.

Acceptance of the possibility of death does not mean you take no precautions. You *take all the preventive measures* you can think of. What could you do to help your father live longer? Call your father; ask him how he's feeling. Go visit him; see for yourself. Ask him if he's been taking his high-blood-pressure medicine regularly. Well, he says, he ran out a few weeks back and he hasn't gotten around to going for more. He feels fine, he says, but he's going to get some more one of these days. Tell him today is the day. Talk him into going now. Or call the pharmacist and have a refill sent around. Or get it for him.

This may not work. In case preventive measures are not going to change the outcome of the dream, *do what you think should be done before* he dies. Tell him you love him. Tell him you appreciate how he never missed one of your ball games, how you always knew he was in the stands cheering and hoping for you even when you couldn't see him. If you've never told him that before, now is the time.

Maybe you haven't been close lately; maybe you've had a falling out that still stands between you. Now is the time to talk it out. Saying you are sorry for your part wouldn't hurt either.

Ask him about his mother's side of the family. You know all the stories about Papa's side, but you don't even know where your grandmother's folks came from. Ask him now. Encourage him to talk. Write it down. When he's gone, there will be no one else to tell you.

Mention to your father that you remember that he once said he was leaving the lake house to his nephew, Harold, who loves the lake. This may be the time to remind him that Harold has borrowed ten thousand dollars from him to start a business that turned out to be a drug-running operation, and now he is in federal prison. Then wonder out loud if your father has thought about changing his will. If so, you'll be happy to pick up the phone and give his lawyer a call right now!

Maybe the stock that was in his and Mother's name before her death has never been changed. Maybe it's time he added the names of his heirs to ease taxes. What other loose ends need to be tied up? Now is as good a time as any.

And to whom did he say he lent that dining-room chair? Better find out now, or you may never get the set of six back together again.

Ask him if there's anything he'd like you to do for him. Drive out to the country with him. Bake a blackberry cobbler like Mother used to make. Bring your young son out to pitch baseballs.

If Dad dies next week, aren't you going to be glad you have done these things? If Dad does *not* die next week, aren't you going to be glad you have made progress anyway? The appropriate response to a psychic dream is almost always the appropriate response, even if the dream does not turn out to be psychic. You have lost nothing and gained much by considering the dream potentially true.

All these acts and mental preparations help *minimize the negative impact* of your father's possible death. Plan what you would do in the weeks following his death so that, in the weeks after his death, panic and uncertainty do not pile on top of grief. For a death dream, it may seem that planning for it is macabre or even disrespectful. People who have lost loved ones, however, tell me that planning for it gives them a sense of peace before the event that lasts through the period after the loss. Planning for death does not mean dwelling on it in your mind constantly. On the contrary, once the plan is made, your mind is free to enjoy your relationship with your father in whatever time may remain, long or short.

Tell someone the dream. This doesn't mean tell your father you dreamed he died. But telling someone may help you. Tell his neighbor. She might confess that she saw your father collapse on the driveway the previous week and helped him up. He might have claimed he just slipped, but she didn't quite believe it. She couldn't decide whether to call you or not. Your telling her the dream is all it took to get her to give you valuable information. Tell your daughter the dream as an explanation for why you are going to see Granddad instead of taking her shopping this afternoon. It will help her understand the change of plans and relieve you of the anxiety of hiding the secret. Together, you will be stronger than alone.

By considering the possible truth of a dream about your

father's death, by preparing for it emotionally and practi-
cally, by doing what should be done *now,* and by telling
someone, you will have made the best use of the dream. You
will realize, as frightening as the dream might have been,
that you are better off for having had it.

Let us look at the individual steps to benefiting from
dreams one by one and see how they might apply to a variety of dream subjects. Some of the actual dream experiences
used as examples proved to be psychic, and others did not.
The responses to both types are what proved the value of
the dreams.

**1. Write it down or record it as soon as possible after
waking.** Dreams are often forgotten very quickly, even
when you think you have them clearly in mind. Many
dreamers say, "My dream was so vivid I have remembered it
clearly for many years." Nevertheless, I have records of very
significant psychic dreams that the dreamers forgot; they
would have been lost except that the dreamer had told
someone else who remembered. Keep a pen and paper or a
tape recorder beside your bed to record your dreams. Don't
forget a light and maybe your glasses.

2. Consider the possibility of your dream coming true.
We all know some dreams are factually absurd. Our subconscious does not distinguish between the absurd and the possible. Half-awake, we don't do much better. Once fully
awake, however, we can often tell which dreams to take
seriously *in a literal sense* and which to consider symbolic.

Some psychic dreamers say there are ways to recognize a
psychic dream. As you have noticed before, psychic dreamers are struck by the vividness of their dreams that come
true. These dreams seem real. Many people mention unusual details. They remember color, texture, and sound, as
well as the emotions associated with the events. Others say
that in psychic dreams they feel more like objective observ-
ers looking down on a scene. Clear memory of the dream
and a sense of its importance are also characteristic.

One dreamer wrote, "I always dream a lot, but the special dreams that occur simultaneously with some event or that come true later are easy for me to recognize. They are very clear, uninterrupted, nondigressive, lifelike, and I am aware that I'm dreaming while I'm dreaming. I'm also aware that this is an important thing for me to remember. These dreams may be very emotional for me, but waking up is always smooth and unconfused."

Some dreams that came true, however, were not so clearly significant. A few dreamers said, "I thought nothing of it and forgot about it until. . . ."

If you do not have a clear sense of reality during the dream, a simple test to apply to every dream you remember when you awake is this: Could the dream happen in real life? Is it possible? If you dream (as one twelve-year-old girl did) that you are flying over your city on a cloud of cotton candy eating your conveyance as you go, your dream is not really psychic. If you dream Abraham Lincoln made you chop down logs to build him a bigger cabin, your dream probably needs symbolic interpretation. Don't be too quick to reject the farfetched, however. If you are actually confined to a wheelchair and dream you are riding a horse, don't rule it out. Consider that there are rehabilitation programs that put physically handicapped people on horseback for confidence building and the pleasure of mobility. Maybe this is the impetus you need to find such a program. If there is any way the dream could come true, accept it as a possibility. The dream may be psychic.

3. Prepare yourself mentally for the realization of the dream. One mother, whose eldest son had gone away to college for the first time, was very fearful something would happen to him. She found herself worrying he would be hit by a car walking around campus or mugged, or die of a fever he had ignored. One night she dreamed he would die in a car wreck. The dream represented her greatest fear and a possible reality. She didn't think she could bear it. She played the dream over in her mind, pictured again getting the news. She cried, turning over the feelings of loss in her mind. After a period of grief, real but less long or intense than she would have felt in real life, she began to feel a sort of peace. She thought that if the tragedy really happened, she could bear it, she would fairly soon return to a healthy, though saddened, life. The dream was not the cause of this mother's anxiety, for she was already fearful for her son. On the contrary, the experience of preparation prompted by the dream soothed her. For the four years till her son returned from college, she always knew anything could happen to him any day, but she was stronger and more at peace about the unavoidable risks than she had been before the dream. The accident never happened.

Many of the dreamers whose death dreams did come true often say they felt more prepared and took the death better than if they had not been forewarned by the dream.

Sometimes an aspect of comfort is built into the dream. It is important to look for these. One young woman dreamed her twenty-year-old sister would die. She saw her in her coffin, looking beautiful. The sister in real life considered herself fat and homely and suffered a great deal of insecurity because of her looks. Her beauty in the dream was a source of comfort to the dreamer, who took her sister's sudden death soon after the dream better than might be expected. The dreamer took the beauty in death as a sign that her sister would find greater happiness in a life hereafter. Many other comforting signs have come in psychic dreams of death, and several dreamers even said, "I have never been afraid of death after that." Without such a comforting sign, the dreamer must simply find strength within themselves in the relative calm before a psychic dream comes true.

Preparing your mind for the realization of a psychic dream is also valuable when the dream is a happy one. One senior in college dreamed he would receive a very prestigious award. In the dream he just took the plaque and happily floated up in the air. He had little idea what his chances were to win such an honor, but after his dream he considered the award a real, if not likely, possibility. He allowed himself to get excited about it, then pictured several different reactions he might have. He even pictured himself making a gracious remark in accepting the award. He felt like a winner. At graduation, he was named as the outstanding student in his department. He was excited but not stunned; he had a warm exchange with the department head when they shook hands, and he really enjoyed the occasion. Sitting back contentedly, he noticed that several other winners of awards in other departments seemed almost ungracious in receiving it. They didn't smile or look the department head in the eye when they shook hands. He knew those honored were pleased. Their response, he concluded, reflected the fact that they had not prepared themselves for the awards as real possibility and were reacting to the occasion as an embarrassing little social demand instead of a moment of glory.

4. Take preventive measures if the dream event is unpleasant. If you dream of a car accident, ask yourself if you have been ignoring the squeal in your brakes that alerts you to excessive brake wear? If so, have your brakes fixed now. Do you drive too fast? Do you take chances? Change your ways.

Suppose you dream someone broke the glass in your back door, opened the door, and came in and stole everything. Call the locksmith today. Put in dead-bolt locks. It is wise to have them on all doors with glass panels so that a burglar cannot break the glass, reach through the opening, and turn the bolt. Taking this one precaution the day after your burglary dream may foil a thief the very next day. And suppose you change your locks, and the dream isn't psychic and no burglar comes? Have you wasted your money and effort? You may discover that your insurance company gives deductions in insurance rates to people who have installed dead-bolt locks and taken other precautions to reduce the chance of break-ins. Since the action suggested by the possibility of a dream coming true is a prudent one, you come out ahead no matter what happens.

A story was published in the Atlanta *Journal-Constitution* (December 8, 1985) about an elderly woman named Lila Mae. The reporter noted that this woman had dreamed a man had broken into her home and beaten her with a baseball bat. That same day her sister called her to tell her she had seen the same thing in a dream. Two are stronger in conviction than one. Together, they decided Lila Mae should move out of her house and into her sister's home for a while. The night after the move, someone broke into Lila Mae's house and burglarized it. The move may have prevented Lila Mae from being harmed that night.

Dreamers have often suggested preventive measures to me that they had failed to take. The dreamers say, "I wish I had . . ." One woman dreamed her dog was shot by a home owner down the street. In real life she normally kept the dog tied up, but the morning after the dream she knew her dog was running loose. "I thought of going to get the dog several times but didn't. *I wish I had* taken the time to go bring him home," she says. The dog died of a rifle shot in the head.

One of the most frequent responses that sometimes prevents a bad dream from coming true is to warn someone, as this mother did after a very insistent dream.

I dreamed I was in a funeral home. All of my son's friends were coming up to me and giving me their condolences. I asked them what for and they said because Chuck, my son, had been killed in a auto crash because of speeding. I started to cry and told them they were mistaken, that Chuck was very much alive even though he was not there. I then noticed in the next room there was a long table. Sitting at the table talking were friends and relatives of ours who had passed on. I went over to them and begged them to tell everybody that it wasn't true, that Chuck was alive and it was someone else in the coffin. They told me that the coffin was a warning of what would happen if Chuck were not careful. Then the door opened and in walked my son. I hugged and kissed him and told him what everyone thought and the dream ended.

The next day I told my son the dream, and I warned him. About two weeks later, he wanted to go to a rock concert out of state. He had no car so he had to hitchhike. A young man picked him up. This young man had been driving for quite a few hours and was very tired. He asked my son to drive for a while so he could get some sleep. My son started to drive at 70–80 miles per hour (70 mph was legal at that time) when my warning came back to him. He immediately slowed down and pulled over to the right lane. He had no sooner done this when a tire blew out. He was able to control the car and pull off the road safely. Had he not slowed down, he would not have been able to control the car, and both boys would probably have been killed.

That dream is not, as I have explained before, conclusively psychic, since it did not come true. Does it matter to the mother whether the dream was psychic or not? Would you not be as satisfied as she to have things turn out so well?

5. Do what you think should be done before the dream comes true. When you dream about a disaster and have done all you can to prevent it, think what you would want done if the disaster still occurs. The most poignant examples of doing something before a dream comes true, as I have suggested before, are found in death dreams. Here is another example.

My mother-in-law was hospitalized for influenza. She had had an angina condition for years. But the reports from Denver, where she lived with a daughter, were encouraging. She was much improved.

However, I had that [death] dream again. I told my husband to go visit her. I was almost seven months pregnant with our third child, and he didn't want to leave me. But he went and had a delightful, satisfying visit with her. When he left, he told his sister that if their mother died, he wouldn't come back for the funeral since he had that wonderful visit with her.

She died about a week or ten days after he returned home. The other members of the family who were all scattered all over the country said they wished they had visited her as he had.

A young lady from Brookline, Massachusetts, wrote of a dream she had while a senior at the University of Michigan. She made a decision that her dream could really be true and acted on that information in the nick of time.

I had a very vivid dream that I was short one credit hour to graduate. In truth, my credits were rather confused as I had two years at Miami of Ohio and one semester in England. However, the previous year I had spent several hours with the registrar, and everything was supposed to be in order. The dream occurred halfway through my last semester. The morning after the dream, I went to the registrar's office to check everything out and I was one credit-hour short. I don't usually act on the basis of dreams, but for some reason I did that time.

This young lady realized that if there was any possibility that she was going to turn up an hour's credit short at graduation, then she wanted to do something about it now. I hope she managed to agree with the administration on some project she could do for one hour's credit. If not, at least she had time to accept being an undergraduate for one more semester, to prepare her parents, and to alter her job search to reflect her later graduation.

One man, who dreamed his house was robbed, went directly out and bought insurance. Soon afterward, his house was robbed, but at least he was insured.

If you dreamed of an automobile accident, shouldn't you check your car insurance? How about hospitalization and disability insurance? If you didn't have a safe baby seat in your car for the baby, you should get one. If you didn't wear seat belts, you should start now. What else would you do if you anticipated the wreck? You could be sure you had identification and insurance cards on your person and telephone numbers in your wallet to call people. There is no end to the things you could do to be better prepared for the emergencies to which your dreams call attention. And if your disaster dreams did not come true, you would have the security of your preparations.

Many precautions are more easily thought of through hindsight. One woman in St. Louis, expecting a visit from her pregnant sister, dreamed of blood dripping and dripping. She worried, but she didn't do anything. She had not lived in St. Louis very long. Now she says, "I wish I had got in touch with a family doctor when we first moved here and found out where the nearest hospital was." As it was, she had put off these sensible steps. When her sister developed pain and bleeding, they wasted precious time trying to get medical help. The baby was lost.

6. Plan what you would do during and after the dream event to minimize its negative impact and maximize its positive impact. Anticipating action is one of the best ways of ensuring the least harm and the most good from the playing out of possibly psychic dreams.

Considering what you might do in a period of relative calm before a stressful event is a major technique not only for effective action but for managing the stress. Countless business consultants teach managers, salesmen, and other personnel how to anticipate situations, plan for them, practice their actions in advance. It is fortunate that many common types of stressful situations can be anticipated. Dreams sometimes give us the opportunity to anticipate less common events.

One man dreamed of darkness all around, except for one spotlighted area. Into the light came a hand holding a gun. The dreamer faced the gun barrel for a few seconds of fear, and then the gun went off. One night soon after the dream, he found himself face to face with just such a gun. Remembering the dream, the dreamer instantly expected his assailant would actually fire, so he swiftly knocked the gun hand away, attacked, and escaped injury. He thinks that if he had not been prepared by the dream, he would have wasted precious seconds trying to decide if the assailant would shoot. The instantaneous action was what made his response successful. The next time you dream of being in a realistic dilemma, consider possible responses, try some out in your mind, choose what seems best, and be prepared to use it.

Notice I say *consider, try out in your mind, choose what seems best.* These are rational processes. Never do I suggest blindly acting according to some voice in the night. I say only listen to the voice in the night, and be prepared to do what makes sense. Here, as an illustration, is an account of two dreams taken seriously. The dreamer considered each dream and thought out what he would do if they were to come true. Responding to real-life circumstances, he changed his plan on the spur of the moment in the first case and took a conservative approach in the second.

Some years ago I was an executive of a corporation. This position required that I travel considerably by auto and by air.

Upon waking one morning, I immediately recalled a dream in which I answered the telephone and a young woman said, "This is Pacific Southwest Airlines. What is your BankAmericard number?" That was all of the dream. After thinking about it, I resolved that, should such a call ever come, I would not give out my number, because I knew that such calls were sometimes a ploy used by thieves to charge expenses fraudulently to other people's credit card numbers.

Two mornings later, I awakened from a dream about an automobile accident. I was driving on a country road. As I rounded a curve to the right, I came upon a vehicle stopped partly in my lane, the outside lane. I crashed into it.

That morning I was at my office when I received a telephone call. A young woman said, "This is Pacific Southwest Airlines. What is your BankAmericard number?" As I was about to tell her it was none of her business, she added, "We have this number . . ." She read my number correctly except for one digit. At that point I recalled charging a ticket shortly before and reasoned that anyone having all but one digit of my number was legitimate. So I gave her the correct number.

A few minutes later I told the company president about the experience and went on to describe my dream of that morning about the auto accident. He said, "That is scary."

A couple days later I drove to Pasadena on the Pasadena freeway, which winds through some hilly and wooded areas in places. Aware of my dream, I was deliberately maintaining a lower speed than normal. As I rounded a left curve in the outside lane, I saw a car stopped in my lane, and going slowly I was able to avoid a collision. However, the car immediately behind me crashed into the stalled vehicle.

Please note that in both instances I anticipated action, although I did not carry out my plan in the case of the credit card call.

No one wrote to say he was sorry he responded to a dream with action suggested by the dream. Dreamers who took the most extreme measures had the most extreme conviction. I think that if the measures they took turned out to be unnecessary these people would have been glad they took them anyway just for the peace of mind they achieved in responding. I do not say believe every dream is psychic. It's not. I say, consider the possibility of a dream being psychic and respond appropriately.

When a dream is about a happy event, maximizing the positive effects can also be satisfying. Melinda, for example, married to a lieutenant stationed at an army base about a hundred and fifty miles from home, had a dream on a Wednesday night that her husband came home for her birthday, which was actually to be on Thursday. She dreamed about his car pulling up and saw him walking up the front walk. She woke up from the dream in the middle of the night feeling very happy. In real life, the only celebration planned for Thursday was a birthday luncheon with her co-workers. Her husband could come home only every other weekend on Friday. The dream was so vivid that the young woman began to think, "What if he came home early for my birthday?" The house, she realized, was a wreck, and the only thing she had for dinner was leftovers for one. So she got up early Thursday morning and cleaned up the house before work. On the way home from work, she picked up two steaks and some French bread. She took a long hot shower and washed her hair. As she was getting dressed, she heard his car in the driveway. She was ecstatic —and ready.

If the dream had not been psychic and her husband had not come home early, she would have been disappointed, she says, but she would have been glad to have things already cleaned up. She had a tendency to come home tired after work on Friday and then have to clean up, so she was often not as relaxed and fresh as she would like to be for his homecoming. So psychic or not, she thinks, the dream would have made her birthday especially nice.

7. Tell someone the dream. Telling someone the dream is the surprise step, because you never know what's going to come of it. The telling of the next dream was simply sharing an idea that had interesting possibilities. A woman dreamed one Saturday night about an advertising page in the Sunday paper. Small ads about the size of a business card were printed on peel-off adhesive labels. Any ad that attracted a reader's attention could be peeled off the paper and stuck up beside the telephone, on the refrigerator, or in a notebook for ready reference.

What a novel idea, the dreamer thought when she awoke. She considered the dream possible and eagerly looked through the paper the next morning. There was no sign of the little stickers. Too bad, the dream wasn't psychic. But wasn't it a good idea? Then she remembered a friend who was trying to get started as a graphic designer in the field of advertising. She called the friend and told her about the dream.

The designer thought it was a great idea and started planning how to sell enough clients on the approach to make a whole page of advertisements. Someday you may open up your newspaper, and there they will be ready to peel. The idea came probably from unconscious blending of experience with advertising, observations of people's propensity to stick reminders around, and the creativity to put it together. It is not necessarily psychic. The only thing that makes the dream of value is the response—telling a friend who could use the idea. Whether the dream was psychic or not becomes immaterial.

Only the telling of the next dream revealed its significance. A Maryland man wrote me:

One night when I had gone to bed early, I dreamed I was floating (I almost felt bodiless) in a funeral home. Below me was a wake; people were crying. I don't remember recognizing any of the mourners. There was a coffin with a man laid out. This same man in spirit, I guess, was also floating above the scene. He was in a panic screaming to the people in the room. No one noticed him. I very forcefully yelled to him that he was all right and everything was fine. I remember telling him not to be afraid. He turned and looked at me and began to smile. Then I woke up.

The dream was so crystal-clear I told my wife the contents in detail immediately. The next morning I related the dream to my mother. It had impressed me greatly, although the dream had no significance to any of us. I didn't recognize anyone in it; nor had anyone we knew died.

After a few days I learned of the death of a close friend's father. I had known he had cancer but had no idea death was imminent. I had not seen my friend, Marjorie, for two full weeks before the death, and I had never met her family.

When I talked to Marjorie about her father, I learned that the last night of his wake was the same evening I had the dream. The time when I awoke, I realized, was about the time Marjorie's mother was breaking down over the death and had to be helped away. I told Marjorie about my dream.

Marjorie passed my dream on to her family and the mother confessed that during these terrible moments she had seen her husband floating over the coffin. She had kept this a secret, fearing the attitude of the family, until my dream was related to them.

The telling of a dream, when it got to the right place, helped relieve someone's burden. This man's dream validated the experience that the friend's mother had during her grief and allowed her to talk openly about it to her family. It was telepathically conveyed to someone, caring but objective, to keep until the right moment. How fortunate that the dreamer responded by giving the dream back.

The serendipitous good that came from communicating the last dream makes me wonder about the potential of every dream not acted upon. Here, for instance, is an account of someone who understandably didn't respond to the dream before it happened and didn't approach the person in the dream after it happened because she didn't know the person in the dream very well. What missed opportunity or significance lies here?

I was about fifteen and a high school student. I had a dream about a girl a class ahead of me. She was not a friend, someone I knew by name only. I dreamed this girl was very ill and in the hospital, and that I was visiting her there. I remember thinking at the time the dream was odd because I did not really know her. Two weeks later, she was in a serious automobile accident and spent several months in the hospital. I did not visit her. I didn't know her well enough.

We understand how a fifteen-year-old doesn't want to barge in to awkward situations. But let's play "what if." What if the student somehow went to the hospital and popped into the patient's room. What if she had the poise to say casually, "You may not remember me because I am in the class below you in school. I heard you were hurt, and since I was passing by. . . ." Where might this exploration of the significance of the dream lead? Might the two have become fast friends? Might she have been the only one who came to visit, the one to save the injured person from feeling painfully alone? I don't know, but since I have communicated with more than four hundred psychic dreamers, I now believe in the meanings of their dreams. I have gone from skeptic to adventurer in quest of significance, and I regret not a single step.

The next dream is a romantic experience that leaves me wishing very hard, "if only. . . ."

Joe and I went together for years off and on. Joe didn't practice his faith and I did. He teased me about it calling me "Gospel Kate." When I'd suggest he get himself straightened out with God, he'd always say, "You always pray for me; no use both of us doing it."

For over twenty years I prayed for Joe every day that he would become a better Catholic. We loved each other, but nothing came of it for reasons I won't go into here. I met someone else one day and got married.

The following year in May, Kate began to have dreams of Joe, vague but disquieting ones. Over the weeks they grew more frequent and the distress more intense. She told her mother about the dream, insisting that something was wrong and insisting that she would not otherwise be thinking about Joe since she was married. On June 28 she had a vivid dream of Joe surrounded by nurses and doctors, and she awoke trembling.

On July 2 she had the following night vision:

I saw Joe walk into my kitchen and I cried out, "Joe, what are you doing here?"

"Kate, I had to come to tell you I died and that your prayers were not in vain. I had a Christian burial."

Joe reached out his hand and took mine. I could feel his hand. We moved from that part of the kitchen to an undertaker parlor. Joe took me over to a bronze casket, velvet-lined, all tufted inside. A man lay there in a dark blue suit, white shirt, maroon, blue, and silver tie. I looked at the man and said, "Well, who is he?"

Joe replied, "That's me. Kate, I really am dead, but I couldn't go without letting you know your prayers were not in vain. And I wanted to tell you I love you very much."

With that, he kissed me and I could feel the warmth of his breath and his lips. Then he faded away. I awoke in a trembling sweat and slept no more that night.

In the morning I told my mother about it. I had to find out about Joe. I called a man who knew us both. He told me Joe died June 28. He was buried that morning. He told me Joe had been in a coma fifty-two days from May 6, the night of my first dream.

Later, I went to see Joe's sister. She said she was sorry she hadn't let me know; since I was married, she didn't know what to do. She often wished she had called me while Joe was in the hospital in a coma. A doctor had questioned the family asking if there was anyone Joe cared deeply about that hadn't been there, a girl maybe, because he felt if whoever it was would speak to Joe he might come out of it. They explained to the doctor about me. He told them to decide soon on calling me because if the coma lasted much longer he would only be a vegetable. Oh, how I wish they had sent for me, but they decided against it.

I then told his sister about the dream and how the body didn't look like Joe. She got chills. She said after the fifty-two days of coma and then the autopsy no one recognized him in the casket. I described the casket lining and the clothes and I thought for a minute she would faint.

Was that dream not a fairy tale gone awry? When the dreamer says, "I wish they had sent for me, but they decided against it," you realize that the dreamer, too, decided against it. She failed to make the response that might have changed the story. We understand she was married, that she could not know what Pandora's box might be opened if she successfully awakened the man who loved her. Nevertheless, we end up wishing with all our hearts that the princess had heeded her dreams, kissed the prince, and awakened him.

SEVEN

How to Interpret Symbolic Dreams

All of us dream. Most of us remember our dreams at least some of the time. Elusive dream images may dart about the edge of our consciousness barely discerned, or intricate dramas may play themselves out in the theater of our minds so clearly that we find it hard to believe they really didn't happen.

The most mysterious of mental experiences, dreaming was not studied in true experimental manner until the 1950s when University of Chicago physiologist and sleep researcher Nathaniel Kleitman discovered rapid eye movements (REM) as indicators of the dream state. This stunning research and subsequent studies have established dreaming not only as a nightly occurrence but as a necessity for healthy mental functioning.

A *psychic* dream, like those discussed in previous chapters, is relatively rare. It is usually a realistic scene; its contents are literal; its message is memorable. It seems real, and sooner or later it actually comes true. A *symbolic* dream, however, is a different, more common experience. It does not come true in any literal sense, but it draws images from our experience, rearranges them in fanciful new ways. Whether we remember them or not, symbolic dreams are uncensored dramas starring our most powerful emotions, with petty attitudes in supporting roles. Without a script or director, it is pure improvisation—sometimes Theater of the Absurd. In any case, there is a performance every night.

In Freudian terms, our *ego* is the sensible part of us that regulates and keeps the lid on the *id,* our unbridled emotions. The *id* is the bundle of emotions that we are when we are born, all desire and no knowledge of the constraints of the world. It is the *id* that runs rampant in our dreams. Our *superego* is the body of shoulds and shouldn'ts that we learn from our parents and from society. At its best, it is our conscience; at its worst, it is a body of obsolete rules and unwarranted guilt. The fear often generated by our most heated dreams is the discomfort of our *ego* caught in the middle, in the conflict between our *superego* and our *id.* The *superego* seeks to repress the *id* and to keep our self-image intact. At the same time, with maturity and growth, the *ego* tries to understand by degrees what little it can of our *id,* to accept its hidden emotions, and to satisfy its desires in a way that will work in the real world.

Dreams are the interface between our *id* and *ego,* between our passions and our rational self. The *ego,* the consciousness of our waking self, both seeks and fears to capture the dream figures. For what you capture, you have to care for while you keep it restrained. The ambivalence we feel about knowing the contents of our subconscious is one reason dream images are usually perceived by the *ego* in disguised form in symbolic dreams. The other reason is simply that the "characters" of dreams are raw emotions. The rational self can conceive, remember, and manipulate entities best in the form of sense images—visual pictures, shapes, colors, odors, temperatures, sounds, for example—and words, the symbols that fix the concepts and make them recordable, communicable. The rational self simply cannot grasp a disembodied emotion. It must give the emotion a "handle," something to catch hold of, a visual image, or a name. So in dreams the emotions may be represented by recognizable people, visual scenes, palpable objects, familiar words, and events rearranged.

Fortunately, we do have words that state abstract emotion. These are words learned latest in language development, the most difficult to understand and use. If you have ever tried to explain an abstract word (like *jealousy* or *chagrin*) to a child, you will notice that you cannot easily explain it except by saying, "It's how you feel when . . .," and you give the child a concrete example with real people and objects. You are doing for the unsophisticated child what your dreams do for you.

Psychic dreams, especially sharply detailed psychic dreams, are usually undisguised reflections of reality that we are ready to face, though sometimes with difficulty. Many, perhaps most dreams, however, are disguised presentations of emotional reality, whose symbols require interpretation.

One dreamer tried to describe to me a recurring dream she has had since early childhood. She told me that the feature of that dream was always the same, that she always recognized it, that she was always terrified by it, but that even immediately after waking in fright she could not hold an image of it in her mind, much less describe it in words. It was something swirling, something following her, slowly, inexorably, through a situation she could not understand. In an attempt to think about it, she had mentally pictured it as an outboard motor, without the boat, coming through water. The motor was following her as she fled, turning when she turned, so that she could not escape. The motor was passing by long strands of seaweed floating in the water like crepe-paper streamers. She tried to remember the real dream, but she always ended up thinking about a motor and seaweed, an unsatisfactory substitution. How could she respond in her waking life to an outboard motor and seaweed? She knew she wanted to do something constructive about the real emotional threat she could not grasp, but she didn't know where to begin. This dreamer did not actually figure this out until the dream symbols changed to something she could grasp more clearly, but then she knew the new symbols represented the same emotions as the old outboard motor and seaweed had.

Most dreams are remembered by the waking mind in their distorted motor-and-seaweed form. We must use special techniques to find out what psychological elements they represent.

You may have seen books or lists that purport to tell you the meaning of certain dream elements. I have recently browsed through two of them, one a booklet distributed as a promotion for a cosmetics firm in the 1920s, the other a modern dream-interpretation book. The first lists several reasonable associations such as a *cradle,* meaning a *child,* and *catching a fish,* meaning *success.* The yellowed pamphlet also suggests associations harder to fathom: *dominoes* means *indiscretion,* an *apricot* means *calamity, nettles* mean *prosperity.*

The modern dream symbol book seems equally arbitrary, instructing us that *donkeys* mean *good luck in love.* The dream image *combing,* according to the same book, means *loss.* Perhaps, however, the author is a man who is losing his hair at every comb stroke, and for him, therefore, combing is a symbol of loss. *Combing,* to another dreamer, a woman, for example, might mean sensuality or sexuality or letting her hair down. It all depends on one's individual emotional experience.

There are words that we all think we understand metaphorically. *Home,* for instance, for most people means comfort, love, or security. I have known people, however, who strongly associate home with criticism and feelings of inferiority. In interpreting these persons' dreams, we cannot simply plug in the values of comfort, love, and security. Home may mean the secure, loving place they want or the distressing situation where they feel the worst about themselves. Only the dreamer knows the emotions he feels about *home* in a particular dream.

To understand dream symbolism, I offer you a method I have developed over the years, by adapting the methods of Freud, Jung, and other psychologists, combining them with my own insights, and, finally, streamlining them to fit the needs of busy people.

Here are the steps in my method of dream analysis:

A. **Tell the dream to someone or record it.**
B. **Identify the elements.**
C. **Apply word association to each dream element.**
D. **Divide the dream into dramatic scenes.**
E. **Divide the word associations into corresponding scenes.**
F. **Interpret each scene according to its word associations to find the situation, the conflict, the climax, and the resolution.**
G. **Make a positive response.**
H. **(Optional) Use personification techniques to further explore a dream element.**

Let us now take one step at a time and see how these steps work for some actual dreams.

A. **Tell the dream and record it.** Tell it naturally and write it down exactly as you are telling it. Let the writing flow like your thoughts; try not to let the writing itself be intrusive. Better still, tell it to someone else who will write it down for you. Include not only main ideas, but sense images, funny little details, expressions, and asides. Allow yourself to return to the dream mood as much as possible and relate as much detail and emotion as you can.

B. Identify the elements. Underline and list separately each dream element, that is, each person, place, action, and descriptive word or phrase.

C. Apply word association to each dream element. Say each element one by one in order or have a partner read each of them to you. Respond by saying the first thing that comes into your mind upon hearing the element. Your response may be a word, a phrase, or a whole story. Do not concern yourself with logic or propriety. Let yourself get back into the mood of the dream and be emotionally affected by it, but do not limit yourself to your dream. You may answer something you think of from your childhood, from the work you plan for tomorrow, from a book you read, from anywhere, even your wildest fantasies. Especially, do not think at this time about the meaning of the dream. Concentrate on your response to the element. Write it down.

For example, a dreamer had told me: "I dreamed I was sitting on the *porch* with my brother. . . ." When I read the word *porch* back to the dreamer for association, the dreamer said, "When we were children, it was cool and nice on the porch, very relaxed." I wrote down *cool, nice,* and *relaxed* as the feel of the image *porch.* Another dreamer who used the word *porch* in a dream analysis responded to the word in a different way: "My porch is falling down; the boards are rotten." I wrote down beside the word *porch* the associations *falling down* and *rotten.*

It is fairly easy to write down an association when it is in the form of a one- or two-word reply. When you relate an entire story, however, you or your partner must pick out the key association from the story. For example, a ladder appeared in one man's dream. An expected association for this element might be *rescue*—a short answer, to the point, and bearing an associated emotion, relief. This man, however, responded in the following way to the word *ladder*.

When I was a small boy, I slept in a loft room and the only way up was a ladder. The people who bought the house from us put in a staircase. I hated that, but it showed that they couldn't use the ladder easily. Neither could my mother or father. I was the only one who could zip up that ladder. That was my special talent.

For the man's *ladder* association, I wrote down *my special talent*. In the dream, the man used the ladder, the special talent, to get somewhere. The real-life useful property of the ladder was not lost; it was just shown to be more specific by the association with the dreamer's special talent.

Another example of extracting a summary idea from an anecdotal word association comes from a dream a man had about an old girl friend, Kay. The word from the dream was *birthday*. The man responded like this.

The last time I talked to Kay, it was just before her birthday. We had broken up, but I still cared for her. I called her for old time's sake and said, "Since it's your birthday, could I take you out to dinner?" She said she'd see—something like "if no one else has anything planned for me . . ." She said she'd call and let me know. She never called. I resented that. She could have just said "No."

The summary emotion of the anecdote was *resentment*, and that is what I wrote beside the element *birthday*.

When the dreamer has described an emotion by name, the deciphering has already been done, and no word association is necessary. For example, if you say, "I was afraid of the dog," the word *afraid*, already an emotion, needs no further interpretation. The *dog*, however—the object of the fear— must be explored through word association. Similarly, when you say, "I felt very relieved, and then I woke up," you are stating the emotion engendered by the *resolution* of the di-

lemma; the word *relieved* does not need to be translated by word association.

The freedom you give your mind to wander while it considers a word allows your unconscious to tell you what emotions are associated with a given symbol without the constraints of moral judgment or logic. You may carry around subconsciously the moral censorship of your parent, your *superego,* that says, "Don't talk that way" or "You *know* you don't really mean that." You may also have been trained by family, education, or profession to show only your rational side. You may be further inhibited by fear of revealing yourself even to yourself. Responding in word association without regard for what will later be the interpretation of the association is the only way to get at the truth.

For illustration, here is an entire dream with the dreamer's word associations. An investment counselor asked me to help him interpret this dream about himself and his wife, Margaret.

Margaret and I wanted to go down the shore across the Delaware Bridge to Atlantic City, but this time there was a tremendous flood on the Philadelphia side. The water was swirling and dark.

Margaret said, "Come on; the water is not that deep."

It was up to my chin. I was afraid we were going to drown.

She said, "It won't get any deeper. Come on." I was leading, but I didn't want to go on and she was urging me.

We were struggling up on the bridge. The water was up to my nose.

When I asked this man to associate with the word *shore,* he told me he dreamed of the shore because his wife was actually there right then and she had called him the night before. He's right, of course, that his wife's call from the vacation spot was probably the reason for the appearance of the shore imagery in his dream. That logical connection does not, however, tell us the meaning of the *shore* as a dream element. Here are his associations, once he got the hang of the technique.

shore   happiness, relaxation
Delaware Bridge   I have to go over it to get to the shore
Atlantic City   wicker chairs, pushcarts, all the women in their furs
flood   I almost drowned once
Philadelphia side   memories, a nice home
swirling   fear
dark water   fear
"Come on"   my wife is being braver than I
not that deep   I didn't believe
my chin   that's when I get in trouble
drowning   it doesn't hurt—that's what I remember about my drowning
struggling   I couldn't fight
up on the bridge   safety

The dreamer's response to *Atlantic City* was three more concrete images. I wanted to dig further here. After I had finished the list, I went back *Atlantic City* and asked him to associate again by saying, "What does *Atlantic City* mean to you?" and "How do you feel about the wicker chairs, the pushcarts, and the women in furs?" The scene of Atlantic City made him think of "the opulence that we didn't have," a phrase that brings up the issue of affluence and lack of it not apparent in the first associations.

Sometimes I make a second list of associations to the right of the first in which I try to put more abstract, emotional associations than those first given. Other times I just ask for an expression of more emotional significance as I go along and add the second response to the first in one column. Some people readily abstract meanings from concrete images, and others have to be led. Often making a second list by asking the dreamer to associate with the words in the first list instead of the words in the dream frees them from the dream content, not in mood, but just enough to stop trying to have the answers "make sense."

An examination of this man's associations with the words in his dream suggested that some old fear of disaster was preventing him from reaching happiness and relaxation, even though his wife was confident. The man said that, as a matter of fact, he was struggling with a decision. He and his wife wanted to retire. He knew he had saved enough money and knew how to make it grow, but an inexplicable fear that something would go wrong and he'd be without money prevented him from making the decision. His wife was confident and was urging him to go ahead, but so far he was clinging to his fear.

D. Divide the dream into dramatic scenes. The meaning of the dream is not often obvious from the word associations, which form a disjointed list of emotions and relationships. The next step after word association, therefore, is to divide the dream and then its associations into scenes like those of a play.

The critically acclaimed playwright Daniel Sklar once said that he chooses the subjects of his plays according to two criteria. One, the subject will emanate from some experience in his life that has stayed with him, coming back time and time again to haunt him. Two, the experience must be one he doesn't understand. One of Sklar's plays, for example, explores fictionally a humiliation he felt as a young baseball player when he misread his coach's signal and foolishly tried to steal home. Another play was inspired by a panic attack the playwright inexplicably experienced in a large supermarket.

Our dreams seem a lot like Sklar's plays. They are dramas with settings and conflicts, acts and scenes. They deal in images from our experiences, ones that have stayed with us emotionally and that we don't understand. To organize them into coherent thoughts, we, like the playwright, have to divide them into acts or scenes.

Here is the dream of a thirty-eight-year-old woman

named Charlotte. I divided the dream, as dramatic as any play, into paragraphs that represent separate scenes.

1 | A good friend had moved to Colorado. I went to look at her house, which was up for sale. I was going to buy it. My husband and I looked at all the rooms and saw the potential.

2 | In one room there were three women. One was Oriental and one was blond, Swiss. The third, a nurse, had a hypodermic needle and was going to kill the Oriental woman by injection. She explained to me why she was going to kill the Oriental and how it was all right; it would be painless. I was just standing there.

3 | All of a sudden I made eye contact with the Oriental woman right at the moment of injection. I try to stop it, but it is too late. She does not die easily as I was told, but with great agony. The whole time she was dying, her eyes were pleading with me to save her. The nurse injected the Swiss woman, too, and I didn't try to help her.

4 | Then we went on calmly looking at rooms.

In dividing this dream into scenes, I used an intuitive feel for dramatic units. I did not interrupt episodes that seemed to have unity. There are other principles and clues to the divisions of dream stories into scenes.

The first scene presents the setting and the initial situation—in this case, looking at a house to buy. An introduction of new characters usually mark the beginning of another scene—here, the encounter with the nurses. Narrative words like *all of a sudden* and *then* usually indicate a shift in scene. These words mark the beginning of scenes three and four in this dream. I had some doubt about whether to begin a new scene with the death of the Swiss woman, but decided that the second death was just another view, an "instant replay" of the death of the Oriental woman. I was helped in this decision by the fact that in the word associations the dreamer made, she identified both the Oriental and the Swiss woman as *beauty.* They were almost the same characters abstractly speaking, and their two deaths were one event played twice. The word, *then,* marked the opening of another scene, similar to the first scene but with a new horror not present in the innocent opening.

All together there are four scenes. In my experience, as in the findings of famed psychiatrist and dream theorist Carl Jung, four is the number of different dramatic scenes in a complete dream. Jung called the four parts the *statement of place,* the *exposition,* the *culmination,* and the *solution.* In theatrical terms, the four parts could be called the setting, the conflict, the climax, and the denouement. For symbolic interpretation, I prefer the terms the *situation,* the *problem,* the *working out to a climax,* and the *resolution.* I use a variety of words to help the dreamer identify the meaning of the parts. Sometimes I call the second scene the conflict, the dilemma, or even the question. The third scene may be the crisis. The final part often contains the answer or the solution. Whatever you call the parts, look for four. Although sometimes I see more or I see less at first, in the final analysis I often find that I have failed to notice shifts that were important or I have not recognized that two parts go together and should be combined.

The last scene, the *resolution,* is the part of the dream that, if taken seriously, holds the potential benefit of the dream, for it contains the suggestion for an active solution or a change of attitude. Symbolic dreams, like psychic dreams, are only as good as the dreamer's response.

You could divide the dream into scenes immediately after you have recorded the dream in writing and before your word association. I prefer, however, to get the word associations first, while the dreamer is in the emotional state of the dream. As in the case of the dream above, I may see things in the word associations that help me divide the dream according to a feel of emotional unity.

E. Divide the word associations into corresponding scenes. The next step is to divide the associations into the same scenes as the dream that inspired them. Draw brackets around associations that correspond to the dream scenes. Here are the associations Charlotte made for her house/nurse/injection dream which I have bracketed according to scene.

1. *friend* soulmate, the bond between us was our agreement on feminist and theological issues

   Colorado I went to college there, wide open, free

   her house on Taylor Road, a more socially correct address, but it was not different from mine—cluttered with bicycles, kids, dogs

   buy it "I'll buy that" means I'll accept or agree to that

   rooms "many rooms in my mansion" or "I am preparing a room for thee in my mansion"

   potential my potential—I was doing cancer research before I married, I might have done great things

2. *Oriental* darker, beauty—beauty that comes from inner strength

   blond lighter

   Swiss beauty, accomplishment and peace. The Swiss manufacture, host peace talks, and maintain the beauty of their country all at the same time.

   the third the one in charge, head

   nurse dependency, foreboding, coldness, correctness, follow the rules. I hate nurses. Women who follow a man's orders regardless of themselves. But also compassion and service. That's another kind of nurse.

   hypodermic lethal

   needle death, mercy killing

   kill murder

standing there   I had potential to stop it but preferred to maintain my composure

3 *eye contact*   intimacy, humanity, communication
at the very moment   time for decision
I tried to stop it   exerting authority, assertiveness
too late   too late in life
doesn't die easily   desire to survive
as I was told   what my mother, society tell me
great agony   great agony
eyes   communication
pleading   making wishes known
save her   cry for help
nurse   the one who followed the rules
injected   killed
Swiss woman   valuable life
I didn't try to help   doing nothing

4 *calmly*   inappropriate calm, acting as if nothing is happening, it's horrifying to me now, but in the dream it seemed to be what was expected
looking at rooms   domestic life, marriage

F. Interpret each scene according to its word associations . . . After you have divided the dream and the associations into four scenes, translate the associations of each scene into a coherent thought, the dramatic point of that scene. I, as the interpreter/partner/therapist, often draw together the bracketed associations myself and present the thought to the dreamer for her reaction. Other times I ask the dreamer to make a thought herself from reading her associations bracketed into scenes. To help her focus the sometimes disjointed associations, I ask certain questions for each scene, which your partner can ask you or you can ask yourself.

The question I ask to facilitate interpretation of the first scene, the *situation,* is "What is this dream about?" The opening of Charlotte's dream is about the survival of her potential within her domestic situation, she thinks.

To interpret the *conflict,* I ask, "What is the dilemma?" Charlotte answers: "The rules of correctness and submission to men are killing what is beautiful in me, the other side of me, my desire for accomplishment and service." If I had asked, "What is the question?" the dreamer would likely have said, "Are the rules of correctness and submission to men killing what is beautiful in me, the other side of me, my desire for accomplishment and service?"

"What happens next?" I ask to prompt Charlotte to interpret how the struggle *works out to a climax* in scene three. "It is time for decision, or it may be too late in life to respond to the cry for help from the beautiful desire within me. This inner need dies with great agony, not calmly as society expects it to. It wants to live, is stating its desire to survive."

"Then what is the *resolution?"* I ask. "I should see the life-as-usual domestic scene as inappropriate passivity," Charlotte concluded.

Charlotte was the mother of three children, one of them a teenager, the others close behind. She had given up a career as a biochemical researcher to have a family. She said she did not regret the decision. Besides, it was not the first time she had turned away from her desired course. Her scientific training had been what her parents and teachers had steered her toward. She herself had always wanted to spend her life pursuing the most important ideas in life—those of God, man, and their relationship. "I have always been a philosophical dreamer," she recalls.

Her desires translated into career with difficulty, however. The ministry was closed to women at that time, and theology did not seem to lead to a suitable career for her. So science had been her course for a while.

At the time of the dream, however, she was discontent with a life of "doing for" her family when they were old enough to do for themselves. It was not motherhood itself that bothered her—she loved her children—it was society's expectations of motherhood. Besides her family, she was intensely interested in social issues and was doing a lot of church work. There was a constant conflict between her desire to do such work in a more formalized way and the pressure to stay home and fix regular meals, supervise homework, and perform other wifely duties. She perceived that the pressure to continue her role of wife and mother in an exclusive way was killing her potential to serve society in a major way and to receive the rewards of such service. The pressure came to some extent from parents, in-laws, friends, her husband, and society, whose consensus was "what I had been told"—that desire for a service career will die painlessly according to the rules of marriage and motherhood.

What the dream showed Charlotte more clearly was that she was *choosing* to let her potential be "killed" rather than face the confrontation with family. The inhibitions were not only pressure from others but also an unwillingness on her part to act on her desire. She was standing impassively by while her desire was pleading with silent eyes to be saved. As Charlotte said in the fourth part of her word association, the calm inaction horrified her.

G. Make a positive response. As is the case with a psychic dream, an interpreted dream without an appropriate positive response is a mere curiosity, a parlor game, a fortune from a Chinese cookie.

The positive response arises out of the lesson of the dream. The dreamer, awake, rational, and able to deal with the realities of life, must decide if and how to respond to the dream lesson.

Charlotte began to think more urgently about how she could save the part of herself that was being killed. As in the dream, she had to consider her time limitations. She was not getting any younger. She passionately wanted to pursue a career in theology through which she could make a significant contribution to society. "This was my authentic call-ing," she said. "It was not just the profession that I wanted; it was the essence of who I am."

Charlotte researched programs that would give her knowledge and credentials to make social impact quickly. She is now, three years after the dream, enrolled in a post-graduate school of theology and has chosen her studies ac-cording to specific professional goals. To attend classes, she has shifted a lot of the responsibilities for the children's care to the children themselves. As a consequence, they seem more mature and none the worse for the change.

Charlotte took her dream especially seriously because she has only had four dreams in her life vivid enough to re-member. Each of them preceded and influenced major changes in her life.

H. Use personification techniques to further explore a dream element. Sometimes the meaning of a dream, even after you have followed the procedures above, will still be unclear. Or perhaps you are still unsure of the significance of one major dream element that seems the most important emotionally or the most puzzling. Perhaps you have ana-lyzed the problem presented in the dream, but it seems to be missing the fourth scene, the *resolution*. To focus better on one part of a dream or to free yourself further from the inhibitions of logic, I recommend a personification tech-nique that I have borrowed from Gestalt psychologists. You simply pretend to be the puzzling or significant element. It can be a person, an animal, or an inanimate object. Choosing to play the unaccustomed role of an inanimate object is es-pecially likely to give you a different perspective of your dream. While playing the part of this element, let yourself go, let your remarks flow without inhibition. Be totally honest about any feelings of which you are aware, including body sensations.

One woman dreamed that she and her sister went swim-ming in a lake. She didn't want to go beyond the rope that divided the shallow water from the deep. Her sister, however, went beyond the rope and she followed. The woman recognized the rope as some sort of inhibition or fear. To get a better idea of what the inhibition was, she played the part of the rope, letting it tell its purpose through her. This technique helped her overcome a habit of unnecessary self-restriction.

Another woman dreamed about this event at a family get-together.

We were all together—my nieces, nephews, uncles, aunts, parents— around a modern spa-like building with a bar. They were touring the building, looking at the showers, etc. Mom was cooking in the kitchen. When older people came, they were sent to the kitchen, and when younger people came, they were sent to the pool area. The young people were hanging up huge lights. One fell. People kept on arriving, the older going to the kitchen and the younger to the pool. I felt weird.

The steps of dream interpretation turned up nothing meaningful enough to explain the weirdness the dreamer felt. I asked her to personify the light that fell. She said, "I'm hanging here, and the others are so straight, but I'm going to fall. Everything is too perfect. Why am *I* going to fall? But I'm not going to break."

This personification technique introduced the idea of too much perfection. The dreamer admitted that she tried to be perfect and was afraid of what would happen if she made a mistake. The pressure to be perfect, she felt, was particularly strong on her in family situations. The lesson of the dream was that if she did fall from perfection once, she wouldn't break, no one would pay much attention, and people would go on much as usual. The sense of relief the dreamer expressed after this interpretation confirmed its meaning.

Sometimes it's hard to know what to say during a personification technique because it's hard to talk to thin air. The solution may be to play the parts of two elements alternately. When the two elements talk to each other in such a dialogue, a tension may arise between them, and then perhaps an agreement. Here is the imaginative dialogue between two kittens, the most vivid elements in a man's lengthy, complicated dream about his girl friend. The man had dreamed that, as his friend was getting ready to leave, she gathered up kittens in her arms. Two of them she had left on the floor were jumping up and down trying to get her to pick them up. Here's how the man personified the kittens.

KITTEN ONE: She's got to take us. We've got to persuade her. Jump higher, jump higher.

KITTEN TWO: She's going to leave anyway. Our best bet is to be independent. Learn how to get along without her. Find some other people here or some food for ourselves. We can be independent.

KITTEN ONE: I'm weaker than you. I don't buy this independence. It's too depressing and scary. I'm going to make every effort to get into her arms and cling to her.

KITTEN TWO: Even if she does take us now, she may leave us later. The dilemma will just go on and on. We may as well become independent now.

KITTEN ONE: I'm so small. She'll think I'm so cute, she'll keep me.

The kittens in the dream, both jumping up, seemed to be of a single mind: They both wanted to go with the girl friend. Obviously, this personification technique reveals the dreamer's enormous ambivalence, a struggle between wanting to be emotionally independent and allowing himself to be vulnerable, in love with this woman.

Ambivalence can also be explored by personification using the two parts of the same person. In Gestalt psychology, this is called the "two-chair" technique. A dreamer named Susan, for example, who had identified two parts of her personality in a dream, used the personification technique to explore the polarity between the proper side of her and the spontaneous side of her. The dreamer sat in one chair as the Proper Susan and talked to the imagined Spontaneous Susan in the other chair. She then changed chairs, became Spontaneous Susan, and continued the conversation.

Thus the personification technique gives the dreamer a lot more information than the dream itself gave while keeping the metaphor of the dream intact. The dream in this way often *works out to a climax* and the dreamer achieves a sense of *resolution*.

The sense of resolution is a sign that you have successfully completed the interpretation of the dream. The interpretation "strikes a chord," "rings a bell," "feels right." You will know.

I often can tell when the interpretation is "right" when I see a certain expression on the dreamer's face or notice a change in the way he holds his body that says, "There. That's it."

Sometimes success does not come easily. Sometimes people become very emotional during the dream interpretation, indicating the importance of an issue that has come out in the open. The point at which a dreamer begins to experience discomfort gives a clue to some issue the dreamer is not ready to face easily. The seemingly fictitious nature of the dream, however, allows the dreamer to discuss the matter without the degree of pain likely to be experienced in a more direct confrontation.

The following dream represents an issue that caused the woman dreamer a great deal of discomfort and could probably not have been discussed except in dream terms.

1   I went to see a psychologist, whom I'd read about in the paper. He was an expert in something like sports psychology, and I thought I was there to get some information for a friend who had need of this specialty. I sat in the waiting room.

When the psychologist came in, I stood up, and he greeted me in a friendly manner.

2 Then, as he passed me, he patted my bottom. That annoyed me less than it amazed me that he would be so unprofessional. He went back to his office, said he'd be with me in a few minutes.

3 I hadn't planned my conversation with him at all. I felt very cool and confident about presenting my request for professional advice on behalf of my friend. But while I was waiting, I thought, "Well, I'll think about how I'll present my questions." I then realized I couldn't remember what area the newspaper said the psychologist specialized in, even though I had the clippings with me. I began to think it had something to do with discipline. I began to wonder why I ever wanted to talk to him. I couldn't remember anything about why I was there and felt very distressed.

4 I thought, "I'll just leave his office and disappear, and when he gets back, he'll never know what happened. I won't be embarrassed by my forgetting, and I'll try to just wipe the episode from my mind." But I wondered if he would charge me for the appointment hour. I also doubted if this solution was right. Then Janet, a friend of mine, walked through the waiting room, and I was going to tell her my dilemma and ask her opinion to ease my distress. I woke up.

The dreamer in real life had been seeing a therapist. The one in the dream, however, seemed to be unknown to her. Here are her word associations.

1 *psychologist*   professional person can help me develop self-esteem
read in newspaper   validated
information for a friend   the old "my-friend-has-this-problem" routine

sat in waiting room I had waited a long time to find someone to help me with my problem.
he came in at last, such a relief
I stood up I was more than ready
friendly he was so supportive.

2 *passed me* unexpected
patted my bottom sexual overtones
not so much annoyed as amazed I was surprised to like it
unprofessional it reduced his value to me as a giver of good advice
to his office he stayed in his professional role
said he'd be with me he was available professionally
in a few minutes on his time schedule

3 *hadn't planned* thought I knew what to do
cool and confident my ability to communicate
plan while I was waiting I realized I needed to think
couldn't remember the specialty the point of the meeting
discipline what I'm weak in
couldn't remember why confused, confidence shaken

4 *I'll leave, disappear* I wanted escape
he'll never know I won't have to face him
avoid embarrassment avoid embarrassment
forget I won't have to face it myself
charge for hour wasted money
not right wrong for relationship
Janet a friend who listens to my problems and is objective—I trust her advice

This dreamer interpreted the *situation* from scene one: "I have been going to a therapist, who is wonderful. I'm so grateful because he makes me feel good about myself for the first time. I'm relieved and sorry it took so long to get help."

The *problem* developed in scene two with the sexual overtones. The dreamer explained to herself: "Actually he has never, ever done anything with sexual overtones. I'm the one who feels the sexual attraction because I can't help it when he is so kind to me. He is completely professional. These sexual feelings are making it hard to carry on the therapy, and I can hardly stand the wait between appointments."

Here's how the problem was *worked out* in scene three. "I am confused. I feel like I'm losing my mind. My original problem seems to be getting worse. I thought I had a handle on it, but I get so distressed and confused. I'm not disciplining myself very well to go on with life between sessions. My new confidence is shaken."

The *resolution* came in scene four. She considered escaping to avoid embarrassment by not facing the therapist with the issue and not facing it herself. That would be, however, a waste of the money being spent on therapy. It was also a dishonest thing to do to her relationship with the therapist, which had been built on openness. Telling her understanding, objective friend in the dream seemed the solution. The dreamer then realized that the friend was, in effect, the therapist.

Telling the therapist about her troubling sexual feelings was a very difficult, humiliating thing to do, but that was the dreamer's *positive response* to the dream. It brought an enormous relief. The therapist was understanding, accepted her feelings, and discussed them unemotionally. The distress, which the dreamer had thought originated in the problem for which she sought help, went away. She then knew the distress about her sexual feelings was the cause of the pain that had replaced the initial relief of therapy. When she discussed the feelings with the therapist, this distress went away; the sexual feelings themselves lingered a while and then subsided.

Interpreting a child's dream with the child can give a parent a clue to some of the issues in the child's life that he may not express otherwise. John, a ten-year-old boy, dreamed the following dream.

1　I was in a football game. I was the quarterback. The head coach said I could be the head coach for the Superbowl instead of the quarterback. We won the Superbowl, and afterward all the reporters came up and asked me all about my life. I told them all about all the sports I had played.

Later, on the TV news, I watched me playing soccer and baseball and running and that season of football. I remembered doing all the things I saw on TV.

2　I was walking somewhere with my friends. We went in somewhere and came out with all these bags of money. We were walking down the street carrying the bags by chains on them. We didn't steal the money in the dream, but it felt as if we had stolen it because we were hiding behind trees and things.

There was the river. We waited for all the cars to go by so no one would see us; then we crossed the road to the river. There was a man who went down the bank to the river. There was a box down in the river and the man put his head in it; there were spikes in the box.

There was a mansion beside the road. We left the money outside and a kid to watch it and went into the mansion. We walked down the hall, hoping no one would see us. Then some people came in, so about three of us jumped up on the chandelier all squooshed together. One hid behind a curtain; I hid behind a chest of drawers.

3　The people started fixing dinner. They served the people in the dining room. The people eating dinner saw my baseball cap on my head sticking up above the chest of drawers and said, "Who is that?" But then they didn't seem to care that I was there. They said, "That's OK."

4 | The telephone rang and someone pushed a button to make it stop. That was a signal. I thought I was hiding behind the chest of drawers, but when I looked at it, it was just a board I was holding up. The board had two eagle posts on it. I went outside, and the guy outside motioned us to come. I began to whistle for the others. The guys jumped down from the chandelier and out of the windows and came with me.

These are the free associations John made with the elements of the dream.

1 | *football*   I played, I like it
quarterback   what I want to be
head coach   what I want to be too. The head coach tells the
   quarterback the plays.
Superbowl   where I'd like to play
reporters   being in the news
my life   it's been fun
sports   all the things I've done
news on TV   an outstanding person

2 | *bags of money*   rich, can afford things
walking down the street   going somewhere
chains   put in jail
hide behind trees   hide and seek
river   fun and scared together
waited for cars to go by   no one like the police could see us
box   a cube, a jail cell
put head in box   in jail
spikes in box   execution
mansion   rich
walking down hall   going in
people came in   scared and want to hide
chandeliers   just chandeliers
chest of drawers   a place to put things
curtain   alert, watchful that no one could get me

3 | *fixing dinner*   something to eat
served it in dining room   I wanted to join them
baseball cap   good times playing ball
"Who is that?"   scared
They didn't seem to care that I was there   relief
"That's OK."   It's OK to be there.

4 | *telephone ringing*   a signal from the guy outside
pressed the button   no one answered it
board   I was trying to look over the top, but since I was holding it up, it just came down.
eagle posts   stands for strength
whistling   signal to others, confident
jumped down, came with me   they were following me

What's the *situation?* "I am a leader and an outstanding person, and this is made public."

What's the *problem?* "I feel guilty like I don't deserve to have what I have. I am afraid I'll be punished. I feel uncomfortable in the place of success, as if someone will find me out. I have to hide."

So *how does it work out?* "When people discover me, that I am talented in sports and everything, they don't mind that I'm in there with the successful people, and they let me stay. I'm relieved. I find out what I'm hiding behind is really my strength."

And what is the *resolution?* "When the time is right, I can be the leader again."

During the discussion, John indicated that he saw great significance in the part about the chest he was hiding behind changing into a board with eagles, which he was holding up. If he were to use *personification* techniques, he would personify this board or the eagles. John observed that passing on the telephone signal to his friends in the mansion was a lot like being a quarterback in the first part of the dream, taking directions from the coach and passing it on to the players. He also observed, when discussing the news broadcast, that some of his friends called his pleasure in his accomplishments boasting.

He felt the dream interpretation really "clicked" in his life and showed him he was an outstanding person and he didn't have to feel his success didn't belong to him. He decided, however, that it might be good for him to refrain from publicizing his success too much; maybe spreading the news was what started the feelings of not deserving success. His *positive response* was a decision for renewed confidence in himself as a person along with an attempt at greater modesty.

John's perception of "clicking" is a sign that the dream has been successfully worked out. An "Aha!" expression frequently lights up the dreamer's face when the interpretation rings true.

In Chapter Six I suggested that any dream that was literally possible could be regarded as a potential psychic dream. A positive response to the content of the dream would prove beneficial whether or not the dream came true. But *any* dream, literally possible or not, can be interpreted symbolically. The overlap between the actual event and the interpreted meaning is often surprising.

Here, for example, is a dream that had the potential to come true in a literal sense. The dreamer, a free-lance writer, could have regarded it as a psychic dream, considered what she could do to benefit from it, and responded accordingly. She could also have analyzed it as a symbolic dream or, better still, done both. She would have discovered that the message of either approach was the same and responded positively.

The writer, who had just turned in a story to her editor, was second-guessing herself, reading and rereading the piece in her mind. She was in agony because in the end, as she was going into the last rewrite before the deadline, it all seemed so terribly wrong, so pointless, so boring, so much like a laundry list. She had, of course, at times during the writing been excited by her own ideas, but in the end she believed she'd failed. She imagined that she would be fired; she wondered if she should give up writing. She called a friend and poured out her misgivings. Her friend said, "After all the experience you've had, and the successful writing you've done, maybe this isn't your best piece, but it couldn't be *bad*. Remember, you always feel this way right after you finish a piece, and they all turn out to be fine." The writer was unconvinced and went home wringing her hands.

That night she dreamed that she went into her editor's office. The editor was leaning back in his swivel chair with his hands clasped behind his head. He leaned forward and took her hand. "I really liked that piece," he said warmly. Continuing to hold her hand in his quite naturally, he went on. "It was good writing. I'm very happy about it." She felt the warmth of his hand, and she was amazed by the warmth of his praise. Relief ran over her.

When she woke up remembering the dream she discovered that her hand was exceptionally warm. She thought this warmth would fade immediately when her hand was withdrawn from under the covers, but the warmth lasted as she went about her morning routine. She remembers consciously wishing the dream were a psychic dream and all this were true. "But it can't be," she told herself, "because the article was really bad. And besides, editors do not hold writers' hands, especially not this editor." She began to torment herself all over again.

Note that the writer thought ever so briefly about the possibility of the dream being psychic and rejected the idea. She also did not analyze it as a symbolic dream. We, however, know enough about dreams to see the meaning of this one.

The editor represents the actual editor, editors in general, or all those people who judge her work and whose approval is the key to her success. His office and his chair are the trappings of his official capacity. The editor's response means acceptance; the warm hand, a sign of warm approval; the length of the hand holding, long-term approval. It is a confidence dream. The response that seems appropriate would be for the writer to relax, take pleasure in her success, and get on with her next project with confidence.

After three days of worry, the writer was called into the editor's office. He was leaning back in his swivel chair, as always with his hands behind his head. He had an unusually cheerful smile on his face. This made her nervous.

"I really liked your story," he said.

"It was awkward in spots," the writer said apologetically.

"No, it was really gracefully written. I am really happy about it."

Gracefully written! she exclaimed to herself, amazed. He has never said anything like that before. She felt embarrassed, as if he were making fun of her, but she recognized the dream. *When is he going to hold my hand?* she wondered.

The editor's hands, however, stayed behind his head as she sat down in a nearby chair. There was a knock at the door and the editor of another magazine came in. She had worked for this editor, too. In fact, she had the same feelings about him as the editor whose office she was in. The two editors were counterparts, equivalents.

The *visiting* editor spoke to her warmly, took her hand in greeting, and didn't let go. He held it in his very warm hand, perfectly naturally, for a long time while he joked with his colleague and with her. She felt wonderful and *accepted.* It was not until she left and was walking happily across the parking lot in the cold that she noticed that her hand was unnaturally warm, with a heat that lingered.

The writer had caused herself three days of unnecessary torment by not accepting the dream either as psychic or as symbolic. She had missed the immediate benefits of the message of the dream—accept your success instead of mentally discrediting your work—and the positive response—relax, enjoy, go forward with confidence. The interpreted message was sound; the actual playing out of the dream reinforced its truth, which the writer is belatedly enjoying.

In another dream, which illustrates the parallel course of symbolic and psychic dreams, a man named Tony dreamed the bridge in his hometown collapsed. That was all. When he awoke, he realized the dream was literally possible, so he asked himself what he should do if it were actually psychic. He rejected the idea of warning the people in charge of bridges in that county because he thought they would not pay any attention to a psychic dream. He decided instead to call a friend in his hometown to advise her to stay off the bridge.

At the same time Tony decided to analyze the dream for symbolic meaning. Here are his associations:

bridge   connection
hometown   old friends
collapsed   broken, death

As a drama, this dream would have to be a one-act play. It's hard to divide something so short into scenes, but the meaning is clear: Connections with old friends are broken. Death lurks in the background either as a reality or as a symbol.

The positive response to the dream's *symbolic* meaning, Tony decided, was to call his old friend and reinforce their connection. Once again, the appropriate response to the psychic dream was the same as the appropriate response to the interpreted symbolic dream.

When Tony called his friend, she said that, as a matter of fact, she had been on that very bridge the night before thinking of jumping. She was considering going back to do it. The dreamer encouraged her to talk to him about her problems. His caring convinced her not to jump.

The dream was not literally *psychic* because the bridge

never fell. The bridge was a strong *symbol* that conveyed a potent message. And yet it was a factor of critical importance in the real-life turmoil of a young woman, which appeared in a dream to a man several hundred miles away.

Question: Was the dream psychic or symbolic?

Answer: Does it matter?

It was through the dreamer's response that the girl's life may have been saved and that the significance of the psychic and the symbolic merge: Without response, the dreams are meaningless.

EIGHT

Where Psychic and Symbolic Meet

Marie Françoise, a Belgian woman living in Brussels, was sleeping warm in her bed on a March night in 1942 when an exceptionally vivid dream came to her. In the dream, the telephone rang. It was a call from the small Flemish town in which she had been raised. Her father had just died, her brother-in-law's voice told her, and Marie Françoise needed to come right away. She was shocked, since her father was not known to be in poor health. She got her things together and went out to catch the bus. It began to rain furiously, and so she stopped in the small city of Louvain and went to a department store to buy an umbrella because she knew she would have to walk a good distance in the rain from the bus stop to her father's house in the small town. She asked for a black umbrella for mourning, but the store didn't have any in black.

"In the dream, I got upset beyond reason," recalls Marie Françoise, "After all, the point was to keep the rain off, and any color would do, but I was distraught not to have black." She finally and with great distress bought a brown umbrella and took the next bus on her way.

When she arrived at the closest stop to her destination, she got out into the rain. "It was a terrible rain; the water was up to my knees," she remembers from the dream.

Immediately, she was accosted by some German soldiers. They asked her who she was and what she was doing there. They demanded to see her identification and questioned her explanation for being in the area. They asked her the same things over and over. They demanded information about the saboteurs who that morning had cut the telephone wires and insisted that she must know about this crime.

Marie Françoise woke up trying to convince the soldiers that she was innocent and had legitimate reasons for being there.

In the morning she awoke feeling anxious from the ordeal. She made herself a cup of coffee and sat down at her breakfast table to think about the dream.

Marie Françoise did not at that time have a systematic method for interpreting dream symbols, such as the one I have explained in this book. But she did understand intuitively the symbols of this dream because these were the major elements of the most important emotional issues of her life.

First, the father of Marie Françoise had seemed to hate her. From the very beginning, he had treated her badly, even beaten her, and by the time she was a teenager his rejection of his second daughter forced her to go away to Brussels to be raised by an aunt. She did not understand why she was rejected and felt that something must be very wrong with her. This was a terrible emotional burden, which for a long time made her feel inferior and deserving of abuse.

So the death of Marie Françoise's father in the dream meant an end to his emotional tyranny; he could no longer judge her unworthy of love. No wonder that when she tried to buy an umbrella in the proper color of mourning she was unable to. She could try to mourn, but she could not do it properly. She had to settle for brown—the dark appearance of mourning, not the real thing. Her failure to get the right color upset her in her dream because she did not yet understand that her emotions were valid; she considered them part of what was wrong with her.

The meaning of the German soldiers that confronted Marie Françoise at the bus stop in the country was easy to identify. She had been a little girl when the Germans in 1914 had overrun Belgium, burned her family's farm, and conscripted her oldest brother. And here they were again in 1942 occupying her country. Germans to Marie Françoise meant two things: cruelty and organization. She would have admired the organizational ability of the Germans if she did not feel that they used it to cruel ends. And so at the bus stop she was met by these embodiments of systematic cruelty.

The questions the soldiers in the dream asked her were the ones she now knew had pounded in her father's head her whole life: Where are you from? What are you doing here?

But only when Marie Françoise had grown up did she finally learn why her father hated her. At the time of her birth, a busybody in the family, a jealous relative, told her father that his wife had been unfaithful and that Marie Françoise was the child of another man. Her father believed the tale; he hated the baby for who he thought she was and for how she had supposedly come into the world.

His wife denied the accusation till the end and protected

the child from the angry father. After the mother died, when Marie Françoise was only five, the little girl lived out her childhood with the great distress caused by this man's systematic cruelty. As her only comfort, she always carried the memory of her mother as her guardian angel.

In the dream, Marie Françoise was accused of something she knew nothing about, cutting the lines of communication. She protested her innocence, but her protestations could not free her yet, for emotionally she had never gotten over feeling unacceptable. While Marie Françoise was having to explain her presence to her inquisitors, proving her identity, legitimizing her arrival, she woke up.

The dream was a clear symbolic representation of a major issue in Marie Françoise's life. But she had not resolved the dilemma in this dream.

When Marie Françoise had washed out her coffee cup and tidied up her little kitchen, the phone rang. It was her brother-in-law from her hometown. "You have to come," the brother-in-law said, "your father is seriously ill; we don't think he is going to live."

Marie Françoise packed her things and got on the bus to the country. Of course, she was startled not only by the news itself but by the news coming right after the dream. Once she was on the bus, rain began to pour down. She got off the bus near a department store in Louvain to buy an umbrella. It seemed the sensible thing to do, but, of course, she was well aware that this act was prescribed in the dream. She looked for a black umbrella but couldn't find one. She asked the clerk, thinking there must be one, because black was the most common color for an umbrella in those days. They were out of black, the clerk said, perhaps brown would do. Marie Françoise took the brown one. Instead of being upset, however, this time she felt a great calm come over her, a deep peace she attributed to the dream. She felt her mother was watching over her and had sent the dream as a preparation and comfort.

As she got back on the bus, she held her head high. *Our time has come, Mother*, she thought.

When the bus pulled up in the small town of her birth, Marie Françoise stepped down into water that splashed up to her knees in its rush down the gutter. Noticing her getting down from the bus, two German soldiers hurried over. Since the Germans occupied Belgium, Marie Françoise was accustomed to seeing them goose stepping around Brussels, but she would not have expected to find them at a country crossroads no longer in dispute. The soldiers demanded her identification; they questioned her reasons for being there; they asked her the names and relationship of everyone in her family. Then they asked everything all over again. Finally they demanded she tell them about the telephone wires being cut. Who had done that? they wanted to know. Marie Françoise answered their questions civilly for her own good, but she felt defiant, and her anger felt good.

Finally, the soldiers let her go on. When she arrived at her father's house, he was still alive, but he could not speak. He died within a few hours.

Suddenly, anger engulfed her; this fiery emotion felt the same as her anger toward the Germans, an anger of long standing that had just been fanned into flame down the road. She suddenly realized that her new anger toward her father was just as justified as her anger against the Germans, who had burned her home, taken her brother, and killed her friends. The punishment she had for so long turned on herself for being unloved and unlovable was changing to anger against him, and the anger felt good. This was the resolution of her dream.

Marie Françoise, in the years that followed her father's death, came to understand how her opinion of herself had been shaped by her father's rejection and that this opinion was in error. The change from self-rejection to anger toward her father was a healthy change. Over the years that anger has subsided. Marie Françoise is today a delightful, confident seventy-nine-year-old adventuress, whom you might meet any day going to town on the Brussels tram.

Marie Françoise's dream—like many I have helped students, patients, and friends interpret—was loaded with symbolism important to the dreamer's life. Understanding such a dream is a step in understanding and resolving issues, large and small, in one's life. The fact that Marie Françoise's dream also came true in the most literal sense in almost every detail confirmed the truth of its message and led to a life-changing resolution. The message of this drama was that it was time for her to end the emotional tyranny of her father, who questioned her very right to exist. The meaning of the dream was dramatically underscored when every part of the dream actually came true, bringing, as it unfolded, the sense of freedom Marie Françoise deserved.

The double role of the dream is curious. When the dream process chose images as symbols associated with various emotions, it chose images, not from the memory bank of recent past experiences but from that of the immediate future. And why not? If future-memory exists at all, as psychic dreams suggest, images from future-memory may as well be chosen as those from past-memory.

Another example of a highly symbolic dream coming true in the literal sense was the dream of the writer in Chapter Seven who was wringing her hands over a manuscript she had turned in to her editor. She feared that the story was a failure and her job was in danger. Then she dreamed her editor loved it and, in telling her so, held her hand long and warmly. The dream was a clear offering of the gift of confidence, spelled out in words, and, in addition, symbolized by the lingering warmth of a hand. The dream, of course, came substantially true, underscoring the validity of the message.

In both dreams, almost perfectly accurate examples of precognition, there are small errors. In Marie Françoise's dream, the news on the telephone was that her father was dead; actually he did not die for ten more hours. But his tyranny was dead; the speechless, dying man held no further terror for her. News of his death and news of his imminent death were *emotionally equivalent.*

In the writer's dream, a certain editor to whom she had delivered a story held her hand warmly while praising her writing. In reality, a different editor held her hand in the presence of the editor who had praised her work. The dreamer had had similar experiences with both editors; they both were associated with the same emotions, both pleasant and unpleasant; they were *emotionally equivalent* characters.

Discrepancies between psychic dreams and the reality they depict thus seem to be substitutions of emotional equivalents, symbolic sleight of hand.

In fact, although the details of the psychic dreams in previous chapters have been close enough to the events they predicted to convince us the dreams were not random happenings, in only a few cases were the details of the dream exactly like the details of the event. The discrepancies in many cases were minor, yet if a dream can predict a future event or know about an event happening far off, why does the dream make "mistakes"?

It is a human tendency to fill in what we don't observe clearly as a means of retaining and communicating a coherent account. It is our feeling for an event that dictates our perceptions of the facts. We also inadvertently substitute one word or image for another in telling people what has happened or will happen. Have you ever told someone you would meet him at such and such a store, saying the name of one store but picturing another one in your mind? Substitutions of one word for another generally mean that the correct store and the one you said have some connection in your mind—a store with the same ambience or goods for sale, the store in your hometown that is the equivalent to the one you really meant, a store with a name that sounds similar, etc. If our waking accounts contain errors, small wonder that our memories of dreams, psychic or symbolic, contain inaccuracies.

Our dream errors, however, are not so much cognitive slips as emotional transpositions. Substitutions seem to be between things you could never mistake in real life but whose emotional impact are the same. For example, a man dreamed an airplane crashed into the house next door. Two days later, an automobile crashed into the house. The dream seems more than coincidental, for vehicles crashing into houses are rather rare events. Yet the difference between a plane and a car is not one a waking observer could ignore. The dream was thus inaccurate as a psychic dream. If the dreamer had reported "I dreamed *something* crashed into the house next door " we would regard the dream as accurate if not detailed. From the point of view of a neighbor or the person who lived in the house, what happened was a crash, a shattering force, terror, destruction, loss. What difference does it make emotionally whether the vehicle of destruction was a plane or a car? Curious readers of the next day's paper will want to know what hit, who was driving, how it happened. The owner of the house, standing in his splintered rooms, is going to wonder only "What am I going to do?"

Have you ever had an ordinary dream in which you found yourself at a party or at dinner with some old high school friends and then later in the dream, without notice, they turned into your office co-workers and the dream went on without missing a beat. You can bet the dream was not about your specific relationship with these particular people; it was about relationships in general, probably current, perhaps your desire for approval or support. The high school friends, symbols of companionship from the past, were interchangeable with your office buddies, symbols of companionship from the present. It is apparently possible in such a dream to see as yet unknown friends, symbols of companionship from the future. Whatever symbols work emotionally will serve equally well for the night-time drama. A related process is one Freud refers to as "condensation". Characteristics of similar emotional valence are "condensed" into one feature.

Similarly, in psychic dreams there are occasional image transpositions that occur during the translation from emotion to associated symbols we can grasp mentally and remember. We might call this "psychic condensation." Where psychic details may differ from the details of the subsequent events, the real-life elements have been replaced by images that are different but symbolically equivalent, just as in symbolic dreams. I have drawn this conclusion not only from my discovery that entire dreams prove to be at the same time literally psychic and symbolically truthful but from the remarks of the dreamers themselves. The following dream involves an airplane that turned out to be a car in real life.

My dream was on the Saturday-Sunday night of March 22–23. I think it was in the morning hours, possibly just before I awoke.

In the dream my husband was going to the aid of his best friend, who appeared to be trying to fly an airplane. He couldn't seem to get over a hill. This part of the dream wasn't too clear in my memory on awaking. What was very clear in my mind was my screaming at the best friend, "You killed him. You killed him."

That same day, Sunday, March 23, I told the friend and his wife and my husband of the dream. I omitted the part about my screaming, "You killed him," to spare his feelings.

On the following Sunday, March 30, my husband and his friend were returning around midnight from a trip to Los Angeles. They were on the freeway, in the area known as Kellogg Hill. The friend was driving. They were involved in an accident in which my husband was killed instantly and his friend was uninjured.

I had forgotten about the dream myself, but on the day of my husband's funeral, the friend's wife recalled it to me. Of course, I've never forgot it since.

I have italicized the remark that points out the part of the dream that was unclear. It is, of course, the part of the dream that was inaccurate. The image of a plane trying with difficulty to get over a hill has a similar feel of speed and danger as a car going over a hill in a dangerous situation. When the dreamer tried to explain to herself what she had experienced in the dream, the plane image was not one that proved to be actually true but carried the same feel of speed and danger. It was emotionally accurate.

The remark, "You killed him," is an expression of raw anger that one normally feels when a loved one is lost, particularly in a situation in which others survive. This considerate woman did not ever say to her husband's friend, "You killed him." But she no doubt suffered the questions, consciously or unconsciously, "Why *my* husband? If he had been driving, instead of his friend, would *he* have survived."

The whole basis for dream interpretation is that one image is a substitute for another emotionally similar. We demand more of a psychic dream because it is by definition a dream revealing a future or distant event in factual terms. But we have seen that both psychic and symbolic dreams can convey symbolic and literal truth. Dreams lie on a continuum from totally literal to totally symbolic truth. Most lie somewhere in between, where psychic and symbolic meaning may not only meet but overlap.

The symbolic interchange of character identities in dreams is one of the most puzzling discrepancies between literal and symbolic meaning. Usually we have to figure out who has been substituted for whom *after* we wake up. In a few accounts, however, I found observations *within* the dream that indicate how even the dreaming mind seems to have trouble casting the players.

A Colorado optician's dreams, for instance, had predicted her brother's sudden death in an accident and other less tragic events, giving her reason to pay attention to dream revelations. She dreamed one night of an old boyfriend, who had moved to another state. In the dream, he kissed her, then told her she was going to China. She argued that *she* was not going to China, that *he* was the one who was going to China. He readily agreed that she was right. The fact about who was going on this trip would have been a major point in real life. In the dream, it seemed little more than a slip of the tongue.

Once awake, the young woman contacted the old friend's mother, who gave her the young man's address. She wrote him several times before he answered—from Hong Kong, where the Navy had sent him well after she had dreamed his destination.

In another dream, the dreamer asks even more clearly, "Are you sure this is the right person?" A Michigan woman dreamed of her own funeral in great detail. She saw clearly the bottom of the grave, and she noticed the ornamentation on the coffin. Although she was not upset in the dream, she knew this was her grave. Obligingly, "I tried to die, but I couldn't," she recalls. Finally, she told the attendants they'd have to get someone else. Within a week, a relative had died, and at the interment she stood where she could see the very bottom of the grave and the coffin was ornamented just as she had dreamed it.

The little arguments the dreamer has about the identity of the main character seem so trivial in the light of the importance of getting the identity right. One can easily see how straightening the identity out, as low key as the efforts seem to be, might by morning be one of the forgotten details. Why the dreaming mind seems to place so little importance on factual identity is unclear.

In the following startlingly accurate precognitive dream, there is one transposition of character. A remark made by the dreamer in the dream is said by someone else in real life. The change made the dream a more impressive precognitive experience for the dreamer because she had no control over what the other person said.

I used to work in a children's hospital as a nurse's aide. One of my duties there was to transport patients to and from our hospital to the one across the street via a long, white, underground tunnel that joined the two facilities. I had a dream one night that I was transporting a little kid, about ten years old, through this long, bright white tunnel.

The kid looked pretty sick. He (or she, I couldn't tell) didn't have any hair left and had a round puffy face and dark circles under the eyes. We were stopped in the corridor, just me and the kid. I had a close-up view of the child as he took his fingers, rubbed beneath his little black eyes, then put his two index fingers into the sockets underneath his eyeballs. He rubbed his eyes as you would if you were tired, except he was actually dragging his fingers around underneath his eyeballs. It was quite shocking, but I remember thinking that I needed to remain professional about it, and after all, they were his eyes.

I forgot about the dream, dismissing it as a horrible nightmare. Then, one day at work, I had to take this little cancer patient to the other hospital for radiation treatment or chemotherapy, I can't remember which. Her mother and I took her through the tunnel on a stretcher. We had just started down that long, white tunnel when that little bald-headed, moon-faced cancer victim started rubbing her eyes. She pulled down her lower lids and stuck her fingers a little under her eyeballs and rubbed back and forth, rolling her eyes to the ceiling. This in itself was a tough scene to take, but having dreamed it before made it even more difficult to deal with. I had to stop in the middle of the tunnel.

I told the mother I had dreamed about her child. She didn't seem too surprised. I think she was too tired from taking care of her dying daughter to let anything shock her. She explained to me that her daughter's cancer treatment caused her eyes to dry out. She was also losing a bit of her vision, which confused her. She rubbed her eyes like that because they were so irritated and dry. The rubbing, of course, only aggravated her condition. The mother told me that some of the nurses had wanted to restrain the girl's arms, tying them to her bed, but the mother had refused saying they're her eyes *and she can do with them what she wants. At that, I inwardly freaked out and rolled the little girl down the tunnel to her treatment.*

This dream is so bizarre and so accurate that I have no doubt it was a future-memory. The one difference between the dream and reality is that the dreamer said, "They're his eyes," and in the event it was the mother who made the remark. This difference was necessary because the mother was not present in the dream—the dream was a soliloquy. That may be all there is to it—the dream was a play with too few actors. But my educated guess is that, even though the remark, "they're her eyes," had horrified the dreamer, part of her agreed with it. She hated to hear herself say it; yet the thought "rang true" as a tempting mental effort to take some of the responsibility for the patient off herself. After all, she couldn't fix these poor patients; she had to relieve her own emotional distress somehow. The dream, accurate in startling detail, may also have been a symbol of an internal struggle. The "error" in the dream was not really an error but a representation of a real conflict between the dreamer's desire to do something for the suffering patients and her desire to let them be because nothing seemed to help.

Frequently, the only discrepancy between a psychic dream and the real event is exaggeration of the seriousness of the incident. An Atlanta woman dreamed that Dan, her four-year-old nephew in Ohio, had an accident and his left arm had to be amputated. When he came home, he kept falling down. When he fell to the left, he was unable to catch himself with his arm. What the dreamer remembers most vividly is the pitiful expression the boy had on his face after such a mishap, as if he didn't understand why he couldn't catch himself as before.

The dreamer awoke crying and upset. In the morning she called her family in Ohio and asked about her nephew. To her amazement, her mother said that Dan had fallen from his bed the night of the dream and had broken his left collarbone. The doctors had taped his left arm to his chest to immobilize the shoulder. The dreamer told her mother the dream.

Two days later, she got a call saying that Dan had lost his balance and fallen. Unable to catch himself with the restricted arm, he had tumbled on his face. The expression on his face had shown his fright and lack of understanding.

The dream, or at least the dreamer's reaction to it, had exaggerated the seriousness of the accident—Dan's collarbone quickly healed—but the dream had portrayed accurately the boy's shock and bewilderment at not being able to save himself in the accustomed manner. What seemed to be communicated—the future emotion—was accurate.

Just as often as a dream exaggerates the severity of a future mishap, a dream may minimize its importance. One young woman had agreed to meet a man at a restaurant that evening. Having a few minutes to spare after work before the date, she took a little catnap. Soon after she fell asleep, she dreamed the man she was to meet was sitting at the bar in the restaurant already. She then dreamed he fell off the barstool and injured his head. Awakening, she made haste to the restaurant, where she learned that, on his way there, her friend had been struck by a car while crossing the street and had died immediately from the impact to his head.

Some of the strangest symbolic changes are little plays on words. One woman wrote that her husband dreamed of encountering Ed Sullivan on the street. The husband in the dream expressed surprise because he knew Ed Sullivan was dead. The next day his wife answered a help-wanted ad. She went to an interview and got the job. Her new boss was named Ed Sullivan.

Another woman dreamed an image that she feels became reality not as the actual visual image but as a play on words.

There was one dream I dreamed repeatedly so much so that I told my mother about it, but she didn't know what it meant either. It was always the same. In the dream I saw a train pull up to a wall, back off, pull up again, back off again, go to the wall over and over and each time back off.

When I dreamed this dream, I never expected to live in New York City. I had hardly heard of a subway and had no inkling that I would not remain in Colorado married to my first husband.

It is my guess that this dream, if analyzed as symbolic, would have something to say about the troubles in this Colorado woman's first marriage—going up against "a wall" over and over is a common emotional dilemma. However, like other meaningful symbolic dreams, this one came true almost exactly. Years later, the woman divorced, remarried, moved to New York, where every day she commuted to her job in town. Every day she got off the train when it stopped at *Wall* Street.

An Oregon artist had a very bizarre precognitive dream; its actual unfolding involved an even more bizarre twist in words. She dreamed of being in a distinctive but unfamiliar two-story building one night with seven other people she couldn't identify. The building was surrounded by lions with guns, and she was very frightened. An eighth person arrived and dispersed the lions. If the dreamer had applied the test for a potential psychic dream, as I have suggested in Chapter Six, this dream would not have been a candidate. Lions with guns are too absurd to take seriously as real possibilities. In any case, she told her psychologist husband the strange dream.

A few days later the artist and her husband went to a housing project in Seattle to a workshop. Her husband recognized the building in his wife's dream and, without mentioning it to her, told a sociologist there about the dream. Several hours later, as their work was about to be finished, the sociologist called her into his office. He wanted to know if anyone in her dream had been hurt. It seems that during the meeting a gang of neighborhood boys had surrounded the building brandishing guns and protesting some political situation. The artist looked out the window, and there, hiding in the bushes, were several boys in white T-shirts boldly printed with the name "Lions." Pistols glinted in the street-light. Everyone was relieved to learn that no one in her dream was hurt, but the seven people turned off the lights, stayed away from the windows, and waited anxiously. They didn't call the police for fear of a shoot-out. After a while, the sociologist's wife (the eighth person) arrived, saw what was going on, and quietly called the police, who broke up the threatening situation without violence.

It is fascinating to me that, while there are many patterns of dreams heard over and over, unique twists like "lions with guns" pop up that I could never have invented in a million years.

Here is another account, with a surprise, from a woman in Drexel Hill, Pennsylvania, which seemed psychic, although almost every element of the dream imagery seemed to be a clearly understood symbol rather than a literal truth; then, to everyone's surprise one of the symbols turned out to be real as well.

At 10 P.M. on a Saturday night, my pastor called to tell me my brother had had an accident on the Delaware River with his boat, which was bringing him home from Wildwood for the winter, and he was presumed to have been killed. My mother, who lived with me, was on her way to bed and I told the pastor I wanted her to get one more night's sleep and would he please come in the morning and help me tell her of my brother's death.

Sunday morning, as we were getting dressed and ready for the day, Mother told me she had had a strange dream. She said she was in a boat with the minister and that she had a bundle in her arms, which someone took away from her. I went into mild shock but stayed calm enough to ask her if there was anything else in the dream. She said she could not understand why, but the boat was full of flowers.

I left her saying I would be right back and went downstairs to call the pastor. When I told him the story, he was also surprised but admitted there are many things we cannot understand or explain.

Everyone who hears this dream comes to the immediate conclusion the bundle in the dream is my brother, who had once been a baby in her arms, and the flowers, like those at a funeral, represent death. My brother was a boatman all his life, so the boat fits very well. My mother was an active churchwoman all her life and very close to the pastors of our church, so it seems natural that a pastor would be with her symbolically at her time of loss.

However, my brother's son called the seashore to notify the neighbors there that my brother had been killed on his return trip from the seashore. After the usual condolences, the neighbor said that my sister-in-law had forgot to dig up all of her plants from her seashore garden for transfer to her winter garden. So they had dug up all her plants and placed them in the boat for my brother to take back with him, and, she added, "It looked beautiful as it moved out of the bay, full of flowers." Needless to say, this information was unnerving to all of us because no one knew of the flowers except for the neighbor in Wildwood.

The overlap between symbolic and psychic elements of that dream is intricate. The dream was primarily symbolic since it did not actually show death; yet it was psychic because it seemed clearly to symbolize an event the dreamer had no other way of knowing. It seems to have been a peaceful scene, as if the flowers represented beauty more than death. And that thought was the truth, as it turned out; the flowers were a scene of beauty and a thoughtful gesture of kind neighbors just before the man's death. It must have been a comfort for the mother to have her mind focused on the beautiful send-off by friends instead of the accident at sea; I think this was the purpose of the dream.

Here is a wonderful example of a precognitive drama with a symbolic setting and symbolic characters, along with very real props and a very touching emotional reality.

I dreamed I was at an estate auction, standing toward the back of the room. Many things had been auctioned off as I stood there, but nothing really interested me. The auctioneer then displayed a small white box with seven rings inside. They were beautiful. As he began auctioning them off, I began to get more and more frantic. I wanted to have one of those rings more than anything, but I had no money. I got a big lump in my throat and began looking around for someone I knew to lend me money. I looked and looked for someone, and I kept looking back at the auctioneer helplessly. Then I woke up.

Three days later, I got a call from an aunt saying that she was throwing a family reunion, since my grandparents were coming across the country for a visit. I later found out my grandfather had terminal cancer and wanted to see everyone while he was still active. The reunion was seven days after my dream.

After an afternoon of outside games and food and picture taking, we all assembled in the living room. My grandfather entered with a large box. He began calling names and handing out mementos—coins, old wallets, books, etc. He pulled out a small white box and gave my cousin a ring, then my grandmother a ring, and my stepmother a ring, then went on to other things. I got a terrible lump in my throat as I felt he had no ring for me and therefore did not love me as much as the others. The disappointment was overwhelming, but at the same time I was angry with myself for feeling so spoiled.

He later called my name and asked me to join him in the kitchen. There he gave me a beautiful opal ring. We gave each other a hug I will never forget, because it was the last one. By the time his little white box was empty, he had given seven rings.

Here was a family reunion and a dream about an auction, yet there is no doubt in my mind that the two are one and the same. Why did the dreamer wake up remembering an auction? Symbolically, the dream is about love, the feeling she had come up short, and finding out she was loved anyway. The dream was the truth. As the dreamer added, "The little white box with seven rings was a very interesting element, but the *feelings* I had in both the dreams and real-life were identical—that's what gave me goose bumps."

But how far can we go to consider a dream psychic when

it has major factual errors, however symbolically correct? When I did my original research to find out how many people actually have psychic dreams, my criteria allowed for very few discrepancies between dream and real life. In dream accounts that I received later, I have been willing to consider dreams psychic if many details and the overall feel came true, even though there were changes as great as the one above, in which a real-life family reunion from future-memory was transformed into a dream auction. Some other accounts contained too much symbolic truth as compared to the literal truth for me to accept the dream as psychic. Yet the person offering the dream felt sure the dream had come true. The test of psychic truth in symbolic form could ultimately be whether an appropriate response to that truth proves beneficial, as it did in the following Biblical account.

The familiar account from Genesis 41 of an Egyptian pharaoh's dreams interpreted by Joseph, the Hebrew slave, offers an example of precognitive dreams whose sense required extensive symbolic interpretation. One dream involved seven skinny cows who came out of the river and devoured seven fat cows. In the same dream, seven fat ears of corn devoured seven withered ears. The pharaoh had no idea what to make of his dream. Learning the reputation of the Hebrew servant as an interpreter of dreams, the pharaoh straightaway summoned Joseph. The future royal adviser told the pharaoh that the seven fat cows symbolized seven years of good harvest, while the seven skinny cows represented the seven years of famine that would follow. The seven lean years would eat up the surplus from the seven fat years. The second part was a repetition of the same warning.

Joseph went on to advise the pharaoh to make the following positive response: The pharaoh would require that all farmers put aside a fifth of their harvest for the next seven years to be eaten in the subsequent years of famine. The pharaoh took Joseph's advice and based his national agricultural policy for the next fourteen years on his dream, as interpreted by Joseph. The pharaoh thus saved his nation from suffering and death. Many other Biblical dreams considered prophetic were not literally precognitive but symbolically suggestive. While I am hesitant to accept all dreams that come true symbolically as psychic, I have seen the benefits of interpretive flexibility.

The following experience is a modern account of how psychic knowledge in symbolic form can help dreamers make difficult decisions. In this case, a literally psychic dream helped a research chemist trust the message of a later symbolic dream. The chemist had dreamed one night that a wise old man with a beard told him that the large progressive company the chemist worked for was going to put a freeze on raises. This news surprised the chemist, who had recently been to the home office and had got no wind of this uncharacteristic business measure. Several weeks later, the company announced the freeze. This experience gave the chemist faith in the wise old man in the dream.

About a year later, the company entered a period of unexpected difficult times and decided to cut back on personnel. The chemist, along with dozens of others, was offered the chance to retire early with good benefits. He thought the offer a fair one, but after more than thirty years with the same company, the prospect of being out in the cold looking for another way to pursue a career terrified him. It seemed safer to stay and work out his days where he had always been. As the weeks of decision making went on, he had dreams of trains and planes and cars going places. He was either going somewhere and leaving others behind or others were going and leaving him behind, but he was no closer to a satisfying decision.

Then one night he dreamed he was delivering papers at dawn. There was a scuffle in the street ahead. He stepped back and people ran past him. He took refuge in a tavern run by the same wise old man with a beard. The tavern was surrounded by an angry mob, and there seemed to be no good end in sight. The wise old man said to the chemist, "Leave now. It's only going to get worse. I'll show you the way out." He guided him to a side entrance the attackers had not yet discovered and sent him on his way to safety.

He woke with a feeling of resolution. The wise old man had come through before; the chemist would trust him again. He signed the early retirement papers and went on to a new and exciting job. After his departure, the management of his old company decided not to develop any new products for an indefinite period, and the activities of the research department became boring and slow. The chemist was relieved to be safely out and in an exciting new career in a different city. His response to the symbolic dream ultimately proved its resolution was sound.

Katie is another dreamer who often dreams symbolic dramas, which, she is convinced, derive their value from psychic elements. Katie was the wife of an Episcopal priest who had recently taken over the leadership of a church in a Northeastern city. The parishioners were ever so friendly. They helped the couple move into the parsonage, gave a pantry shower, and convivially put away canned goods on the new minister's wife's shelves. Everything augured well.

Shortly afterward, however, Katie dreamed of the church building. Out of crevices in the stucco, huge black spiders swarmed, surrounding her. Katie, who had a long history of dreams that came true, awoke saying to herself, "This is not good."

Soon after, Katie had another dream about an orange streak in the water of a swimming hole where some youths were swimming. The orange streak, when it surfaced, turned out to be a marmalade-colored cat. She was struck with how unnatural it was for the orange cat to be in the water with the young people, since cats do not like water. Later, in the same dream, Katie was in church where an old-fashioned bath tub had been placed in the center aisle. *That's got to be a baptistry*, Katie thought. Then she saw in the bottom a streak of orange grease. She felt repulsed. *That's got to be cleaned up,* she thought, *but I don't want to be contaminated by it.*

When Katie woke up, she made an instant association with the orange cat and the orange grease in the water. This association was the equivalent of word association in my dream interpretation method; only Katie did it instantly and spontaneously. "It's Mrs. Walker's dyed hair," she said positively. The red-haired Mrs. Walker was the wife of the pillar of the church, who currently worked with the young people.

Next, Katie dreamed that Mr. Walker was connected with the Mafia. Katie and her husband, Everett, filling up their car at a service station, were discussing how Mr. Walker was good with the young people, but his criminal connections made him undesirable as a youth leader. Just then a big, black Mafioso car pulled into the station. Mr. Walker, a passenger in the car, started shooting a spray of bullets toward them. Katie feared that one would hit Everett.

After that third dream, Katie began to say to Everett at the end of each meeting, "How are things going?" Everett always swore everything was great. Katie observed that her husband seemed to be very popular with the parishioners, and the once struggling church had begun to attract new communicants. Still, she knew that something was wrong and that it had to do with the Walkers not being what they appeared to be.

When she told Everett that her dreams suggested there was something negative about that nice Mr. Walker, Everett thought she was foolish. Her continued concern even caused friction between them. Her pessimism was frankly annoying.

When Katie dreamed of being covered with black things like strips of electrical tape, she cried out, "These are lies being told and I can't get them off me." The faster she pulled the black things off, the faster they stuck to her. Everett was not impressed.

Soon afterward, Katie and Everett learned that Mr. Walker and his red-haired wife were spreading malicious and untrue rumors about them on the one hand, while treating them politely whenever they met. Mr. Walker, the head of the vestry, had run the church single-handedly before the arrival of Katie and Everett. Katie supposed that Mr. Walker was disgruntled by some differences of opinion between him and Everett and jealous of the new priest's enthusiastic following.

Everett responded to the threat publicly—too openly, Katie thought—but Everett was confident he had things well in hand. Katie wished Everett would take the crisis more seriously.

Again she dreamed. This time she was driving a car along a black asphalt road across the tops of mountains in the dark. She encountered great holes in the road and places where the road bed was slipping off the edge. Worried, she kept going until the road finally stopped at a sheer drop. The only way out was to back up over the holes in the dark. She knew she'd never make it, but she tried. At some point, the car started to slip. She tried to get traction but failed. She knew she would be killed. Then a clear thought came to her, "There is no *external* thing I can do to save myself. The only way to survive is to have the *right attitude.*" The moment she woke up, Katie inexplicably *knew* her husband's enemy had succeeded in ruining him.

The same night Everett had a dream. In it, he heard scuffling behind a door. Frightened, he pushed the door open. There he saw a blackboard with a row of feet dangling behind it. He looked behind the blackboard and discovered the entire nine-member vestry hanged. That was the dream Everett recalled when his wife woke him because, she said, he was panting in his sleep.

The next week Mr. Walker called a meeting with the bishop to present accusations against Everett. The vestry neither supported the charges nor spoke out against them.

They had been paralyzed. As the bishop and Mr. Walker conferred, supporters held a vigil outside the church, bearing candles and drinking coffee. The bishop listened to the charges and summarily dismissed Everett from his position. After that, many members left the church; it is now a skeleton parish, Katie says.

She took to heart immediately the words, "There is no external thing I can do to save myself. The only way to survive is to have the right attitude." It gave her courage to rise above the humiliation and the actual privations that followed during Everett's eight months without regular employment.

Katie says that the long series of dreams were preparing her, over a period of time, for the disaster that otherwise would have devastated her. They gave her the emotional means to deal with it. "Every time something really bad has happened in my life, I have had such dreams. Good things just sneak up on me and surprise me. I *need* preparation for bad times. I had my dreams because I needed to prepare. Everett is just the opposite. He had his dream because he's so laid back; it was high time he did take the trouble seriously."

Katie went on: "I rarely and reluctantly tell people my dreams are psychic because there is no way they could believe that these symbols surely represented those later events. But *I* know. I *know.*"

I have come to understand how Katie feels, especially since I, the once-skeptic, had *my* dream. Mine did not come true at all, but it had a psychic element because of its emotional connection to a real event.

I don't often remember my dreams, so it surprised me to awaken one morning with sharp dream images still penetrating the surface of my waking thought. I had dreamed of being a boy again, going to the movies with my parents and my brother and sisters. We were all coming out of the theater with uninhibited boisterousness. My father was jovial and seemed to enjoy our spontaneity. Thinking about the scene, I was filled with a sudden and deep sadness, a hollow in my stomach.

I was puzzled to experience such strong feelings about the dream's content. I supposed the sadness was my realization that my father had never been jovial, and we youngsters in the family had rarely allowed ourselves the luxury of exuberance. But the clashes I had with my father and the lingering resentments faded once I was grown. My father moved to Israel, and I did not think about him much at all. Still the vividness of the dream and the intensity of the sadness disturbed me.

I was disturbed enough to tell a friend, another clinical psychologist, about the dream that same morning. As I was talking, tears filled my eyes, my voice quavered, and sadness engulfed me. I dream little; I cry less. I consider myself emotionally reserved. What was happening to me?

I calmed down and went about my business, leaving town for a four-day trip. On my return, I received a phone call from my brother telling me that our father had died in Israel four days before. The news caused a palpable emptiness in my stomach, a grief that I recognized as the same intense feeling of loss I had felt at the end of my joyful dream, the same distress I felt in recounting the dream to my colleague.

I asked about the cause of my father's death and the time. He had died unexpectedly, early on the morning when I had been dreaming.

For the first time I felt a personal kinship with the individuals whose experiences I had been studying. Indeed, later I heard other stories similar to mine, which I now call *leave-taking* dreams, pleasant dream visits with people who are at that moment actually dying.

I am glad that I started out with a narrow view of psychic dreams, holding them to strict criteria of literal truth, in order to demonstrate to the scientist in me that they undeniably exist. I am equally glad that I have come to know the range of psychic dream experience, the dappling of symbolic emotional truth against a background of literal reality.

NINE

Dreams Beyond Life

"I was sixteen when my grandmother died in my arms," remembers Dana. "I felt that maybe I should have done something to save her." Dana's grandmother had lived with the family and been a second mother to Dana. The young girl went into an emotional decline after her grandmother's death.

"My grief took the form of going over in my mind every bad thing I'd ever done, every ugly thing I'd ever said. These were trivial things, since I really was a good child, but I tormented myself with these petty wickednesses until I was about to have a nervous breakdown."

One night Dana dreamed her grandmother was standing

in the archway of the hall as real as in the days she was alive. Her Afghan sheepdog, however, was lying on the floor quietly as if he did not know anyone was there. Dana felt a rush of grief because she knew her grandmother couldn't stay long. As she rushed to hold her, the grandmother warned, "Don't touch me," but it was too late. Dana put her hand on her grandmother and a shower of sparks engulfed her and knocked her backward. She found herself sitting on the edge of her bed again. Her grandmother was gone.

Dana blamed herself. In touching her grandmother, she had done again what was forbidden and had banished her grandmother's spirit forever.

In a few moments, however, her grandmother reappeared beside the bed, saying, "Nonsense. I came to tell you that I love you and that I know you love me. Now stop tormenting yourself with this nonsense and get on with your life."

Dana's self-destructive thoughts seemed lifted by this advice, and she no longer blamed herself for the loss of her beloved grandmother.

Dana's dream, more lifelike than most, is typical of a whole group I encountered in significant numbers in my research. It featured a visit from a person who had actually died; it occurred during the night but was so vivid that the dreamer did not think it was a dream; the person speaking from beyond death seemed self-assured, loving, and content with the state of death.

It is easy to explain many such visits from the dead by using ordinary psychological principles. The mental and emotional trauma following the death call for an adjustment to the lost emotional closeness and for a resolution of the feelings of guilt that may exist in any close relationship. Just as the body adjusts and mends following trauma, so do the mind and emotions heal following a death. Dreams are a natural healing process. Thus, dreams like Dana's may not represent a distinct category.

Indeed, the dead appeared in all categories of dreams from precognitive to purely symbolic to shared dreams. A sleeping mind can conjure up a dead person's image from memory as easily as any other image. Therefore, the appearance of a dead person in a dream does not require fancy explanations. Still, some of the dreams of the dead are striking enough that I have pulled them together so we can take a closer look at the phenomenon.

Do you remember the woman who, though married to someone else, had been dreaming of her former sweetheart's increasingly serious illness, which was otherwise unknown to her? The dreams, it was revealed later, were simultaneous with the progressive steps of his deterioration, until he was finally in a prolonged coma. The man's family considered calling the dreamer to ask her to come visit him but decided against it. Finally, the man paid the dreamer a visit, a psychic leavetaking, just as he died. His appearance came during the night but seemed more real than a dream. He touched her arm palpably and led her to the kitchen, where he kissed her good-bye after showing her his body in the casket, since she was not convinced of his death. The dream proved substantially accurate as the dreamer realized when she finally contacted the family of her former sweetheart.

My own dream of a pleasant family outing, after which I felt terribly sad, was also a psychic leavetaking I discovered when I got news that my father had died suddenly.

I have found that the leavetaking dreams of other people have also been presentations of pleasant scenes. For example, a woman named Ann Boon R., early one morning in 1962, dreamed about her parents, who were to return to Atlanta later that day from Paris where they had been touring museums with a large group of patrons of the Atlanta arts. Ann does not remember anything in particular that happened or was said in the dream, only how happy her parents seemed. What she particularly remembers is how vivid her parents were in the dream, from the color of their clothes to the wrinkles of their smiles. Ordinarily, she notes, characters in her dreams are more distant and faded. It was this vividness that made Ann become suddenly wide awake and look at the clock. It was 6:05. She was not, however, surprised to have been thinking of her parents in her sleep, for later in the day she was to meet their plane.

But in the end there was no plane to meet. Near six A.M. (EST) in Paris, at the time Ann Boon R. was dreaming, the charter plane had failed to lift successfully off the runway at Orly Airport. It crashed, killing one hundred and six passengers, including her parents.

Ann's dream did not predict the future; there was nothing in it about death. Only the feeling of vividness was unique. It was a dream of truth: an intense physical image of people she loved that signaled the physical end of the loving relationship. This leavetaking remains a special comfort to her.

I believe this kind of dream is psychic, although the message may not be clear until later. In the following, more elaborate leavetaking, there is a clear psychic element because the dreamer did not previously know anything about the dying person. The leavetaking is unique in that the person was not calling on a loved one, as in the dreams above, but was making a last appearance at a *place* where the most important and devastating event of her life had occurred.

In 1980 I attended college at Lees-McRae in Banner Elk, North Carolina, located at the base of Beech Mountain. I lived in an old stone dormitory for girls, on the second floor across from the stairway. I had a very small room and no roommate. In early December during exams, I decided to take a nap about three in the afternoon. While I was asleep I had a horribly frustrating and frightening dream that still bothers me today. The dream I remember goes like this:

I was lying on my bed, and a nurse came into my room and tried to get me up. She said my name over and over and kept pulling on my arm. I wanted to stay where I was and kept pulling against her to stay in bed. She kept calling my name during our struggle and saying, "Please, come with me. I have to show you; I have to show you."

The nurse was very vivid. She was dressed in an ankle-length skirt, a blouse, and cap. She had brown hair, a pleasing face, and large brown eyes. She was relatively petite, and I kept thinking how strong she was for someone so small.

During this whole struggle and her pleading with me, there were flashes of the dorm I was living in; only I was aware that it was about forty or so years ago and the dorm was a hospital. I saw the hallways with pipes running along the ceiling, black-and-white tile floors, carts along the walls, but no people. I saw a dining room with table cloths on the tables, everything placed for dinner, a large chandelier, candles lit, water glasses full. Everything was in full color and vividly real, as if I were standing right there looking at it all. All of these flashes were entwined with my struggle with the nurse.

Then there was another flash. I saw the nurse falling down the stairs across from my dorm room and landing at the bottom of the stairs unconscious.

I woke shaking and sweating, physically exhausted, as if I had actually been in the struggle with that nurse. I walked down the hall to a girl friend's room and told her and some other friends about the dream because it was so strange. We laughed it off.

Later that week, these same friends and I were sitting in the lobby studying for an exam when our dorm mother walked in. For a reason I cannot recall, one friend brought up the subject of my dream and asked me to tell our dorm mother. As I told the dream, she became more and more anxious, and her eyes showed astonishment and a little fear. She kept interrupting me and asking me specific questions about the details of the "hospital" I'd seen and about the nurse.

Mrs. K. finally told us that, a long time before, our dorm had been the Banner Elk Hospital and that every detail I had described about its interior was correct. Until Mrs. K. told us, I had no idea the dorm had originally been a hospital. Mrs. K. went on to say that she recalled hearing about a nurse who had fallen down the stairs in the hospital and been paralyzed. I went home for Christmas break and soon forgot the whole incident.

When I returned to school, Mrs. K. told me she had been talking to some other people who had been around at the time the dorm was a hospital and found out that the nurse who fell had fit the description I had given. One of Mrs. K's friends told her that on the day I had my dream this nurse had passed away . . . I will always remember this dream as if it happened yesterday; it was that real.

Almost all psychic dreams are described by the dreamers as being exceptionally clear. The leavetaking dreams are described as the most vivid. The people who are passing are often, as in the above dream, *palpable.* I never intended to be getting into the subject of ghosts in my research, but here I am describing the appearance of a dead or dying person appearing at the actual place of a great trauma in that person's life: What is that if not a ghost?

Another phenomenon similar to leavetaking involves a visit by a dead person on some anniversary, a sort of commemoration of passing. It is dismissed as a simple memory of that person unless it contains some information not otherwise known to the dreamer, as in the following dream.

My uncle Al, who has long been dead, was a favorite of mine, but I did not see him often. He lived in another city and only came to visit on special occasions, like Thanksgiving and family weddings. He was a jovial man but formal in some ways. For example, I never saw him except in coat and tie.

So I was surprised one night to have a dream about him coming down my stairs in his pajamas and bathrobe. Everything was very clear. I even noted the particular plaid of his robe. I asked Uncle Al if I could get him anything, a cup of coffee or a bite to eat. He said yes, what he'd really like to have was a cream puff. I got him one (dream larders sometimes have goodies real fridges do not), and we had a pleasant visit while he happily ate the cream puff.

The next day I was so taken with this dream visit that I called my aunt in Texas. I asked her if Uncle Al had ever had a maroon and gray plaid bathrobe. She answered yes, he'd had a very fine wool one in maroon and gray plaid, which he had worn for many years. I asked her also if he had a favorite dessert. "As a matter of fact," she said, "he was exceptionally fond of cream puffs."

At that, I told her the dream. She said it was strange because the night of the dream was the twentieth anniversary of his death, a date I myself could not have recalled, since I was very young when he died.

This pleasant experience, as if Uncle Al had a hankering for his favorite dessert in the company of his niece to celebrate the anniversary of his passing, could easily have been seen as a simple dream memory of a beloved man, with some symbolic frills added to the scene. Only through the sharing of the dream did the dreamer discover that it was more than a memory; it was a psychic experience as well.

When a dream of the dead has any element of knowledge the dreamer could not otherwise have known, it can be considered a psychic dream like the others. I have gathered the dreams of the dead together, however, to see if we can consider whether the dead actually play a part in the dreams in a way different from other psychic dreams. It is possible, for example, that the following dreams from Broken Arrow, Oklahoma, are ordinary memories of cautioning grandmothers, or that they are simple psychic dreams or some other complex apparition in which the real grandmothers seem to take an active role in the care of their granddaughter.

On two different nights the dreams occurred. On the first night, my favorite grandmother, who had died about three years before, appeared as if in a framed picture. She was very concerned and repeated twice, "Nancy, be careful. Nancy, be careful." On the second night, my other grandmother, who had died two years before, appeared in exactly the same manner and said exactly the same thing. I awoke each time and thought it strange I should dream about them, since I had only dreamed of each of them once, following their deaths. (During those dreams they let me know they were okay and happy.) But in these warning dreams, I didn't know what they meant.

On October 5 I had a horrible auto accident in which I was almost killed. The doctors didn't believe I would live the first week after the accident. The first conscious thought I remember a week after the wreck was of the dreams. So that's what my grandmothers were warning me of, *I thought.*

When a deceased person appears in a dream with accurate information not previously known to the dreamer, it is tempting to characterize that person as some form of spirit rather than as a product of the dreaming mind itself. In the following *simultaneous* dream, the departed husband seems to be coming home to keep things in order.

My husband passed away on July 26 of this year. I had a dream about three weeks ago in which I saw him inside his coffin and he made a motion with his lips as if he wanted to kiss me. I kissed him on the forehead and then I saw his grave. (We had planted some begonias around the grave the week before and had left it looking very nice.) Well, the grave was all in disarray and the plants I had planted were not in place, so I called some men who were at the cemetery and told them to fix it, which they proceeded to do. My dream then came to an end.

The next day my daughter happened to be going past the cemetery with her boyfriend and stopped to visit her father's grave. It had a large hole in it, and several of the plants were out of place. She told me what she had seen, and I had already described my dream to another daughter, so of course we were really amazed at the accuracy of my dream. I went to the cemetery the next day and fixed my husband's grave as well as I could. I am now wondering whether my husband was communicating his concern to me through a dream. Being a very precise person, I kind of think he might have.

In the next experience a deceased father seems to be expressing his concern for his youngest daughter. The only question is whether the father's image makes these *visitation* dreams or whether he was a symbolic product of his daughters' minds. Some psychic process seems involved because both daughters, thousands of miles apart, received the same strange visit the same night.

A young Atlanta woman, Ellen, had two sisters—Marilyn, her twin, lived in Germany with her husband; Della, the youngest, had been in a lot of trouble with drugs and a general lack of responsibility. Once Della swore she was going to turn over a new leaf, and so Ellen invited her sister to live with her until she could straighten out. But Della was soon back into her old ways, including manipulating Ellen. One evening Ellen had had about all she could take. She threw herself on the bed to sleep, saying she would do no more for Della. Suddenly, she saw her Dad's face—he had been dead for several months—and though his lips did not move, she "knew" his message. He angrily demanded, "What are you doing?" and berated her for giving up on her sister so quickly. She felt helpless and ashamed for being so weak. Her father kept demanding "What are you doing?" until Ellen promised to keep trying to straighten Della out. During the days that followed, Ellen struggled on with her sister.

About a week and a half later, Ellen took a long-planned trip to visit Marilyn in Germany. In the car on the way from the airport, Ellen started to tell Marilyn her dream about their father's appearance, although she describes it as clearer than a dream.

Marilyn nudged her husband, "Does this ever sound familiar!"

When Ellen had finished telling the dream, Marilyn said she, too, had a visit from their father. In Marilyn's dream, the father had demanded more specifically, "What are you doing about Della?"

Unlike her more easily intimidated sister, Marilyn replied she wasn't doing anything about Della; it was Ellen who was taking care of Della. She also confronted him, saying,

"You didn't do anything about Della when you were alive, so what are you jumping all over *me* about?"

Her father demanded of her three times, "What are you doing about Della?" Each time, Marilyn said, "You need to talk to Ellen." Apparently, he did.

Ellen, who has had other psychic dreams, ends her account, "I need an explanation."

I cannot give Ellen an explanation for this *shared* dream; I can only point out some possibilities. One possibility is that Marilyn, concerned about her sister, dreamed about what her dead father might say. She rejected the message she associated with him. About the same time, his image appeared to her twin in the States, who was also wondering what to do about their sister. Ellen perceived the same image but, being more docile, accepted the message and resumed her role of caretaker for her sister.

A second possibility is that the dream came to Marilyn first, and she rejected the responsibility implied, sending the dream telepathically to her twin as a way of getting her father's image off her back.

Here is another poignant story of how a dead person appeared in a dream, first to one family member and then to another, trying to pull them together in time of need.

Arguments between my mother and her father would often cause them to have long periods of silence between them. During one such period, a dream came to Mother. At that time my mother, little brother, and I were living in a basement apartment in Chicago. We were all very sick, and Mother had been warned by her doctor to get out of that climate before the winter set in. I had bronchial asthma and wasn't expected to live through another hard winter. So Mother planned to move us to the West Coast, but we were so sick and in extremely bad shape financially.

One night, as Mother slept, she dreamed someone knocked on our apartment door. Mother got up and answered it. There was her deceased grandmother, who began begging, pleading with her to patch things up with her father. Her words, as my mother remembers them, were, "Bill will help, if you just let him know. Call him."

Mother replied, "He'll have to make the first move. I won't."

When she awoke, she thought how strange it was, since all her life she had never heard her grandmother call her father Bill as everyone else did. She always called him his real name, Wilbur.

Two days after this, Mother received a special-delivery letter from her dad, urging her to call him. She called, and they reconciled their differences. My grandfather and grandmother came to Chicago to move us. He pulled the trailer with our belongings all the way to Houston, and we rode in the car with my grandmother.

In the car on the trip, Mother asked her mother if her grandmother had ever called her father Bill. "Yes, about three months before her death she finally started calling him Bill," her mother told her.

At that reassurance, Mother told her mother her dream. Her mother responded that the same night Bill's mother had come to him in a dream, urging him to contact my mother, since we were going to move without his knowledge. In the dream, she told him how desperate we were. She also said that he would have to make the first move because Mother wouldn't. My grandmother said Granddad got out of bed before daylight and wrote the letter and went all the way downtown to the post office to mail it so that letter would reach us before we moved.

We cannot know if the plight of this family and the young mother's unwillingness to ask for help was communicated to her father telepathically by the image of the grandmother, a figment of the subconscious and a symbol of their underlying family unity, or if the grandmother herself in spirit intervened. In any case, the fact that the grandmother appeared in a dream to each of them seems to involve some kind of psychic communication. The use of the unfamiliar nickname, which the grandmother had only recently begun to use, is also a psychic detail. I am not a particularly religious person; I am skeptical about life after death. But after hearing dreams such as these, I ask myself: Is it not just as reasonable to conclude that the message of reconciliation was the urging of the psychic persona of the grandmother, as it is to conclude that the message and the image of the grandmother were concocted in the minds of two different people at the same time. If time and space can be suspended in ways we don't understand, why not the limits of life?

The strong imagery of the interceding grandmother makes the reality of her spirit seem convincing. As such, dreams are a strong indication of life of the spirit after death. In any case, it is reassuring to know that in most of the dreams of dead people the nature of the visit was helpful, and the impression of life after death has been a happy one.

Note that in any case the value of the dream was not automatic; its ultimate worth depended entirely on the positive response of at least one of the dreamers. Notice the young mother, in her pride, refused to respond. Only the father graciously overcame some hard feelings to reach out and change the life of his daughter. Think what would have happened if the father, too, had failed to act. The daughter and her sick children would not have been helped in their time of need; in fact, neither of the dreamers would ever have known that they had shared such a significant dream.

Another dream, whether psychic or not, was instrumental in achieving a reconciliation; again the success of the dream message was dependent on the dreamer's committed response.

My grandfather has been dead for almost seventeen years. In October of last year, after my uncle died, my grandfather came to me in a dream and told me my aunt and her family needed me. After this dream had come to me several times, I contacted my aunt. I started taking her to church and helping her with financial problems. Then I called her children, who had not been speaking to her, and I succeeded in getting them together as a family. It was hard, simply nerve-racking.

Each night I'd dream I saw my grandfather in a plastic cage. He would

*tell me to keep on "just a little longer, just a little longer." Then in
March of this year, my aunt died. I feel I did keep on, as my grandfather
asked, and that my aunt died in peace of mind.*

Here is another strong example of effective advice ostensibly coming from a deceased family member.

A woman remembers how her brother Philip, the baby of the family, had been spoiled and kept close to their mother's apron strings so completely that he remained an emotional adolescent well into adulthood. Philip married a nice young woman, and in the years following the marriage, he led his life as if she were last on his list of priorities. He was never cruel to her in any active way, but he did not pay any attention to her unless he happened to have a little time left over after attending to his business, his pleasures, his mother. The wife was naturally quite unhappy, to the point that the family wondered how long she would stay with the inconsiderate man. Various members of the family talked to Philip, pointing out the wife's obvious distress. The sister went so far as to take him to a therapist, who explored Philip's priorities with him without achieving any change or desire for change.

Then, one night, Philip had a dream in which his father appeared to him. The father had been dead since Philip was a small child, and he did not consciously remember the influence his father had had on him in those early years. In the dream, however, Philip's father addressed him in no uncertain terms, telling him he had better change his ways and give his wife the attention she deserved. He was stern and authoritative. Philip listened and heeded his father's words. The metamorphosis was astounding. Philip became, according to his sister, if not a wonderful husband, "as good a husband as Philip had it in him emotionally to be."

Philip's dream resembles an ordinary symbolic dream, in which a problem comes to resolution in the mind of a dreamer. There is no reason to consider it psychic, but who can say for sure?

One of the best deeds a dream visit by a dead person can do is to comfort the bereaved. This comment by a Canyon Lake, Texas, mother, whose twenty-seven-year-old son was lost in the crash of his F4 fighter plane, is typical: "Since his death, he has come to me in a dream, in which he told me he was happy and tried to console me."

Such reassurance in a dream can make an enormous difference in how a bereaved person deals with grief. One mother, whose only daughter was killed in a car wreck, simply could not recover from the loss. A year after the young girl's death the mother still could not bring herself to go out of the house. She had made the girl's bedroom into what amounted to a shrine, where she wept daily. The father, however, was coping much better. Asked what had sustained him in his grief, he replied that he had had a dream two weeks after his daughter's death, in which the girl had appeared to him, saying, "I am so happy here, and I don't want to come back." Because of this dream, the father said, he had accepted his daughter's death in a way his wife could not.

The message of comfort from the dead is particularly effective if the death of the loved one was also foretold in a dream. When the psychic power of dreams has been proven personally and dramatically in this way, the subsequent message of comfort is thus validated, as it was for a woman from Canton, Ohio.

My husband and I retired early, since he was tired. My sleep was normal until I dreamed he had died. I awoke with a start and looked at him; he was sleeping well. I went back to sleep, grateful it was only a dream. I dreamed the same thing again. This time I selected the pallbearers. The dream passed and I slept till morning. He seemed perfectly all right when he arose, so I went on the beauty shop. I did not tell him what I had dreamed. . . .

I returned home and was making plans for Easter, which was the next day. My husband came in and said he didn't feel well and started to bed, but fell with a massive heart attack and died almost immediately. He had had no previous trouble, in fact, he'd had a physical exam the Saturday before and was given a clean bill of health. He was only fifty years old and had never smoked in his life, and didn't drink coffee or alcohol in any form. I immediately thought about my dream the night before. I did not choose any of the pallbearers I selected in my dream. I did ask one, and he was going out of town. I didn't want the others. I had never paid any attention to dreams before this; in fact, I seldom dream.

I have had several dreams about him since his death, however, and my visits with him are so real. He seems so happy; in fact, in one he told me he was happy but misses me and our son.

The wonderful thing is that no one in my extensive research who has appeared in a dream after death has ever spoken of fire and brimstone or expressed any dismay at his condition. The reassuring if undescriptive word *happy,* as you have seen, is the universal opinion of the deceased when they make their opinion known.

One man, however, let a loved one know he was still around with feistier words:

In 1974 my brother died. He had been in the hospital six days. I arrived at the hospital several hours after he died. For some unknown reason my sister-in-law and my nephew did not let me know. I was so hurt and angry. My brother and I were very close.

About a week later, he came to me in a dream and said, "Don't cry for me, Ellen, I'm not dead. I don't know who that old goat is they buried." I've had peace of mind ever since.

And finally, I like the matter-of-fact way that Aunt Emily let Angela, an Atlanta housewife, know everything was fine where she went. Aunt Emily used to tell Angela from time to time that the dead come to people in dreams. When Aunt Emily herself died, Angela stayed awake several nights waiting for a visit from her. After a while, when no visit had materialized, Angela forgot about it. A year later, however, she dreamed the telephone rang and she answered it. Aunt Emily was on the line.

"But you're dead," objected Angela.

"You can be dead in one place and alive in another," explained Emily. "I'm very happy. I just wanted you to know."

The call was "very real, very supportive," says Angela, who understandably has a more comfortable view of death since her dream.

Are all of these dreams a manifestation of wishful thinking? Logically speaking, these dreams do not prove life after death. When otherwise unavailable information is imparted by an image of the dead, the revelation may be explained as "just another psychic dream." Emotionally speaking, however, visits from the dead are among the most positive of dream events.

TEN

Life Themes I

EDDY'S STORY

As you have seen, individual dreams followed by changes in attitude or other constructive response have had positive effects on the lives of dreamers. Series of dreams have helped people through times of indecision or conflict by showing step-by-step solutions. In much the same way, whole lives have been illuminated through related dreams that mark, validate, and even cause growth.

In many cases, a coherent series of dreams is remembered, especially by a person whose emotional equilibrium is influenced by a major life-issue. All of us have things we are trying to overcome—shyness, a less-than-stellar academic background, jealousy of a more successful sibling, an exaggerated need for financial security, whatever. People who have exceptional needs or unusual determination to change something in their lives have particularly strong life-issues. For them, dreams may come forth very dramatically or very persistently.

Marie Françoise, the Belgian woman who was not accepted by her father, is one example. It took her more than forty years to achieve a resolution to her problem of self-esteem. When resolution came, it was through a single very dramatic dream experience. Other people achieve growth bit by bit through many successive dream revelations and subsequent adjustments in attitude or active responses.

When a life-issue is strong, many dreams over a period of time reflect the same theme. The conflict appears over and over; only the symbols change. Other times the same symbols and variations return frequently through the years in recurrent dreams. When the dreamer recognizes the setting of such a dream, he says, "Here it comes again." Sometimes it insists, sometimes cajoles, but the feelings are repeated each time. Occasionally, a new element breaks into the familiar scene; finally, at a moment of growth the theme yields to a new feeling. It is important to find a resolution to recurrent dreams and dreams whose themes are repeated. These are signs of the issue's ongoing importance.

In the case of Eddy, now a successful thirty-three-year-old editor/producer, a dream with a set of recurrent images seemed to show up each time life took a tough turn—or was about to enter a new stage. The dream made him face misfortunes, but, as time went on, it also showed him he had the necessary strength. The repeating theme of his uniqueness, in conflict with his desire to belong, were eventually empowering. Seeing the conflict in concrete images and rising above it within the dream enabled Eddy to succeed in real life.

Eddy was four years old the winter of the first dream. The gray drabness of the coal-bearing hills seeped into every corner of the tall rooms of the old house his family rented. His mother, abandoned by his father shortly after Eddy's birth, had little to smile about; the struggle to feed herself, Eddy, and his older brother was wearing her out.

One night, when he had rolled himself up tight in the blanket he shared with his brother, he fell into a deep sleep. He dreamed he stood on a mountaintop under a strangely inky black sky. He was fixated on its disturbing, vast fluidity. When he finally looked down, he saw two red moons in the lower sky. In the valley below, luminescent waves rippled like wheat in the wind. At first, he found the wave patterns interesting; then he began to feel apprehensive. He began to realize the waves were people swaying as they looked up at him, staring. They were humming a word that he would later think of as a mantra. The humming became a deafening roar. Then it faded and faded until he could not hear the people's voices anymore. He strained to hear them, but he could not.

Eddy was impressed by the power of this dream and its imagery, but at age four he had little means of interpreting the experience. A week later, he fell sick with a painful throat and a pounding head. Because of the family's poverty, they hesitated to call a doctor until after the home remedies had failed. One night, Eddy recalls, he was lying feverish in his bed. He turned his head to look at his brother, but his brother was not there in the expected place beside him; only familiar carvings of stylized leaves on the crown moldings on the ceiling met his eye. He was floating. Looking down, he saw his bed, postage-stamp small, his brother's dark curls silhouetted on his pillow. There beside the older boy was Eddy himself, blond, bony, his limbs sprawled out to the cool of the night. He felt light and free.

The feeling of taking a vantage point outside of himself was what is usually called an out-of-body experience. This phenomenon is reported most often in near-death situations, which this may have been for Eddy. The idea of the mind being free of the body to travel psychically is very like the way the dreaming mind feels itself an *observer* in *simultaneous* dreams. Indeed Eddy's experience may have been a *simultaneous* dream, in which the scene observed was himself.

The next thing Eddy knew, he awoke, his mother screaming at him in terror. Then it was night again, and he awoke in the blank whiteness of a hospital. This time he heard no screaming, no voices. The lips moved, but the voices had faded. Eddy was deaf.

Even as a small child, Eddy had felt the emotional importance of the theme of his first "sky, mountain, and valley" dream. Only later, however, when he had had his second dream with these same images, did Eddy realize that the fading of the voices was predicted in his first such dream.

Eddy soon realized that he was going to be very different. But he didn't want to be. He knew what that meant. He had already felt set apart. In his brother's hand-me-downs, he was already just about the shabbiest kid around, and his mother had undergone the shame of abandonment, the suspect state of divorce. Now this.

Kids said things to him he couldn't hear; so he tried to guess their meaning and to respond appropriately. His answers didn't turn out to be the right ones, and the kids laughed. After a while, the kids didn't seem to understand what he said at all. They made fun of him, and he fought back with fists.

He had dreams every night of being trapped—in a room, in a cage, in a box. . . . After a while, in defense, he became reclusive, transforming his silent confinement into a private chamber lined with books. He read for hours every day. He learned words his mother didn't know; he discovered realms his friends had never imagined. When he found he knew words his teachers didn't know and followed arguments over their heads, he began to think his world was superior to theirs and that he was someone special, someone rich, a master of his own domain.

Teachers sometimes thought he was retarded because he couldn't answer questions. To Eddy, their treatment of him seemed sadistic. Through all this, he retained a strong sense of being intelligent. In some ways, his superior world seemed to make up for his deafness. Yet he was filled with rage at being different.

When he was eleven, the "sky" dream returned. He was on the mountain again. He recognized the black, black sky. Again he saw the two red moons. He recognized the people swaying in waves. This time they hummed out to him, "What do you want us to do?"

In anger, he answered, "Burn!"

The rhythm of the people became more agitated. They were upset. He felt a sudden power because he had disturbed the rhythm of these people. Then he felt ashamed and frightened at their alienation. He had wanted to be able to get their attention, but he was afraid of their reaction.

He tried to join them, but something stopped him. He could not become a part of them yet. He knew his anger would flare up again, and he felt protective of them. He withdrew—for his sake and theirs.

In his waking mind in the weeks after the dream, Eddy contemplated its importance. By this time, Eddy had a pretty good idea what some of his dream symbols meant. He recalls knowing even then that the sky in his recurring dream represented the "backdrop for my life, a frame of reference." The blackness "represented a void—that's how I felt about my life. Out of the void, I created my own world, but the black sky always framed my dreams." The two burning moons represented his ears burning with fever, his hearing burning away. The valley was "the repository for my yearning, the pit of my desires for a normal life." The waves were energy patterns, a sense of movement, things working together, people who seemed to "have it all together." The ridge on which Eddy stood in his dream was his vantage point. "I'm always in a superior position, looking down, never up. Unwilling to leave the ridge for the valley, still I yearn to belong among the people in the valley."

The feelings of explosive danger, fear, and power (and fear of using power) caused him great anxiety; he realized he was a disaster waiting to happen, if he did not manage himself with judiciousness. With typical precocity, he set himself the goal of learning to control his anger so that someday he might join the people in the valley. That was his positive response.

When he was about thirteen, his mother got him a hearing aid. The sounds that came flooding into his ears—though never as pure as they had been before he was deafened—made conversation possible. He tried it out at home with his mother. He finally got up the nerve to wear the device to school, even though the kids pointed and talked about it. The new experience of being tuned in was worth the embarrassment. If Eddy could only learn how to join in, he could make up for lost time. But after just a few weeks of auditory communication, the hearing aid disappeared, lost in the careless shuffle of school days. There was no money to replace it. Eddy was back in his world of silence.

The taste of possibilities, however, had tantalized Eddy. He turned the radio on loud, stood in the corner of his room where the converging walls could reflect and amplify the sounds on both sides, and tried to mimic the muffled words of the radio announcers. He strained to hear the little unaccented syllables, to figure out the missing consonants, to repeat the words with the confidence and clarity of a sportscaster or a news anchorman. For hours and days, he worked on auditory perception and speaking.

As years went by, Eddy's mother told him that to grow up a normal boy, he had to play sports. She signed him up and pushed him out the door. He tried baseball and basketball. He had good coordination, a good eye, and enough height. Though he was next to last on the list, he made the

B team in basketball. Predictably, the years of relying on himself alone, the lack of practice at group interaction, resulted in good one-on-one moves but little facility with teamwork. He played, but more often he sat on the bench. Still, sitting on the bench with a bunch of other guys was closer to being "in" than he had ever known. It was being somewhere on Friday night, being watched by supportive crowds, feeling friendly hands on his shoulders, being treated the same as the others, being noticed for something positive instead of for his deficiencies. Eddy gained confidence not so much in basketball as in being a part of a group, being proud to be *himself.*

Basketball meant a great deal to Eddy, but it was a lot of work for a little play. Besides his lowly status as a substitute player, he sprained his ankle several times and missed entire games. He didn't know if his ankle would ever be completely right again. Although basketball had brought him into the world of regular guys, he just didn't know if it was worth it. One evening, after warming the bench through most of a midseason game, Eddy quit the team. He had made the decision, but he was miserable with it. He went home, slipped gloomily up to his room, telling no one what he'd done. He flung himself on the bed to sleep away the emptiness.

Eddy dreamed he had sprouted enormous wings and could fly. But, although the wings were graceful, his takeoff was awkward, difficult. After repeated attempts to get airborne, he finally soared into the dark night sky. He flew over his brightly lit high school gymnasium, where there was a basketball game going on. He hovered over the game, cheering his teammates on.

"I felt light and free," he remembers. "No one really noticed me. I felt good, as if I did not need that anymore."

As in the valley and sky dreams, Eddy was once more high above the people. The wings represented the means to rise to success, the awkward takeoff his difficult beginnings;

but the waves of people in the valley, who had been abstract and distant, were replaced by the basketball team. He had been among them; he had belonged. Now the basketball team had served its purpose. He had grown and was ready to go on to something else. He no longer needed basketball as an arena to prove himself or as a means to get attention, but as a spectator, he cheered them on.

When Eddy awoke and thought about the dream, it helped him feel good about his decision to quit the team. The embarrassment of being last-chosen, the shame of quitting, and the agonizing prospect of facing his former teammates disappeared. He felt in charge of his life and ready to seek another area of activity more suited to his talents.

About this time Eddy's mother again scraped together several hundred dollars and bought him another hearing aid. This time Eddy wore it without self-consciousness; he had achieved a sense of worth that transcended any sense of deficiency. Although understanding group discussion remained difficult, he could follow one-on-one conversations well. Public school speech therapy, along with the new aid, helped him master the mechanics of talking so that only a hint of a lisp revealed that he had ever been impaired. He had, for the most part, overcome his deafness. Nevertheless, the isolation he felt from having missed normal social contact for all of his formative years lingered.

With money provided by the state vocational rehabilitation program and from an on-campus job, he managed to arrive at the state university where his academic ability could be challenged and where, among his intellectual peers, he could feel a sense of belonging. He reveled in it, honing his abilities. He especially nurtured those skills that had once been the most out of reach. He took to entertaining his friends with stand-up comedy routines; he was a member of the debate team and the student newspaper staff. Whatever anger he may have still harbored against those waves of people in his past found an acceptable outlet, acceptable at least to his friends: He became a student activist, a political protester. Besides all that, he had a girl friend.

Then one night the old dream returned. The same mountain ridge, the same weird black sky, the same two red moons, the same valley. Standing on the ridge, he recognized in the dream the juxtaposition that symbolized his isolation, the dream situation that had preceded disasters. There was a sudden outcry from the waves of people in the valley, as something divided them, cut the flow in two like the parting of the Red Sea. He felt the fear of separation.

Eddy was awakened by his roommate bursting into the room bearing empty cans of spray paint and boasting of spraying the ROTC building and the administration building with anti-Vietnam involvement slogans. By morning, the dean of students and the chief of police had descended on the dormitory. They took Eddy in their car and questioned him for hours. Eddy denied being involved in the vandalism, but he would not break the code; he would not defend himself by accusing his roommate. Both boys were enjoined to leave the campus. Gone was the newspaper work, the debate forum, the camaraderie of activism, the girl friend, the belonging. His world had been cut in two just as the people in his dream valley had been separated.

Eddy eventually came back to college, but those later years were not the same as the first ones, in which he reveled in the intense shared experiences of ardent freshman and reckless sophomores. He was back for the degree. He received his degree in psychology and set about earning a living.

One January, Eddy began a new relationship and a new project. He met a video producer named Michelle, and they embarked on the creation of a television production called "The Lifeforce," which would be the opening of a multimedia campaign to promote healthier life-styles in an area of the country known for its poor understanding of nutrition, its high alcoholism rate, low level of education, and the debilitating absence of self-esteem that characterizes such segments of society. The work would reflect Eddy's and Michelle's mutual interest in people who had not realized their physical, mental, and spiritual potential. The project had the backing of numerous state officials and nationally known fitness experts. Michelle and Eddy would travel the state together documenting situations and putting them together visually in ways that would appeal emotionally to people wanting to make changes in their lives. Michelle was to seek out the people and scenes that best presented their message visually. Eddy was to commit the spirit of their subjects to words. The video project would later be incorporated in seminars as part of the larger campaign.

Eddy and Michelle spent hours and hours discussing food and philosophy, past relationships and ambitions. They traveled and worked together. They took walks in the park; they were playful together. They began as friends; soon they were lovers.

Over the months, disagreements and uncertainties about the project arose; long hours of work and money frustrations frayed the bonds between them. He had seen signs that too much togetherness could ruin either the project or their relationship. She had considered going on the road without him, getting another writer, with his approval. He too had considered not working day to day with Michelle; he felt the distancing would be good for their personal relationship. She waited for him to decide; he hesitated. "I was sort of numbed," he says. "I didn't want to go with her, but I didn't want to decide that." He asked her to give him a few more days before seeking another writer.

By summer the results of Eddy's aggressive promotion were falling into place. Several good corporate sponsors promised help; school districts and governmental agencies agreed to use the program; details were ironed out. For the first time, they were both convinced that the project was definitely going to fly. Relief and excitement took the strain out of their relationship; they were enjoying each other again. In this flush of optimism the matter of whether Eddy and Michelle went on the road together seemed just another detail to work out.

One night he dropped her off after a shoot. "I'll see you tomorrow," he'd said with easy comfort. That night Eddy had this dream.

1   In a big room there were scores of people related to our project—politicians, sponsors. It was all so vivid. A big glass-topped table was covered with smoked salmon, roast turkey, salads. Everyone was toasting with Korbel natural champagne. They were congratulating each other on how well it was going, how happy they were that we had come to this point.

2   I felt strange because the celebration was premature. We had letters of support, intent to agree, but no signed agreements. I felt nervous about it.

The banquet room had a picture window that opened up right on the beach. I felt uneasy. Michelle was sitting on my right. I turned around, hearing waves. The sky was inky black; the ocean waves seethed with energy.

Michelle was staring expressionless ahead. It was a weird stare, and I couldn't get any reaction from her. All the other people were whooping it up beyond reason, but Michelle was in a trance.

One of our sponsors stood up and offered this toast, "To Michelle and Eddy, who know a good storm when it is about to break." At that moment, a monstrous storm arose over the water as if a tidal wave would sweep us away. Across the black sky an even blacker funnel was advancing.

3   Michelle looked at me with an incredible stare, then took all of her clothes off. She said, "I've got to get my eyes" (she

called her video camera her eyes) and, stark naked, ran away down the beach toward her car.

I ran after her. The crowd said, "Let her go; that's what artists do." But I ran out into the middle of the storm. She was having no trouble running on down the beach, but I was being driven back at every step by the storm. Finally, the funnel sucked her up. Oh, my God! She's dead. Gone. I had an incredible sense of loss. My face was hot with tears.

4   Then all of a sudden I felt warm all over; I felt I was back in my valley. That rhythm, that murmur. I felt I had control. All I had to do was raise my arms and emit that sound I had known since childhood. I raised my arms and the sky lightened. Michelle came floating down. I took her in my arms and took her away from the room, away from her car, away from the project. I felt good.

Although Eddy had always intuitively understood his dreams, my method of dream analysis gave him a finer understanding of the steps he had taken and made him confident that future misfortunes would offer opportunity for further growth. Here are his word associations divided into the four dramatic scenes of the dreams.

1   *big room*   lots of people, a challenge: I've always been good one-on-one, but in a big room of people the ambient noise in my hearing-aid keeps me from following conversation.

our project   the project and the relationship began at the same time. It was a symbiotic statement about our political beliefs, our complementary art, our sensitivity to people. The project was bringing it all together.

politicians   policy-makers, mouthpieces

sponsors   enablers, partners

glass-topped table   transparency, nothing holding anything up

salmon, turkey, salads   food has been a real issue in my life since childhood, and still I am a "starving artist."

Korbel natural champagne uneasiness, it reminds me of a woman I was engaged to, we used to sit on the levee drinking that good cheap champagne; she committed suicide.

2 *letters of support*   supportiveness but only promises
picture window   could see clearly the storm was brewing
beach   place both lovely and frightening. When I was twelve, I almost drowned twice. It's renewal and fear.
Michelle on my right   my partner, very different from me, not much emotion, distant, self-protective; someone I needed to understand to understand myself. That is also a numbness in me that I have covered up with camaraderie, doing debate and stage acting, something I needed to touch.
waves   forces in valley, people I could never be a part of
expressionless stare   I don't know who I am, what I'm doing here, or why we came this far.
toasting   it was so weird that the guy toasting Michelle and me had, in real life, made a pass at her. I was disappointed in him. Disappointment, deception.
a good storm   culmination of wave pattern
funnel   all the energy focused

3 *took her clothes off*   she's usually so self-protective. Here she opened up, but it was just a superfluous gesture. It's as if she said, "When I open up, you still can't see me" or "Vulnerability wasn't important after all."
her eyes   her camera. She uses it as a defense. She sees her subjects, but they don't see her.
she ran away   abandonment, like my dad
sucked up by the funnel   by the immensity of the task

4 *warm all over*   voice from valley
in the valley   but not of it, strength from it
murmur   energy
raised my arms   gesture of power, control

> *carried her away* I could have her, but only away from the project

In the first scene, the *situation* is plain. The big challenge of Eddy's life, "getting it all together," is symbolized by the project that brings together in one package the possibility of artistic success, love, and food on the table.

The *problem,* found in scene two, is that Eddy is uneasy about celebrating the project's success, for in the very acts of celebration he sees only possibilities of disappointment, loss, and pain. (The first hint of a problem is actually revealed in scene one when Eddy associated the image of Korbel champagne with loss by suicide.) Eddy does not identify Michelle as an object of his love, as we might expect; rather he indicates that she represents his own self-search. Notice *her* "expressionless stare" becomes in word association *his* failure to find himself. Again "Michelle on my right" evokes "someone *I needed to understand myself.* That is also *a numbness in me."* Michelle, as a dream element, is a sort of alter ego, personifying his efforts to see behind his own self-deception.

In part three, we look for the dilemma to *work itself out to a climax.* Michelle takes her clothes off, runs out, and is sucked up—a climax, certainly. Self-revelation has not been the big deal he thought it would be. Finding himself is still ahead of him, and he is overwhelmed by the "immensity of the task." He feels the pain he has felt so keenly at other times when his identity has been snatched from him by misfortune.

The *resolution* is swift and clear. The images of his life theme return. He is *in* the valley for the first time, if not *of* it. He feels the voice from the valley. He chooses to take control. The sky lightens at his command. He renews his search for identity with confidence, but it is clear that knowing who he is does not succeed or fail with "The Lifeforce Project"; he takes his desire for identity away from the project.

This dream itself probably did not *give* Eddy the power to be in control of his own life, but it *made him aware* of the position of strength at which he had arrived. The dream reminded him that he could be in control, validated his decision to distance himself from Michelle and accept a diminished yet valuable role in the success of the project. He felt the burgeoning strength and, as a positive response, decided to take the initiative in changing his status in "The Lifeforce Project."

But before he could call Michelle, she called him. She had made a decision for him, she said. He wouldn't be going on the road with her. She had decided to get another writer. He was, of course, a full partner in the project as always; he would be in charge of marketing as he had been. And, she added, their personal relationship was over; she didn't love him anymore, probably she had never really loved *him* so much as the *idea* of working with a lover.

Eddy was shocked. Just when he thought things were going better than ever, the love relationship was over. He felt the blow of disappointment. But unlike other such disappointments in his life, Eddy did not feel this rejection was the end of the world. He knew his dream. He accepted the strength from the valley. His new-found resilience felt as strange and startling to him as Michelle's revelation, and he wrapped himself in it as in a new and magical cloak.

Several nights later, another dream came to Eddy. He was in the valley; the familiar waves were flowing rhythmically around him. There was a wall to one side of the valley. Something was closed off, but the wall was not especially foreboding. He walked over to it and found a letter stuck in a crevice. Somehow he knew that the note was for him, and he opened it. Although in the dream he was not ever aware of seeing the actual contents, he knew the communication was from Michelle. The dream ended with Eddy holding the letter, feeling neither joy nor sorrow but having a strong sense that everything would work out all right concerning the contents of the letter.

As a symbolic drama, the dream is fairly straightforward. Eddy confirms that the valley was the same valley. The wall, he says, is a barrier; something is closed. The letter is a communication, but not face to face. The crevice is a chink in the barrier, a device for limited communication. Eddy identified Michelle as the chance to put his career, his desire for an intimate relationship, and his search for himself all in one basket— "The Lifeforce Project." That was now out of reach, but his feelings of satisfaction at the end were "businesslike" and made him think that it was time to go on with other matters.

The dream problem, like the real-life problem, reveals that a barrier has formed between him and the realization of his goal—to find a harmonious place in life. Then a communication comes from Michelle about the project, but it is from a distance, not intimate. The project is now a business deal, a career step, not the coming together of all the desires of his life. The resolution of the dream is that he accepts this arrangement and feels satisfied and optimistic.

The dream helped Eddy to put the project and recent events in perspective and to get on with his part of the project with a more limited objective. He considered the dream as classic symbolism, thinly veiled at that.

The next day, however, he was startled to receive a letter, a communication from Michelle, indirectly, through her lawyer. It stated that it was necessary to put the project arrangements down in clear contract terms, to define their roles in writing. The letter gave Eddy a bad start. He had been accustomed to defining their roles according to their personal relationship and by their recognition of each other's talents and aspirations. Now he had to consider the impact of the barrier between them on his career. He had visions of paying hundreds of dollars for a lawyer to fight for the fruits of his work up to that point. It seemed like a bad dream. Then he remembered that the dream of the night before, which seemed to foretell this letter more exactly than he could have guessed, had been a good dream, not joyful but satisfying. Its message was clearly that things would work out. Eddy decided to accept the dream. Yes, he got a lawyer to handle the issues, but he did not let the matter torment him.

Things did work out. The project was funded and completed, although it never led to the full-scale program that had originally been planned. Eddy is currently involved in another project with a satisfying theme and magnitude. "I still feel tugs sometimes, thinking about what might have been," Eddy says, "but mostly I've gotten over it.

"After all that, I am also—finally—confident about some future relationship. Yes, I'm still vulnerable, but now I know that to open to someone, to risk, and to lose is not the end of the world. I'm in control of *me;* I'll still be *me* at the end of the storm."

The life theme of Eddy's dreams—the ups and downs in his struggle to belong while still nurturing his uniquely superior talents—marked Eddy's growth in a symbolic way. In addition, the predictive aspect of some of the dreams, which preceded setbacks Eddy did not anticipate, seems to be psychic knowledge presented in symbolic terms. The psychic value of his experience gives Eddy faith in the dreams: He feels confident that he will keep his vantage on the mountain, jutting into an ever-lightening sky; endure the remnants of his burning moons; and become more harmonious with the rhythms of the valley.

ELEVEN

Life Themes II

ADELE'S STORY

Like Eddy, Adele had many disturbing dreams over the years, which she felt reflected troubling themes in her life. Unlike Eddy, she was never aware of any psychic content in her dreams, but she felt they symbolized insights she had not fully realized consciously.

I first met Adele when she attended one of my dream workshops to learn my method of dream interpretation. Later, she made an appointment with me for private counseling. She told me her general impressions of her childhood in the 1940s and 1950s and the major points of her current problems; then we spent some time talking about her dreams. I soon realized she had learned to interpret her own dreams very effectively. Though she later went to another therapist available without charge through school, she came back to visit me periodically to give me "progress reports" and to share especially important dreams with me. She gave me permission to publish her story because we both felt that dream interpretation facilitated her growth over a period of years, and we hoped a detailed account would be instructive to others who are puzzled by the insistent but veiled messages of symbolic dreams.

The way Adele described her childhood situation to me, she felt like the "boy" of the family. Born first in a string of four girls, she had the feeling she was different from the others. She was more serious, more inhibited, more responsible than her sociable younger sisters. She was the high achiever; they were more dependent, lighthearted, and lovable, she believed. Their characteristics Adele considered feminine; hers more masculine. She had been led somehow to think that masculine was better, so she prized these characteristics. When someone, admiring her logical thinking, told her she thought like a boy, she took it as a compliment. Even so, though she was the closest thing her parents had to a son, she made an inferior boy. Her parents seemed pleased with her only for her achievements. Except at report card time or awards ceremonies, they seemed to take little interest in her. Her sisters, however, were clinging, winsome, giggling girls, perfect examples of what girls were meant to be. They were, all three of them, her parents' favorites, the ones with whom they preferred to spend their time. Adele's independence meant not only that she did not seem to need her parents' attention as much as her sisters did, but that they did not feel needed. Adele and her parents developed little intimacy. Adele believed all this from the beginning, but she learned to articulate her beliefs and to put them in perspective only in recent years.

Adele went on to explain how, from her earliest years, she had confidence in her ability and expected to accomplish great things. She had expected to be the achiever of the family and have a career, whereas her sisters, she thought, would do just average and get married and have families early in life. Her family was proud of her academic achievements and her talents, but in more personal ways she could not seem to please them. She could hardly wait to grow up and leave home to pursue a life of independence and adventure. The careers she pictured for herself were very much in a man's world.

But as each choice came along, a choice of colleges, for example, she chose the least independent, the least adventurous. She was accepted at three medium or large coed schools at some distance from home, one several thousand miles away, one in a big city. She was also accepted at one small, all-girl school in a town nearby. She chose the small, protected, and protective girl's school nearby. She had toyed with the idea of the school more suited to her dreams, held on to the option for a while, then let it go. She ended up being one of the most confident girls in her freshman class; perhaps she preferred that to being one of the least confident in a more socially challenging school. She did outstanding work there, as she had expected.

In her next big decision, she chose to marry immediately after graduation and to go with her husband where his job took him. Rick was a bright young college graduate, raised in a very conservative, traditional blue-collar family. He picked out their first car, their first apartment, their first furniture. She was with him, but he asked the questions, and she limited her influence to agreeing with him. She was pleased with whatever he chose. She learned to cook and determined to be a wonderful homemaker just as she had been a great student.

Soon she was offered a job when a large corporation contacted her college and one of her professors recommended her for a position. She considered the job wistfully, realizing it exactly fit her original career plans, but she found she felt

extremely apprehensive when it got down to the real prospect of having a job in the business world. She turned down
the job and decided to have a baby right away instead. That
kept the prospect of accepting any job offers safely out of
the question.

She had been happy with her husband and her baby girl
and the two baby boys that followed, but she had been
unhappy with something else. It didn't ring a bell with her
that she should do something about her emotional situation
because she had long been accustomed to the feeling that
she was waiting for something that was missing. However,
she had spells of depression that were new: extreme fatigue,
long naps, periods of despair, in which she sobbed until she
was exhausted without being able to articulate a single specific complaint about her life. All this napping and sobbing
kept her from housekeeping, which had never been satisfying anyway. Housekeeping, however, was important to
Rick. The more he complained about the way she kept
house, the more she hated keeping house, the more she
moped. She kept all this to herself, perking up when her
husband came home. She served dinner, listening to his
tales of business, the challenges he faced, the people he met,
the sales seminars he attended.

She didn't do anything about her daily malaise because
she could not put her finger on what specifically made her
unhappy, and she and Rick never talked about that kind of
thing. She had once asked Rick why they did not have long
talks about their feelings, conversations like those she had
with her close girl friends. He replied, "I'm just not that
kind of person." She once approached him calmly and constructively about some of his behavior that made her unhappy, and he wouldn't talk about it. He went on as if he
had never heard what she said. She brought it up again later
more plaintively, and he just called her selfish. She argued
and he became enraged. She was discouraged, frustrated,
and afraid to bring up that matter again or any other con-

cern. As years passed, hostility and a feeling of helplessness built up.

She found that certain types of experiences, however, did make her happy. She found herself gravitating toward the conversations of career men and women at parties, instead of her housewife friends in their usual crowd. She found herself becoming very animated discussing certain topics where stimulating intellectual ideas were being applied in the "real" world. At the same time, she began to notice her husband becoming irritable whenever she became animated and socially independent of him. It made her feel guilty to enjoy so much what made him irritable. He criticized what she said and told her to "calm down." She began to feel rebellious but afraid of his displeasure. She liked to be on the other side of the room from him. She recognized that her relationship with him was very like her relationship with her father. She couldn't love him because everything—his financial support, his approval, the tranquillity of the household—depended on his pleasure. And he was so hard to please!

About this time, Adele began to read material in magazines on women's issues. It didn't take very long for her to recognize that she was suffering from a very common woman's syndrome—the high-achieving woman becomes housewife: end of story. She read and she read; she talked to other women, tentatively at first, then ardently. She became angry, angry that men had all the challenges to fulfill their potential, that women only provided the nest for them to come home to. She became specifically angry at her husband for what she perceived was his punitive attitude toward her lack of interest in her assigned role. She became angry at her father for having been that way toward her mother. She became angry at her father-in-law for having raised her husband to be the way he was. She became angry at all the men who were not actively trying to change this. She had been having nightmares, she said, that seemed to show her fear of men and their power and to explain her anger toward the threat men represented.

She had actually been having the same nightmare since childhood, but in recent months recurrences had become more frequent, more and more frightening, and increasingly urgent. She felt that the stepped-up intensity of the dreams was a significant and illuminating factor that she needed to explore right away.

The expression "sweet dreams" was a mystery to Adele; nothing sweet had ever happened in her dreams, she said. Instead, she remembers as a young child waking up from her dreams shaking and frightened. Always there was a man chasing her, lurking and chasing. A faceless man who might harm her, he was no particular man with no particular weapon. She ran and she ran and she ran. He lurked in halls of strange dark houses and suddenly stepped out to confront her. She ran up staircases, out windows, across roofs. He waited behind bushes in woods to pursue her. She stumbled down paths, leaped across streams, climbed giant rocks. Her greatest dream decision was whether to hide in a closet or thicket and hope he would pass or to keep a distance between them, always running.

She told me the man in the dreams was beginning to come closer and stay longer than ever before. In fact, he was beginning to stay after the point when she awoke. He would be blocking her path through the woods, for example; she would wake up, and he would be standing in her bedroom. He stayed, it seemed, for several seconds until her conscious reason overpowered her perception of him. She felt particularly helpless because in the past she had been able to escape at least when terror succeeded in waking her. Now even waking did not bring immediate relief.

I said, "Tell me about this man. What is he like?"

He had no particular physical features, she said. "He's powerful, sure of himself. He takes the initiative. He doesn't specifically threaten me with harm, but I know he is strong, and I am deathly afraid of what might happen."

I said, "This man is the masculine part of *you*. Part of you is powerful, sure of yourself, assertive. You do not know what danger this part of you poses. You only know you are strong, and you are deathly afraid of what might happen."

Adele was astounded, then relieved, then tearful. I did not realize until later how important this dream revelation was to her.

Adele agreed immediately that the traits of power, confidence, assertiveness, and strength were indeed traits she considered masculine. If these traits she had so prized as a child had to be personified in a dream image, the image would have to be a man, she agreed.

With Adele, I had followed the method of dream analysis described in Chapter Seven. My directive, "Tell me about this man," was the equivalent of asking Adele to associate with the dream image. Interpreted part by part, the setting or *situation* of each recurring dream was simply "where I am," and the *problem* was her fear of the man, who represented the so-called masculine traits of power, confidence, initiative or assertiveness, and strength. Running and running until her pursuer cornered her was the way the dream *worked out to a climax.* Like most recurring dreams, there was no *resolution.* The dream repeated itself, asking over and over for a resolution.

This interpretation made an immediate difference in Adele's attitude. She had supposed that the man in the dream was all men—her father, her husband, and all the men who did not share the challenges of adulthood with women. When I told her that the dream man was *part of her,* that she was afraid of her own power and initiative, she realized suddenly that she was afraid, not of men, but of letting the masculine part of her succeed. Men, including her husband, *might* react negatively to her ambitions, but her own inhibitions were equally or more controlling than their negative reactions. Her choice of school, and her choice of a husband, too, kept her from having to face her ambitions, to risk initiative. As long as she turned down jobs, had children, and stayed married to this man, she would never have to face the masculine part of her, which in the past she had admired.

But why had the child who admired and counted on her ambition and ability to achieve become so fearful of the traits that would allow her to achieve in adulthood? "I don't know," said Adele. "I was just afraid that it was the wrong thing to do."

It became apparent that Adele's fear of the masculine part of herself stemmed from the threat it posed to her relationship with her father in the past and with her husband in the present. Independence had cost her her father's affection, it seemed, and, if pursued, was likely to change her husband's feelings for her, too. No wonder her recent expressions of a need to be stimulated outside the family had frightening repercussions. But now that she knew what she was afraid of, she was freed of her general hostility toward men for having denied her the opportunity. It had been largely *her* choice to deny her "masculine" qualities; the choice to enjoy them could be hers now. She had only to accept her desires as valid, work out ways with her husband to meet these desires in an open, constructive, nonjudgmental way.

Soon after Adele's decision to stop regarding men as the enemy and to accept the fact that she herself had chosen to deny an important part of her personality, she had another dream. Unlike the simple chase scenes of the past, this dream had more details, more complexity. The added detail seems to amplify the basic theme that Adele had heard over and over in the original recurrent dream until she finally understood it. Like the pharaoh's dream interpreted by Joseph, it had two parts. The second part was just a repetition of the first, with different symbols as if for emphasis.

1 I dreamed I lived alone in a house in a college-type community. There was a party with some of my high school classmates.

2 After the party, I was trying to rent out a room in the house for money. A strange middle-aged man applied, with whom I felt no rapport. I didn't want to rent the room to him, but he wouldn't go away.

3 I finally pushed him out the door, but he kept trying to get back in. I tried to latch the door then and he used a nail and a screwdriver to open the lock. I tried to hit him with something, but it didn't bother him.

4 I knew it was hopeless to keep him out. I felt very anxious.

1 I was watching kids play on the hill, and a horse came galloping down the hill. I liked that.

2 But the horse came to my door and put its head in.

3 I tried pushing the horse's head out nicely, then I had to get something to hit the horse in the face, but that was ineffective. It was the same scene as with the man.

4 I knew I couldn't keep the horse out much longer. I was scared, but less scared with the horse because it was less sinister. It was more directly forceful and less cleverly manipulative.

Adele recognized immediately that the strange intruding man was the same man who had been chasing her in dreams for most of her life because her feelings about him were the same. She easily made the following word associations with the other elements of the dream.

1. alone   taking care of myself
   house   protection
   college community   self-contained unit
   party   not arranged by me; I didn't invite them
   high school classmates   I was not close or secure with them

2. rent out a room   the traditional way single women, without profession, made ends meet
   money   necessary for independence
   strange - didn't know him
   older   too old to be attractive
   man   my "masculine" side
   no rapport   no rapport
   I didn't want to rent the room to him   I was uncomfortable with him and didn't want him around
   he wouldn't go away   insistent

3. I pushed him out   I was determined
   kept trying to get back in   determined, not polite, not normal
   latch the door   a safeguard (when I was a child, I tried to lock a door against a molester but was overpowered)
   he used a nail   men can do things mechanical
   then a screwdriver   same as the nail
   tried to hit him   matched my power against his
   it didn't bother him   my power was insufficient

4. I knew it was hopeless to keep him out   same

1. kids play   fun, sociable
   on a hill   pleasant, I like hills
   horse   beautiful, strong
   galloping   graceful, free
   down the hill   easily, wonderful feeling
   I liked that   pleasure

2 ⎡ *to my door*　threat of danger
　⎣ *put his head in*　intrusive

3 ⎡ *I tried to push*　struggle
　⎢ *nicely*　I try to be nice
　⎢ *hit the horse*　I had to get tough
　⎣ *ineffective*　I was powerless

4 ⎡ *I knew I couldn't keep him out much longer*　it was just a matter of
　⎢　　time
　⎢ *less sinister*　natural, not sneaky
　⎢ *more directly forceful*　honest opposition
　⎣ *less cleverly manipulative*　more open

Adele, interpreting the *situation* from the first scene, understood that she was taking care of herself but in a protected situation like college. The *problem* was that in her efforts to support herself without a career, an unwanted male, strange and more mature, was trying to get in. As she *worked the problem out,* she succeeded temporarily in preventing his entry, but he was using his masculine skills to get in anyway. The *resolution,* frightening though it was, was that the intruder would gain entry and she would have to face him.

Since she had learned, through interpretation of her recurring dreams, that the intruding male was that masculine part of herself she feared, she understood the new dream message: that she would have to accept this part of herself and learn to use it, instead of wasting her efforts in vain to exclude "him."

She interpreted the second version of the dream in the same manner. The *situation, problem, working out to a climax,* and *resolution* were the same. But she noticed that in the second version, with the horse as the intruder, everything was less intimidating, easier to deal with. She could relate to the children better than to the classmates they replaced, and the horse, unlike the strange older man, was beautiful. The qualities of the horse—strength and initiative—she saw as admirable, free, graceful. The horse seemed more "open" and forthright in his efforts to get in; she knew better where she stood with the horse. The second version of the dream uses symbolism Adele was more ready to accept. It was a presentation of the message she could respond to with more confidence. Such is the nature of dreams: They paint a picture to help the dreamer deal with a problem at her current emotional level of readiness.

Adele realized that the time was past for asking herself would she or would she not let the threatening male part of her in. The matter was settled. She knew it would upset her way of life, force her to be more confrontive, cause her feelings of guilt. She knew it would upset Rick because it would upset his way of life. She did not think it would upset her children, because they were flexible, but Rick would think it was detrimental to the children or at least he would use their needs as a reason to keep the status quo. She expected resistance from him, the one person above all whom she was afraid to face with her newly accepted side.

As a response to the dream, she made up her mind, nevertheless, to value instead of fear the masculine side of her that she had valued as a child and had expected would lead her as an adult. She made up her mind to give that suppressed part of her a chance. And for the children, she decided to serve as a model of an active, assertive adult who went out and made her own destiny, who didn't settle for the unsatisfactory for fear of the discomfort of change. She would deal with the consequences as bravely as possible.

Adele began to make small attempts to do things "men do"—make independent decisions about money; go places alone; talk to mechanics about her car, make inquiries with several businesses before making purchases instead of always asking Rick. She took karate lessons and gained a new confidence in her body and in her ability to take care of herself physically. She found herself jubilant at the feel of her new independence, then scared of her husband's reactions. Her fears, she knew from her dream insights, were partly her own inhibitions, but these were reinforced when he put down each of her efforts, second-guessed her decisions, redid things she had done so they'd be done "right." Sometimes she anticipated his reactions—correctly or incorrectly—so she became secretive about what she did. Naturally, this made him suspicious and negative.

As the struggle between her desire to lead her own expanded life and his resistance became more intense, Adele began to have a new kind of nightmare from which she awoke shaking and sweaty. She dreamed over and over that during each night a military-industrial complex took over her basement. Long missiles were assembled there and rolled on huge-wheeled carriers to racks on the wall, where they were stored for some dangerous event that was imminent. The activity was both exciting because of its energy and high-technical level and frightening because of the enormity of the coming event. The scariest part was that in the dream Adele knew she was responsible for this activity. What she could not figure out was if there was an attack coming for which she was preparing a defensive program like a SAC center or if the program was an offensive operation that was going to start a hostile activity. Until she figured out which, she didn't want her husband to know about it. When she awoke from each dream, her main fear was that her husband was going to find out about the nocturnal industry in the basement.

An analysis of this dream very quickly revealed that the clandestine industry was Adele's new independent activity. The question was whether, in carrying on this activity, she was heroically preparing to face the enemy or if she was the enemy. She was half-convinced she was doing the right, constructive thing and half-afraid she was doing the wrong, destructive thing. She did not resolve this question for herself for a long, long time.

Adele started reading self-help books, especially about becoming more assertive. She tried out some of the techniques. She found they worked fantastically well. She began to feel more and more confident dealing with sales people, repairmen, doctors, friends. The people she dealt with responded to her more positively than ever. She began to feel like a different person—but somehow the person she always knew was hidden inside and had fantasized she would become. She became a more confident, more open, more receptive mother to her children. They responded in kind, and she found herself enjoying them more. She encouraged them to be more assertive, more self-expressive, more independent.

Again Adele had a dream:

1 ⌈ I was in a clearing in the woods where some children were playing.

2 ⌈ All of a sudden, one of the twisted trunks of a small tree nearby began to split open. An arm emerged, then a leg, a head, and so forth. I was horrified. Finally, this entire misshapen child was standing there just freed from the tree trunk. He was thin and twisted like the trunk he had hatched from, and I recoiled from him.

3 ⌈ But, as he moved, his limbs filled out, and he straightened up and began to look normal, even beautiful.

4 ⌈ Then he went and played with the other children.

Adele woke from this dream with a deep feeling of peace, which contrasted intensely with her anxiety following the dreams of the military operation in the basement. She easily associated with this one.

1 ⌈ *clearing*   a secret place
  | *woods*   where I loved to play as a child

> *children*   fun, charm, no responsibility
> *playing*   carefree, youth

2 ⎡ *twisted*   distorted
⎜ *trunk*   natural form
⎜ *small tree*   nature
⎜ *split open*   showing something inside
⎜ *arm*   active part that does things
⎜ *leg*   part that goes places
⎜ *head*   part that thinks
⎜ *misshapen child*   long-term, difficult handicap
⎜ *thin*   from restrictions
⎣ *twisted*   distorted by form

3 ⎡ *he moved*   alive
⎜ *limbs*   of a tree, of a boy
⎜ *filled out*   healthy
⎜ *straightened out*   pride
⎜ *to look normal*   natural, accepted
⎣ *beautiful*   beautiful

4 ⎡ *played*   happy
⎣ *with other children*   acceptance

Adele determined the dream *situation* was one of carefree, childlike lack of responsibility. The *dilemma* was how to react to the horrifying emergence of an active, moving, thinking body, twisted by long restriction. It *works out* that the boyish body is really healthy, normal, and beautiful. The *resolution* is that he can easily be accepted by others as normal.

No wonder Adele had a deep sense of peace. This dream was a sort of answer to the problem posed by the military industrial dream. The emerging masculine personality—active, moving, thinking—is healthy, beautiful, and accepted—a positive development.

Adele responded with renewed confidence in her new

techniques of assertiveness and independence. She tried to use a new approach at home with Rick in the same open, caring way that she did with others, but old hostilities made a positive attitude difficult if not impossible. Rick misunderstood her new personality and responded with anger. When he saw her being more assertive, more outgoing with their friends, he told her she talked too much. The very characteristics she was beginning to love in herself were upsetting him. She started to feel a lot happier when he was not at home.

Adele fantasized about having a career. She imagined having a career in business because it seemed to be where the action was. She knew that her talents lay in communication and interpersonal skills. Adele looked at graduate school catalogs and found a program leading to careers in counseling in business environments. There were, she discovered, jobs as trainers and corporate counselors who helped employees with personal problems, such as substance abuse, tension, hostility, and lack of confidence, and taught employees positive skills needed in management and sales. With training, she would become a competent counselor that businessmen would respect.

Adele signed up for the basic counseling class at the university. Secretly. She didn't tell Rick. Her new ambitions could not survive his objections, she feared.

Three days a week, while her boys were in school, she took the bus downtown to her class. (Her daughter Stephanie by this time had grown up and left home.) Sometimes Rick would call and find her gone, but she told him later she was doing this or that errand.

She loved going to school. She loved the stimulation of the course work; she loved being ambitious and outgoing. She loved discussing ideas and hearing about what books people had read. These students were not like undergraduates who read what they were told to read, but people who read all kinds of things that led them on into life.

Not that Rick was dull by comparison—he was, in fact, an interesting, intelligent person. Rick had always been full of ideas—about his work, colleagues, politics, philosophy, world events. He had just never seemed quite as interested in her ideas as she had been in his. Now that her world had expanded, Adele had many exciting ideas on new subjects and wanted to share them with Rick. She disguised the origin of her recently acquired interests and brought them up. He did not share her enthusiasms. His reactions to her opinions were negative, and she soon decided to keep them to herself.

Rick, of course, sensed a withdrawal. He had long noticed her lack of sexual interest, and he knew it was a symptom of a more general dissatisfaction. He began to act even angrier at her absences, the dishes she occasionally picked up at the deli instead of making from scratch, the times she let the boys take care of themselves. Adele loved being out on her own during the day, she also enjoyed coming home in the afternoon, elated, to her boys after a day of pursuing her goals. Fulfilled herself, she could give more to them emotionally than before. More and more, she found her heart sank when Rick came home.

After a while, Adele found the other graduate students in her program getting ahead of her because she was taking only one course per quarter. That's all she could take without Rick knowing. Her good school friends, with whom she had started out, were signing up for summer internships. She was not yet eligible, and even if she had been, an internship was full-time work. That would disrupt her comfortable routine of a couple hours of class and study at school, picking up groceries and other errands before the boys got out of school, and returning home with them to the routine of housewife and mother. It was a good life, filled with both intellectual stimulation, family participation, and security. She realized her hiding the fact of her graduate work from Rick was cowardly, bizarre, destructive behavior, but it gave her some of what she wanted without confrontation with him. Except for a certain level of anxiety about her withdrawal from Rick, she was comfortable.

Then she had this dream:

1 In a country like India, they were paving the narrow roads or paths from one house to another in a village or rural area. The women laid down their husbands' dirty dress shirts (laundry) along the paths and sprinkled it with "bullfight dust," the fine cinderlike material they put on running tracks and walking paths—but this was what was used in a bullfight ring. I stood on the porch of one house and watched the Indian women lay the shirts along the path and sprinkle bullfight dust over them as pavement.

2 I noticed that the women within the homes tossed the shirts out their front doors to be used for the road; only a few would be distributed out along the roads farther away. I pointed this out to them, saying, "Isn't this a problem when so many shirts are right by the door? The shirts are so thick there and much thinner far from the houses." I hoped they would see and make the effort to take the shirts farther from the house out into the parts of the roads where they didn't often go.

This dream seemed very strange to Adele because of its exotic setting and the bizarre activity of the women. She could not wait to analyze it. Here are her word associations:

1 *India*   unhealthy country, repressed women
paving   urbanizing, improving
narrow   narrowminded, not liberal or liberated
road   to get some place
house   a base to operate from
village   community, interdependence
rural area   natural resources close by
women   work

> *husbands*   power, decisions
> *dirty*   sweat
> *dress shirts*   offices, power
> *laundry*   women's work
> *paths*   a way out
> *sprinkled*   careful, moderate
> *bullfight*   useless violence, macho
> *dust*   dry, old, death
> *running track*   healthy sport
> *walking paths*   fitness
> *bullfight ring*   macho sport
> *porch*   where you can watch the world
> *Indian women*   dutiful, trapped

2 > *tossed*   disdain
> *out their doors*   openly
> *used for*   recycle, positive act
> *road*   road to the city
> *distributed*   even sharing, fair

The dream, interpreted from the opening scene, is about an unhealthy *situation,* in which repressed women are improving narrowminded ways to get somewhere. As a community, they are carefully using power and decision making and fitness and other "manly" possessions to pave the way out.

Adele clearly labeled the *dilemma* in the dream itself when she said, "Isn't it a problem . . . ?" She was concerned that, even though women had acquired some power, too much of it was spent close to the house because it was easy. It was not really paving the way *out.*

The dream dilemma did not *work itself out to a climax* nor arrive at a resolution. Adele wanted a resolution, and she wanted to know to what extent to identify these women with herself, so she used the Gestalt technique to work out the rest of the dream drama.

ME: For this to work you have to spread the shirts out so they don't pile up in front of your house. Instead of building roads out, you are creating mounds, obstacles, right outside of your own houses.

WOMEN: It's too much trouble. We'd have to leave the house and walk so far. We'd have to leave our houses empty while we were gone. Someone else might get in our houses.

ME: Who?

WOMEN: Someone. We don't know who.

ME: No one. The men are away working, and there are always some women at any given time who watch out for the houses.

WOMEN: Okay, okay. We *like* to stay at home.

ME: *Yes.* That's fine, if you want to stay at home. Then there's no need to pave the roads anyway. You're not going anywhere.

WOMEN: Then we'd just wash the men's shirts and hang them up to wear again.

ME: Right. There's nothing wrong with that. If that's what you want to do, okay. But if you want to build roads out, do it right. Make them good, even roads, without piles of stuff to get bogged down in. You'll have to get out of the house regularly and make the effort to go down the road.

After her dialogue with the dream women, Adele saw that the *working out of the dream* followed a familiar theme. She saw that her desire to get out in the world and achieve still conflicted with her desire to take the easy way out and stay at home." The climax was the point of decision that she had stated to the women in the Gestalt dialogue: "That's fine, if you want to stay at home. . . ."

As a resolution, she forced herself to make the decision. She decided to "build the roads out, do it right." Her response consequently was to pursue her preparation for a career openly. With great difficulty and apprehension, she told her husband she wanted to get a graduate degree in counseling. As expected, he pointed out all the pitfalls, especially her duties to her family, and asked her how she was going to deal with each. She answered as best she could. When she did not have an answer, she said she would do her best to work it out. "Where there's a will, there's a way," she reminded him. She had the will. He did not think that was good enough.

She signed up for twice the load she had previously carried but not without feelings of guilt and anxiety, which clung to her every morning as she left the house and took the boys to school. By the time she got downtown, however, she felt free.

She had fallen in love with the downtown area where the university was located. The people and their life-styles were so much more varied than those in the suburbs. There were people of all ages and of different races. There were people who broke all the stereotypes she had heard—for example, a middle-aged wife of a blue-collar factory worker had read every piece of literature Adele had ever heard of and was maybe the brightest person she'd ever met. A young homosexual man she found positively delightful. She could joke more comfortably with the young black women in the counseling program than she had ever been able to with her college roommates.

Adele was enchanted with the restored town houses and apartment buildings. She was delighted to meet people who were not married but living together; she was even more delighted to meet women who had men housemates with whom they were not romantically involved, because it proved that men and women could be friends and associates without being sexually involved. She met people who went to the main downtown library, to the old marble-front downtown banks, to the theater, shopping, and to the airport without owning a car. The in-town environment was a community of active people who could get around independently.

She began to find her suburban home that Rick had worked so hard to provide unadventurous, their activities unimaginative, their children pampered to the point of dependency, and their friends cut out of a terrible sameness. Suburban people talked about different things: cars, real estate, tennis. They were so glad they didn't have to go downtown where there were muggings, and black people, and gays.

Rick began to verbalize more and more principles about what families *should* be like, what people *should* do. He pressed her to redecorate the house, to entertain their old friends more. His racial slurs increased. He made derogatory remarks about people who were living different kinds of life-styles from theirs. Adele realized suddenly that they had different values. She thought perhaps hers had changed, then she remembered that the ones she now espoused had been, though never well articulated, the values of her youth, before her marriage. Rick had never known about them. He seemed to feel that because he was in love with her, it followed that they shared the same values, which were the right values, the only ones nice people had. She had subjugated her values to his when they married, to please him, to be the perfect traditional wife. Her values were just now being expressed. She had not known any more than he what had happened.

She kept her growing dissatisfaction mostly to herself until she became desperate. She wanted to get out of the marriage completely. Yes, she wanted the boys, but she felt more urgently that she had to experience being independent. She was afraid that if she said anything to Rick, she would say everything—then there would be a horrible confrontation, after which she'd find it impossible to live at home. She'd lose the boys; she'd be out on the street. She wasn't sure what she was most afraid of, but she wasn't yet ready to face it. As much as she didn't want the ultimate confrontation, she was equally reluctant to attempt a campaign of bit-by-bit, imperceptible progress. She didn't feel she had the self-control for that.

About this time, Adele had the following dream:

1 There was to be a family reunion of Rick's family. Some had already gathered at a lake.

2 I did not want to go to the reunion at all, but I was expected to. I did not feel I could express my reluctance.

3 I was sailing with Ed, a cousin of Rick's, but in my own boat alongside his on the inland waterway, part of the ocean several hundred miles from the lake. It was cool, refreshing, just right.

4 I called to Ed, "Let's try to get them to come to the ocean where it's cool. The lake would be too warm." I did not want them to come where I was either, but it was a compromise to say, "Let them come here where I am."

These are Adele's word associations with the features of the dream.

1 *family reunion*   conformity to the will of others, which I resent
Rick's family   he puts an enormous priority on family and all other conservative values. I value family but not above individuality, freedom, etc.
some had already gathered   the power of the institution
lake   dull, bland compared to ocean

2 *I didn't want to go to the reunion at all*   I didn't want mutual goals
but I was expected to   No one thought to ask, "Are these your goals?"
I did not want to express my reluctance   I feel selfish displeasing

Rick, and there's no good way to say, "I don't care about family or I don't share your goals"

3 *sailing* smooth, cool, wet, challenging sport I excelled at; I wanted my own thing

in my own boat *I* was in control of self, independent

Ed conformist, does not excel, I didn't want him here, but he could serve as a messenger to the family

inland waterway a route somewhere, a goal

ocean home, knowing where I am, self-realization

several hundred miles from the lake Rick and I are that far apart in what we want

cool healthy, not pampered, rugged

refreshing stimulating

just right happiness

I called to Ed I didn't want to face telling Rick and his family myself

4 *get them to come here* teach them my ways

to the ocean to adventure

where it's cool stimulating

lake too warm for unadventurous, bland people

I didn't want them to come where I was I didn't want them to change because then I wouldn't be alone, unique

it was a compromise compromise keeps you from getting what you really want. It ruins your determination because it makes life bearable.

to say, "Let them come." it keeps the peace because they can't say I didn't invite them

Adele interpreted from scene one: "The dream is about being in a family and conforming to family expectations.

"The *dilemma* is that I want to give up family requirements, which I have been good at fulfilling but resentful of. I want to do something different to seek happiness, but going my separate way is going to cause a problem, and I haven't told them yet.

"I have *worked it out* by choosing to withdraw from the family to my own place, where I can do my own adventurous, challenging thing.

"The *resolution* is that I invite them to change if they want to be with me. They will either change or not, but if they don't, they can't say I didn't invite them. I am reluctant for them to change because they will be with me in my chosen adventure, and I won't be free, independent, alone. But I must issue this invitation to avoid a complete rift."

At this point Adele, in real life as in her dream, wanted to leave Rick to pursue more wholeheartedly her career goals and to live a more untraditional life. The only solution she had been able to think of was divorce. The dream resolution suggested to her a compromise: Instead of leaving him, it was only fair to Rick to tell him what her needs for change were and, however reluctantly, to invite him to fulfill them.

Adele's response to the dream was to invite Rick to go to counseling with her to explore this compromise. He resisted at first but finally went.

In joint counseling, he explained to her that he had been hostile to the changes she had made because they threatened everything he had based his life on. She explained to him her need for independence and challenge. She told him how she could raise the boys well and manage her career, too. The boys would accept the change very well, she thought. Her values would help them grow up healthy, tolerant, and flexible. She wanted Rick to become less rigid and follow her in the direction of independence.

I would like to say that Rick agreed to meet her halfway, and they found a common ground where they could both be content. It did not turn out that way. Rick heard her out, then told her that he understood her values, that they were wrong, that his were right, and he had no intention of changing.

She took a quarter off from school to think things out. Among the many things that went through her mind was this dream.

1. A black man in some primitive culture was getting ready to make a human sacrifice of a young boy by throwing him into the turbulent water below. I could see the water like the ocean behind them. The man was doing some ceremony in which he held the boy in his arms in front of him. The man stretched both their arms out to the side and then pulled them back, leaning forward and backward with the boy, doing ceremonial calisthenics. This was done before a crowd of that black culture; the water was behind the man and the boy. I was standing where the crowd was but off to the side.

2. I was wondering what the boy was thinking: Was he terrified and heartbroken, or did he accept the rightness of the religion and believe he was going to a better place? What did he even know? *I* was sick about it. I also wondered what the man thought. I saw him as a father of the boy, if not the real father, at least a tribesman who knew him, perhaps loved him, perhaps chose him to sacrifice.

1. *black man*   strange, not understood, somewhat threatening
primitive   emotional, not rational
culture   values
human   special, intelligent but vulnerable
sacrifice   giving up what is dearest
young boy   Peter, my son, beloved, growing more independent, but I relate to the boy as if he is me.
throwing him   forced loss
water   danger, power, pleasant if you can stay on top and control it, but death if you can't
ocean   infinite water
ceremony   not the real thing, important to society, part of its
   bonds

his arms   loving but controlling
stretched   open, growing
pulled them back   restricting growth, control
leaning forward   growth
and backward   helplessness
calisthenics   ritualized exercise
crowd   society, people you know, who observe you

2 *rightness of the religion*   a point of view I was questioning
father   my husband, Rick, loving but someone who keeps me
  dependent

Adele read the *situation* from scene one: "Someone or something not understood and somewhat frightening, something emotional not rational, with different values from mine, is throwing away, killing something. What is being killed is something special, intelligent yet vulnerable, something loved, growing better and more independent. This force, supported by society, is alternately loving and controlling, freeing and restricting growth as a ritual prelude to the killing.

"I am wondering how the special, intelligent, yet vulnerable loved one is taking this? Is he willing to die without a struggle? Does he accept it or not? Does the father/man know what he is doing, or is he doing it deliberately? Is he doing it especially *because* he loves this one, in a warped sort of favoritism? These all seem to be the *questions.* This dream is situation and questions. There is no working out to a *climax* or *resolution.*"

Adele had associated herself with the boy, her husband with the man, family and society with the crowd. But because the dream did not seem finished, she decided to use the Gestalt "two-chair" personification technique to explore further the troubling relationship between these elements. She talked first as the child to the man.

CHILD: What are you going to do to me? Tell me! I know, but I want you to confirm it.

FATHER: I'm going to throw you into the water.

CHILD: And I'm going to die?

FATHER: Yes, but you will then be in the hands of the gods.

CHILD: Why did you choose me, the one you loved the best?

FATHER: The gods will be the most pleased with you.

CHILD: It's not a good god who would ask for the life of your most loved.

FATHER: Gods don't have to be good.

CHILD: I don't believe in any god that isn't, above all, good. I won't be sacrificed.

FATHER: You must be. Our family, our tribe requires it; it has always been done this way.

CHILD: Then I reject the family that requires it.

FATHER: You can't. I will have to force you.

CHILD: I'm going to struggle, but in a struggle I know I'll lose. I'll die anyway, fighting you and the crowd that supports you.

(Adele draws the crowd into the discussion, getting into the mind of the crowd as well.)

CROWD: We can't watch. This is so sad. But we're afraid of what will happen if we offer you to the gods and then take our offer back. The gods are so much more powerful than we.

CHILD: You are nothing but weak and worthless if you don't stand up for what you believe in, even before the gods. You are dependent on the gods, helpless, slaves to their whim.

CROWD *(calling out):* Is there any other child who is willing to be sacrificed? *(The children all cower, hide.)*

CHILD: You see, they won't. I was mentally prepared for this; that's why I have come this far to the sacrifice. But they didn't expect to face it, and they won't come forward unless chosen and prepared as I was.

CROWD: Okay. Don't make the sacrifice. Let him go. We'll work something out. It's not safe, but we'll just hope the gods don't punish us too badly. *(They disperse.)*

FATHER: You are the object of my humiliation. They have no more respect for me. Now I don't have the gods' respect or the tribe's respect. And I don't care about you any-more. I loved you, I chose you, but your association with my failure has cooled my love for you. I see that you are stronger than I am. I resent that, and I don't love you anymore.

CHILD: I'm sorry. But I also don't respect you as I once did. You say you loved me but not so much that you wanted what was best for me, for me to exercise my strength, to be a leader. Yes, I was a leader just now with our people. Now I have to decide whether to just go my way as a free person or to take up the role of leader in your place.

Through this role playing, Adele found answers, a *resolution* to the dilemma the dream posed. The boy knew what was happening but had not confronted the man till now. Though the boy had cooperated and prepared himself men-tally for death, he did not want to die. The father knew what he was doing but thought it right. He was sacrificing the boy to retain his own position of authority and respect. What had seemed like love would not survive beyond this purpose. His desire for this position kept him from allowing the child to enjoy life and freedom, much less leadership, which he wanted to retain for himself.

What this meant to Adele is clear from her associations with the words, man, boy, and crowd: her husband; herself as a lovable, growing independent person; family and soci-ety. Adele was perfectly aware that her perception of her husband as the chief who was willing to sacrifice her to his need for authority was not necessarily an objective truth but *her* perception of him and their relationship. The dream showed her how deep this conviction of hers was, how much her desires for freedom were equivalent to life itself, and how asserting her need for freedom could win her that freedom and the option of leadership of others but at the price of the man's love.

She was in a sad dilemma, but she knew her response must be divorce. The bravery the boy-part of her had shown in the dream crisis waned, however, as she contemplated the reality of divorce, and she was afraid.

Again she dreamed:

1 There was a group of skyscrapers close together, very stylized, at least twenty stories tall. I didn't see anything around the buildings to even know where it was. Just those buildings. They all collapsed and fell down together like demolition. I knew all the people in them were killed.

2 Then I realized my daughter, Stephanie, lived there with her husband, and they were killed. It wasn't like I saw them killed. There were no bodies or blood or people rushing in to save the half-dead ones. They were just all neatly killed. I didn't dream anyone told me. I just saw the buildings fall, and I knew they were killed.

3 Most of the rest of the dream was my thoughts. I was hurt and shocked. I was grieved at the loss of my only daughter— but I thought, "This is not the end of the world." I was impressed with how strong I felt. I would always be sad about the loss, but I could manage without her. So my dream was just thoughts about dealing with my grief.

4 The only other thing was me at the funeral looking at the wood and brass of the casket and thinking, "I'm not falling apart now, but will I later?" There was grief and strength.

Adele brought this dream to me to help her analyze it. I read out her images, word by word and she made the following associations.

1 | *group of skyscrapers*   very substantial, massive structures
close together   belong together, like a family, same architect
very stylized   like an architect's drawing, not real, a prototype
at least twenty stories tall   tall is strong, but tall is also dangerous because if it falls, people get hurt
I didn't see anything around   no neighborhood, anonymous
I didn't know where it was   I didn't know these structures
collapsed   it was all over
fell down together   in a heap to be swept
like demolition   destroyed carefully, on purpose, so other
things around are not hurt
people killed   like a disaster in the news, you know people are
hurt, but you don't know them
my daughter, Stephanie   near-perfect, conservative, ideal, values family unity
lived there with her husband   traditional, committed marriage is
what good people have

2 | *neatly killed*   I had always hoped my estranged father would
die "neatly" without a prolonged illness during which he
might ask me if I loved him. He did die suddenly. I felt
guilty at my lack of sorrow and at my gratitude for his
tidy death.
"This is not the end of the world"   I would recover.
at the funeral   wrapping up grief, last thing before new beginning
hurt, shock, grief, loss   those same emotions
strong   I felt amazingly strong

3 | *looking at wood and brass of casket*   same wood and brass orna-
ment of my mother's casket, I remember looking at hers
and saying "What a waste." She had suffered so long and
at the end her body was in such terrible condition, and
here they were trying to preserve these miserable remains
in satin inside of wood and brass. How in vain to try to
preserve something in as bad shape as this woman's body.

It would have been better to have turned it to ashes
quickly and returned it, uncontained, to the earth.

4 *"I'm not falling apart now, but will I later?"*   I never quite trust my
confidence
grief with strength   that's the message

I have recorded here the whole answer associated with
each dream element. In my analysis, I often jot down just
the summary words. I was glancing over the long associative
response to the "wood and brass of the casket," trying to
find some summary words. I had noticed that Adele's throat
had tightened, and she was close to tears when speaking of
her mother's funeral, so I expected some strong emotions
about her mother to tie in with the rest of the dream. Then I
noticed in the response the juxtaposition of "mother's casket" and "What a waste." On a hunch, I asked, "Adele, did
you consider your mother's life a waste?"

"Yes," she blurted. "She devoted her whole life to her
marriage, doing what she was supposed to do. She never did
anything for herself or toward her own growth. She had
talents she never developed. She was a servant to a husband
and four children. And they all grew up thinking a wife
should be a doormat for a man. All us girls became door-
mats. I blame my mother for not doing better for herself,
and I blame her for not giving us an example of a woman
who's a grown-up."

The intensity of Adele's answer helped her understand
the *situation* this dream was about. Reading again from scene
one, she said, "The dream is about the death of ideal marriage, ideal family. It seems that the prototype, the plan, is
too good to be real—the taller it is, the more it hurts if it
doesn't last. But the demise of this impersonal family
doesn't make me feel bad." She had been wanting divorce,
she added, thinking about how traditional marriage stunts
growth, and admiring single parents and other kinds of rela-

tionships. "I don't believe in keeping-the-family-together-no-matter-what."

"The *problem* is," she said, reading from scene two, "that when I see that this collapse involves my family and hurts the people in it who count on it, it becomes a different thing. My desire has been for the marriage to be 'neatly killed' with 'no blood, no bodies, and no half-dead people' like in the dream. But even in the dream I was aware that this neat end is not real, it's my fantasy.

"As the dream *worked out*," Adele said, interpreting from scene three, "I would personally grieve for the loss of an intact family for Stephanie's sake and the others' sake. I value that. Still, the overall feeling, after I faced the death of the ideal that my daughter represents, is of strength. I know I could face the end of my marriage and feel strong.

"The *resolution* is that even though there would be hurt for others and grief for me, I am angry about devoting my resources to the ritual of a dead marriage and unwilling to waste the trappings on what's not really there in spirit. At the climax of grief, I am ready for a strong new beginning, even though I realize that the long haul later might be even tougher. The resolution is that I will have grief and the strength to endure the grief."

Adele decided to get the divorce. Her decision itself relieved her frustrations, so she was no longer desperate. Feeling unsatisfied but no longer desperate, she put off getting the divorce. Then this:

I had a long dream about a nice older couple with whom we were staying as guests. They gave us our own bathroom, abundant towels, good meals, and took us to their club for a dinner party. Everything was very comfortable and pleasant. They showed us pictures of their children and grandchildren. Later, one of their children visited with the grandchildren and we met all around. We went through a lot of meals and conversations I can't remember. I think there was a scene of trying on our children some nice clothes their children had outgrown or vice versa and having them fit nicely. Also, there was a scene outside looking at a tree or a garden in the yard. We were very polite. The mood was of uniform pleasantness, temporary contentment, and I had the idea that it's very nice, everything is nice, as long as I know I don't have to stay here very long.

older couple   what we will be in a few years

bath, towels   security, comfort

meals   security, being taken care of

dinner at club   affluence, limitation to one place, one society, sameness

pictures of children   family support and obligation, ambivalence between fear of loneliness and resentment at being restricted by children

trying on hand-me-down clothes   sadness at children growing up, I have kept all my children's little outfits, I cling to them, yet they take up room. I'd have to give them up to move. Saving clothes means staying in the same house, same institution, not moving on.

we were very polite   nice, but not completely at ease

tree, garden, yard   I'd have to give up my yard with the trees and the garden to move. I love this place. (She cries.)

It's nice as long as I don't have to stay here very long.   I don't want to stay. I can't bring myself to leave.

As told, the dream offers a lovely picture *(situation)* of family comfort and happiness. Only the last line, "Everything is nice as long as I don't have to stay here very long," has a hint of the negative. In the word associations, however, the *problem* shows up much sooner: "limitation to one place," "sameness," "ambivalence between fear of loneliness and resentment at being restricted," "sadness." How the dream dilemma works out is expressed in the line, "I'd have to give them up to move."

The final line of the dream has the feel of a *resolution*. It was not a happy one. It was a particularly acute face-to-face encounter with the truth that to move on Adele must give up much. The dream is simply an opportunity to accept the loss and to grieve—or to turn back and decide to stay in the pleasant home with the comforts, the meals, and the mementos of children who have grown up.

Adele stayed on and the dreams continued to come.

1 My children and I were in an open area, an extension of a large courtyard, like my high school quadrangle, a lawn open at one end.

2 We saw a small plane look as if it were going down. It curved as if coming our way.

3 I got the children and led them out of the way. It turned and got close enough to the ground that I thought it would crash before it could circle back to us. I thought, "Hurry up and crash, so we won't be in any further danger."

4 It crashed and I felt safe.

Adele's word associations were as follows:

1 *my children*   dear, enthusiastic, free
open area   free, but exposed, unsheltered
large courtyard   formality, open but restricted
high school quad   pageantry, restricted
a lawn open at one end   only one way out

2 *small plane*   not scary size, neat, sleek
going down   end, disaster
curved   change
coming our way   could hurt us

3 *I got the children*   they are mine to take care of
close enough   could jump
go ahead and crash   get it over with
circle back   repeating cycles. I go from deciding to leave and

feeling happy about it, to thinking of the problems in leaving and feeling depressed, then deciding to leave again and getting happy again . . . I want to get off the cycle.
hurry up   I don't want to waste any more time
crash   end
danger   tension, waiting for end

4 *safe*   after you've gone through the worst, then you don't have to fear it anymore

In 1985, Adele got a divorce because of her sense that the desire to be independent would never go away, would always haunt her days and her nights. She stayed with the boys in the house they had lived in. Rick supported her and the boys for a year while she finished her degree (four years after she first started work on it). She did most of her schoolwork while the boys were in school, so she could be with them more than Rick, with his full-time job, could be. She now has a part-time regular job with a large company. In the afternoon she does training for other companies on a contract basis. This gives her the flexibility she feels she needs while the boys are still at home.

When she first was divorced, many things were painful, but she often felt joy in achieving independence and the confidence she had hoped for. She has found the difficult things, for the most part, satisfying challenges.

At first, she felt no particular desire to have a relationship with a man. Having long engaged in sex according to Rick's schedule, which was much more frequent than she wanted, she had developed a distaste for sex. In addition, their sexual relations at best had been unimaginative, out of ignorance and rigid ideas of what one was "supposed" to do. She had never been comfortable with what she considered her very imperfect body and with her latent sexuality. She decided to learn sex over from the beginning. She read books about successful sex, imagined it with a loving partner, and began to explore her body in a new way. Through masturbation, she discovered a lot of things she liked about sex and about her own body. Freed from previous inhibitions, she imagined how she would relate sexually to the right man.

She had many dreams during her period of transition, but she remembers the following one as a milestone, a dream in which many aspects of her life were brought together.

1 I lived in a city apartment. I looked out the window and saw someone with a gun shoot one or two people on the sidewalk across the street.

2 I went out and walked up the street till I found a woman policeman, off-duty, carrying her small toddler, a chunky little boy. I said, "I'll take care of your child while you go do something about this shooting." She did. I took the child up the stairs to my apartment. I enjoyed the feel of holding him. I played with him and cared for him.

3 Then an attractive blond young woman came to my apartment and suggested having sex. She was so forthright and not coy that the idea seemed good to me. What she did sexually was what I like, very intimate. After a while, I got up and closed the blinds so no one could see in. I preferred privacy, but I wasn't upset at the possibility that someone might have seen us. We contentedly continued our sexual interaction.

4 Later, the policewoman came back for her child, recognized the sexual relationship, and regarded it as natural. The three women were together very comfortably.

1 *city* exciting, sophisticated, free
apartment private, free
out the window in the middle of things
a gun danger

one or two people   random victims
across the street   danger close, but not too close

2 *a woman policeman*   strong, in charge, brave, professional
   off-duty   retaining authority, power while actively mothering
   her small toddler   family, caring
   a chunky little boy   attractive, cuddly
   up the stairs to my apartment   voluntary caring
   holding him   warmth, affection
   played with him   making effort

3 *attractive, young, blond*   someone desirable
   have sex   it seemed normal, natural, healthy, enjoyable
   forthright   honest
   not coy   honest, playing no games
   what she did sexually   uninhibited, mutually satisfying, bal-
      anced—we were equals
   closed the blinds   I was aware that our activity was not ac-
      cepted by society, but I did not feel ashamed, just discreet
   privacy   something I desperately need
   possibility that someone might have seen us   family, associates who
      are not especially friends, society
   contentedly continued sex   I have a right to these feelings, my
      sexuality, my desire to be free

4 *policewoman came back*   everyone was getting together that
      should be together
   for the child   responsibility and caring for children
   recognized the sexual   it was no surprise, right
   regarded it as natural   as it should be
   the three women   the assertive, strong one who acted, the nur-
      turing one who cared for the child, the sexual one who
      initiated sex and fostered honest sexual relationship
   all comfortable together   they each accepted and respected the
      others' roles and fit together harmoniously

"I was living alone, free, in the thick of things, just the *situation* I had always wanted," Adele said, interpreting the word associations. "There was the possibility of danger, of course, in my much-wanted independence.

"The *question* is: Can I successfully have my assertive, active, strong part take charge out in the larger world, and at the same time have my caring, motherly part care for the children at home?

"It *worked out* that there was a third part of me, my sexuality, to consider. I had become more expressive, less inhibited, more comfortable about my sexuality, and had found the means to satisfaction. The question of coexistence of my parts needed to be broadened to interweave my sexuality with my qualities of initiative and nurturing.

"The *resolution* is that the assertive, active, professional side of me benefits from my motherly, affectionate side and is content and comfortable with my sexual role. My motherly side is grateful for the assertive side for taking care of things outside the home and is happy and unashamed of my fully expressed sexuality. (At last my assertive side is represented by a woman instead of a scary man and then a boy as in the past.) It's a feeling of new-found respect for all the aspects of my life. I guess it's a broad self-esteem. I feel really good about it."

For Adele, this dream marked a point of self-acceptance where she considered she no longer needed therapy. She is now seriously involved with a man she hopes to marry. She is putting off the wedding until she has had a period of time to be sure that she knows how to maintain her independence lovingly while giving her share in the relationship. She wants to be sure she can commit herself completely without resenting any interdependence that will and should ensue. She expects that, when she reaches that stage of growth, it will be verified by a dream of great joy and peace.

TWELVE

Using Dream Interpretation to Develop Intimacy

"You tell me your dream and I'll write it down," one person says.

"Well, I dreamed I was eating a sandwich and . . .," the dreamer says, as the friend scribbles furiously.

"Now what do you think of when I say *eating a sandwich?*" the friend asks, after the dream has been completely recorded.

"The old brown-bag days when I was just an hourly employee before I got this supervisor's position," the dreamer says. "A time of less responsibility."

When two people interpret a dream together, many good things can happen. One is that an objective listener can hear things the dreamer doesn't even realize he is saying and point out to him important self-revelations. A second is that one person can learn the emotional history and the personal symbolism that form another person's current point of view. A third is that the dreamer and his companion can be led gently into a discussion of something important they would not have dared talk about without the protection of knowing "it's only a dream." All three of these products of dream interpretation—listening closely and objectively, understanding another's point of view, and talking out difficulties—are critical factors in developing intimacy.

An example of objective listening occurred between two good friends. Tina told Becky about a dream she had about traveling abroad with her husband, Todd. In the dream, Tina and her husband were having an unpleasant argument in some foreign country. "I couldn't figure out what time it was in that country, and I couldn't read the train schedule with that military time that goes on to 1300 and 1400 hours, and I couldn't figure out the money. Todd was trying to help me, saying he would take care of all that, and I felt so angry with him. I felt so insecure about myself."

Later, when Tina had done her list of word associations for Becky and Becky had divided the dream drama into scenes, Becky began to interpret. "You feel insecure about yourself when Todd tries to help you," Becky said, repeating Tina's exact words from the associations.

"No," Tina disagreed sharply. "I feel very secure about myself."

"You seem to be very secure to me," Becky agreed diplomatically. "You seem as happy with yourself as anyone I know. But *you said* that you felt insecure about yourself when Todd helps you." She showed Tina what she had recorded verbatim.

Tina was stopped cold. She had to consider that she did have a chink in her self-confidence. She realized for the first time that her self-esteem suffered when Todd tried to take care of her too much. That explained the source of a lot of their arguments. Tina would find herself inexplicably angry and quick to snap at him. She only got angrier when he explained to her that she was unjustified because he had, in fact, been especially helpful at the time. She now understood that the source of her anger was her insecurity and the perceived implication of his helpfulness—that she couldn't take care of herself. Understanding the basis of her touchiness, she could recognize when an unpleasantness was brewing and head it off.

This understanding might never have come about if Becky hadn't recorded and read back to Tina her own dream evaluation. Besides the benefit of the dream interpretation to Tina and Todd's marriage, the discussion between Tina and Becky demonstrated and nourished the intimacy between these two friends as well.

Learning the emotional history and personal symbolism of each other is also a step toward further intimacy. I remember a couple in therapy for marital problems who were, during one session, at odds over buying a rider mower for their lawn. Alice said she was embarrassed by how long the grass was allowed to grow in their yard and suggested that her husband Harry get the rider mower, and she would do the trimming around the edges. Harry agreed, but he never would buy the machine. Every time she suggested that today would be a good day to get it, he got irritable. The more Harry balked, the longer the grass grew, and the more impatient Alice became.

Harry said that he was eventually going to get the mower. The problem was that Alice was nagging. If she quit nagging, he would buy the mower. She claims to have stopped nagging, but Harry didn't get the mower.

Later, Harry had a dream involving some heather plants. When he told Alice about his dream, she asked him why in the world he dreamed about heather. He said he didn't know; he hadn't thought about heather in a dozen years. He went on to tell her about his grandfather, an old Scotsman who migrated to Canada and finally got together enough money to buy a house with a spacious lawn, where Harry and his family also lived. On a trip back to Scotland, the old man got some sprigs of heather from his ancestral home and planted them in rocky areas about the yard. Intent on creating a Scotch moor, he transplanted every tiny sprout that came up in the lawn to the place where he intended for the heather to grow. The heather patch spread and bloomed, not only in purple but in white. It became almost a sanctuary the old man tended like a monk.

It was Harry's job to cut the grass with a hand mower, but he was not allowed to cut it until he had gone over the whole lawn on his hands and knees looking for new heather sprouts. He was paid a penny a sprout if he found one and marked it for transplanting. He remembers once, however, mowing without having made the ritual search, counting on seeing the sprouts ahead of the mower. He found a few and he missed a few. He was severely punished by his grandfather for taking this shortcut.

"No wonder you don't want to buy a rider mower," exclaimed Alice. "You were punished for cutting the lawn the easy way."

Harry saw Alice's point. He began to recall how the lawn was almost sacred ground because it was the incubation place of these little plants, the link to Grandpapa's native land. He was made to feel selfish and unfeeling for not personally caring if he snipped the sprigs' little heads off. He resented having to search for them and being told he couldn't be counted on if he missed one. The whole task of lawn care became a threat to his self-esteem.

In recounting all this, Harry actually burst into tears. Then, relieved, he went out and bought a rider mower. He now happily and with a vengeance slices off the top of any plant in his path.

Without the dream, neither Alice nor Harry would have

realized that to Harry lawn care was a symbol of an old resentment, an old failure. Who could have guessed? The revelation was a very pleasurable experience and the new understanding made them more patient with each other.

Each of us has his own heather plants, his own experiences that represent something not obvious to other people or even to ourselves. Dreams employ these images from our past (and from our future) to convey emotional issues to us. The process of interpreting dreams with a caring person increases intimacy by entrusting to that person our previously secret symbols.

When two people interpret their dreams together, they sometimes end up discussing topics that are important to their relationship, but which they would otherwise avoid talking about. The dream is told before the dreamer realizes what he's getting into, but once in it, he finds that talking about it is not so bad. Besides, talking about issues in symbolic terms is less scary than talking about the same issues in real you-and-me-now terms.

One young woman named Peggy, for example, dreamed she was at a party with her parents, where she ran into an old boyfriend, who was now married. She went over to him and greeted him cordially. They had a nice conversation until his children came up. She talked to his children with pleasure until her parents beckoned to her to come with them. She said good-bye to him, and she hoped to see him again. Secretly, she was relieved her parents had called her because, even though she liked her friend's children, she got tired of making polite conversation with them.

Peggy told Burton, her fiancé, the dream, and they decided to analyze it together. When the word *children* came up, Peggy quickly said the names of Burton's children. Seeing the implications of her answer in a flash, she could have balked, but she valued their openness enough to be honest. Through her word associations, it quickly became clear that the old boyfriend in the dream represented her fiancé. She

liked Burton's children very much but became tired of making polite conversation with them. Her parents in real life,
she noted, had tried to discourage her relationship with
Burton because they didn't like her marrying a divorced
man or being an instant mother to his children.

Without the dream, Peggy would never have discussed
any negative thoughts with Burton for fear of damaging
their relationship. But once her concerns came out in the
dream, they engaged in their first real discussion about her
relationship with his children. The fact that the subject
came up in a dream, rather than in an emotional crisis,
helped keep their remarks constructive. Peggy learned that
even negative issues can be worked out. If they had found
they could not discuss the issue productively through this
indirect approach, perhaps they should have rethought their
marriage plans. As it was, Peggy and Burton agreed that she
would learn with practice to have a "real" relationship with
his children, instead of an exercise in party politeness. Any
insight he gained into her anxiety about her role as his new
wife could only help relieve inevitable tensions.

This particular dream also points out the fact that, if you
do not want to be intimate with someone or you are not
ready to be honest, you shouldn't share your dreams with
him, because dreams honestly interpreted often result in a
discussion of intimate issues.

Susan and Mike are an example of a couple who were not
as intimate as they would have liked. A discussion about a
dream helped open up some areas in which they could become closer.

Susan married Mike, a campus leader, president of his
fraternity, and student council member at a university in
New Orleans. After college, he became a management
trainee at a large manufacturing company and was headed
for success. He seemed self-assured in his leadership role
and comfortable in any situation. Susan, on the other hand,

was very self-conscious in a lot of situations, so she admired and envied his confidence.

Susan had to talk Mike into interpreting their dreams together. He was at first reluctant, and when he did agree, they analyzed only Susan's dreams. One morning when Mike said he'd had a disturbing dream, she insisted they analyze it together, that overcoming his reticence would help make them more intimate.

Mike's dream centered on one very common dream element—the dreamer's nudity. Mike dreamed he was naked behind a podium before a large meeting. After the meeting, he hoped the crowd would disperse so that he could come out from behind the podium unseen. But the people stayed and stayed. Mike finally made a dash for it, and the crowd saw him and ran after him. He ran down the streets of the French Quarter in New Orleans to get away, but certain ones were determined to follow him. Finally, Mike ran into a souvenir shop and grabbed several of the ceramic masks offered for sale to tourists as symbols of Mardi Gras. He put these masks over the parts of his body he wanted to hide. He thought he had solved the problem but still felt uneasy. The crowd gathered and stared at him for a while, then went away.

Then Mike had to decide what to do with the masks. He wondered if he needed them to go home with or if he should give them back to the store clerk. He wondered if the clerk would make him buy them because they had been "used."

He finally said he wanted to put them on lay-away. He felt relieved because he could go home without completely giving up the masks.

Mike told his word associations to Susan. Nakedness in Mike's dream—as in the dreams of most of us—meant vulnerability and fear of being seen with his defenses down. The podium was his position as a leader. The store was his work as in the expression, "minding the store." The masks, he said, "hide who you are." Home was where he and Susan were together. His dream *situation* was that he was expected to be out in front of people as a leader, but he feared exposure. He only wanted to show his uncovered self when his audience had gone. The *problem* was that people never left him alone to be himself; they pursued him. *It worked out* that he hid behind a mask, an image that seemed to protect him fairly satisfactorily. The question remained whether he would have to keep the elements of his image all the time just because he had "used" them before. The *resolution* was that he could keep the image available when needed, *but he didn't have to take it home.*

Mike and Susan talked about how this resolution related to real life. Mike said he had to keep up an image at work, and in fact, it wasn't that easy, just as it hadn't been that easy in college. He said sometimes he wanted to just relax and be himself. He wanted to forget about all those principles for dealing with higher-ups and subordinates, for resolving conflicts, and for selling his point of view. He just wanted to be spontaneous. The dream resolution was that he could be spontaneous at home and let his defenses down, keeping the image available "in the shop down the street" for when he needed them.

Susan said that, as a matter of fact, she had felt that the demands of his job were somehow interfering with their intimacy. She said she wanted his real, spontaneous personality back when they were together and that the desire for a deeper level of intimacy was one reason she had wanted to interpret their dreams together.

He said that maybe she was one of the people in the dream pursuing him when he was naked, that maybe she was one of the people he feared seeing him as he really was.

What she had seen through the dream interpretation, in fact, was that he was not the cool, ever-confident, always comfortable person she had thought he was. He'd had to fake a lot of that image that assured him the role of big man on campus. But, far from hurting their relationship, the revelation of his vulnerability drew them together. Susan felt more his equal, and she was attracted to his vulnerability. She promised to be more supportive in his struggle to maintain his professional image while being himself at home. After the shared interpretation of Mike's dream, they agreed Mike need not feel any longer that being open with her was dangerous.

Notice that the dream interpretation led from pure dream symbol to more abstract word associations, to application of the dream meaning to their lives, and finally to an open discussion of general issues related but not exactly tied to the dream. The dream led step by step, at a rate the couple could handle, to a free discussion of previously troublesome areas of their relationship.

Rachel and Jerry are an unmarried couple who also used dreams to develop intimacy and to learn better what each of them was looking for in a relationship.

Rachel is a successful young computer systems analyst. When I met her, she was in the process of figuring out what to do about her floundering marriage to a man who had retreated into a cloud of marijuana. She wanted a divorce, but a debilitating fear of something was holding her back. Rachel thought understanding her increasingly troublesome dreams would help her find out why she could not go through with the divorce. She enrolled in one of my dream workshops to learn to unlock the secrets of dream revelations. She found the analysis method I taught her helpful in understanding her fears and dealing with them. Soon thereafter, Rachel filed for divorce.

It was in her first relationship after the separation that Rachel began to use dream analysis to enhance intimacy and to enrich the relationship.

When Rachel met Jerry some months after separating from her husband, she was immediately attracted to his intellect and wit. His extreme openness made him seem self-assured. There was an instant communication between them that she had never before experienced in a male-female relationship. She was "curious to explore it," she says, even though her divorce from her first husband was not final.

Jerry also felt a level of intellectual sharing with Rachel that he had experienced only with men in the past. He was very satisfied to have his need for intellectual stimulation fulfilled in the same relationship with emotional and physical intimacy.

Rachel was reveling in the new-found comfort of deep communication. Jerry, though cautious, was wondering if Rachel at last might turn out to be the woman he would want to marry. Still, as with every relationship, there were times when something was not quite right.

"One evening we had issues bothering us," remembers Rachel, "but we didn't quite know what. We talked around them but did not resolve them." She was disturbed by the impasse, remembering how she and her first husband had developed an abyss between them, which had grown from small cracks like these. Nevertheless, Rachel and Jerry spent the night together.

In the morning, Rachel awoke from a dream and felt Jerry reaching for her. In the hazy, early morning light they made love softly and silently. Afterward, as they lay in each other's arms, Jerry said, "I had a dream . . ."

"Tell me," Rachel said, "before you forget it." Jerry told her his dream, and when it was finished, Rachel said, "I had a dream, too. I was dreaming when you woke me." She told Jerry the dream while the details were still fresh in her memory.

Both Rachel and Jerry realized that the dreams had a significance to their relationship. Because they were intrigued by the details and even laughed at the absurdities, they did not feel intimidated by the content. Rachel suggested to Jerry that they analyze the dreams, using the method she had learned in my workshop.

As Jerry told his dream again, Rachel wrote it down, marking the elements. She then urged Jerry to free-associate with each of these images, which she underlined as in the dream text below.

1 | You and I were *walking* in a *city,* not this one. The city had a *European* flavor more like in *Old Town.* I felt as if I were *home.* We were both very *hungry.* We walked the *streets* looking for a place to *eat,* but at each *restaurant* there was some reason not to stop. Finally, we found a cozy *café,* where a *plump, motherly* woman brought us a *cornucopia* of delicious-looking *fruit.*

2 | Then we were in a *bedroom* of *high-tech* design with *light* from large *angular windows* filling the room. We had just got out of *bed* when suddenly a large group of your *friends* and *co-workers* —*beautiful, young,* and *vivacious* people—began *crowding* in the room. They were all eager to *talk* to you, to tell you something, to receive *your approval.*

3 | You were in charge of these people; you were in control.

4 | Yet no matter how hard I tried to talk to you, I couldn't *get your attention.*

1 | *walking*   not going anywhere, just amusing ourselves
city   romantic, adventurous
European   Old World, traditional
Old Town   home, where I was raised
home   comfortable
hungry   wanting something I don't have
restaurant   place to get food
café   social
plump   motherly
motherly   nurturing

cornucopia plenty, all you want
fruit sensuous

2 *bedroom* living together, sharing life
high-tech modern
light enlightened
angular windows Nadine and Michael, they have a very modern, enlightened relationship
bed sex
friends not my type of people
co-workers high-tech types (negative)
beautiful young
young what I'm not anymore and it bothers me
vivacious sparkle
crowding pushing so other people can't get in
talk communicate
your approval acceptance or rejection

3 *you were in charge* assertive, powerful woman
you were in control somewhat scary

4 *no matter how hard I tried* I called to you but I didn't go up to you among those people
couldn't get your attention that's the way it really is

Rachel marked the dramatic divisions of the account as shown above and pushed the paper toward him. "What is the dream about?" she asked him, explaining that he was to look for his answer in the "real" meanings in the right-hand column in part one.

"It's about looking for a place to settle down in a traditional, romantic relationship that feels comfortable and is satisfying."

"And what is the *problem?*"

Jerry moved for his answer to the second scene. "This is a *modern* relationship," Jerry answered from the symbol meanings in scene two. "It's intellectually honest, open, analytical, like Nadine and Michael's, or any enlightened modern couple. That's good, but being modern means that you have all kinds of demands on you that a old-fashioned woman didn't have—demands from your job, your graduate study, your children, your ex-husband, other men—some of them more attractive interests to you than I am."

"And how does it *work out?*"

"You are an assertive woman with the power to control all of these relationships. You are in a position to approve or reject. I'm waiting for you to choose me. That is scary."

"What is the *resolution?*

"I can't have your attention, unless maybe I go up to you and clamor like those other people.

"Usually in the past," Jerry added, "I have made women fit into my life, into my schedule, my demands. I can see in this dream, that I may have to fit my life into yours. I see myself having to compete with other people and other things for your attention a lot of the time.

"I have to decide if I am willing to compete. I have to determine if I can get enough of your attention out of this relationship to be satisfied."

So this was the issue that was bothering Jerry. Why was it easy to see in the dream? Interpreting the dream was like reading a book. The elements were there to see but just fictive enough to be nonthreatening. Now they were out in the open.

Why was the issue so hard to see in real life? The answer came out easily, now that the cards were on the table. Jerry had not felt he had the right to demand more attention, he said. It was the same way with his mother, he recalled. She was always very busy running the family deli. The customers seemed more important to her than he was. He didn't feel he had the right to ask for her attention. It seemed presumptuous even now to say to a busy person, "I need more of your attention."

Rachel pointed out that the other people in the dream had got her attention, her approval even, by going up to her and asking for it. Only he had stayed on the outside watching. Rachel gave Jerry permission to do the same as the other figures in her life. "How do I know you need attention or that you are feeling neglected if you don't tell me?" she asked. "I *am* so busy that when you don't seem to need my attention I concentrate on other things. Try being assertive about it like those other people in the dream," she advised Jerry.

Jerry felt relieved to have this issue out in the open and very close to Rachel after she had accepted his expression of it.

It was then Rachel's turn to tell her dream.

1   I was home with my family, packing and preparing to leave for a new school term. My father came into the house from the mailbox with a folded note in the box; he thought it was for me, although there was no name on the outside.

I opened the note and read it, a mere two sentences from a recent lover: "Pam wants me to tell you that we are planning our nuptials. We expect our future together to be bliss(less)." I threw the note away and continued packing.

I was then at school at the university, where I did most of my undergraduate work. Trying to register and find a place to live, I moved around the college town efficiently and quickly, taking care of business.

2   On one part of the campus, there were animal cages, like a small zoo, and a pool for dolphins. One dolphin followed me the length of the pool, occasionally nudging my hand to be petted.

Toward the end of the day, I met a young man. I felt an immediate kinship to this man; we talked intensely and at length about our futures, our expectations, our fears and feelings. The sexual attraction between us was very strong. Then I noticed that the man had no use of his arms; they hung limply at his side. He was not capable of holding me, of hugging me, of placing his hands on my face as we kissed.

3 ⎡ Then we kissed anyway, and the dream became very erotic.

4 ⎡ As we kissed, I made a decision not to think of his limitations until they became a problem. That's when you woke
⎣ me up.

Jerry read off the elements to Rachel and she free-associated with them as follows:

1 ⎡ *family*   closeness
packing   preparing to leave
new school term   a change
father   good relationship
mailbox   communication
folded note   privacy respected
former lover   if I'd married him, I would have stayed in my
   hometown
Pam   immaturity
nuptials   traditional rituals
future
bliss(less)   happiness is what you expect, but it wouldn't be
   happy
threw away   I rejected the traditional, hometown relationship
university   belonging
register   making it sure, official
place to live   finding my place
efficiently   I was confident, capable, could take care of my
⎣   business all by myself

2 ⎡ *animal cages*   zoo
   ⎢ *zoo*   confined
   ⎢ *pool*   a different environment from me
   ⎢ *dolphins*   beautiful animals
   ⎢ *one dolphin*   good feeling, flattered to be chosen
   ⎢ *following*   a friendly dog, dependable companion
   ⎢ *nudging*   couldn't tell me, couldn't reach out to me
   ⎢ *petting*   affection, stroking
   ⎢ *toward the end of the day*   at last
   ⎢ *young man*   naïve
   ⎢ *kinship, talked intensely, expressed fears, sexual, other feelings*   all pos-
   ⎢   itive emotional factors
   ⎢ *arms*   very useless
   ⎢ *limply*   couldn't respond
   ⎢ *holding, hugging,*   affection, not so much sexual
   ⎢ *putting his hands on face*   sexual initiative
   ⎣ *kiss*   sexual

3 ⎡ *kissed*   sexual relationship
   ⎣ *erotic*   erotic

4 ⎡ *decision not to think of limitations*   a limitation is what you make
   ⎣   of it

"The *situation* was that I was leaving the emotional comfort of home, rejecting a marriage in the old hometown
whose traditional happiness was doubtful, and instead trying to find my place in a new place with a confident sense of
learning new things, being assertive.

"The *question* was how to respond to a friendly, pleasant
creature who wants my affection but is limited in how he
can ask for it or express it.

"The theme of that question is played again in my dream;
this time it is more clearly a potential *problem*. The man offers
all the emotional factors I care about, except that he can't
reach out well and his responses are limited.

"We go ahead and give a sexual relationship a try, and *it works out.*

"The *resolution* is that I can, for the time being, just ignore the limitations and enjoy the good parts."

In applying the dream interpretation to her real life, Rachel acknowledged she was happy to be leaving the traditional expectations of her hometown and family to try her wings at being an independent career woman and part-time graduate student. For the moment, she didn't want to be tied down by another marriage. She admitted, however, that she was disturbed by his lack of passion, both physical passion and reciprocating verbal expression of love. As in the dream, she said she had not drawn any conclusions about it, but she knew something was missing. She thought he was capable of responding more ardently, and perhaps he would learn to let go. If not, she recognized a potential problem.

Jerry admitted that he felt something like the man with no use of his arms. He cared for her, but he was withholding something; he was not letting go. He thought perhaps he was simply not as sexual as she was, and he also agreed he was afraid to "let go."

Jerry's dream view of Rachel as self-sufficient was also validated by her dream. Her statement— "I felt confident, capable, able to take care of my business and *get it all done by myself"*—concurred with his view of her as a leader who did not need him for self-esteem. He admired her confidence and self-sufficiency, but he also found it threatening. He would like to have felt more needed.

Rachel's dream, nevertheless, reassured him of his attractiveness to her. He was indeed fascinating and exciting. The episode of the useless arms brought out into the open that his passion, his expression of affection as well as his need for it, was severely limited.

Jerry received permission to assert himself for Rachel's attention, while she was made more aware of Jerry's vulnerability. She began to see him as less self-sufficient than they both had thought he was, and she paid more attention to making herself more available to him.

The experience of analyzing their dreams together had created an atmosphere of openness and sharing. They had lifted the lid of their unconscious and had shown each other the contents. What they could not quite articulate even to themselves, they revealed to each other. They accepted the revelations without being judgmental and felt a remarkable peace.

Both Rachel and Jerry say they cared more for each other after they began to share dreams. Rachel professed her love without restraint, sent him gifts, and bared her soul to him. Jerry, however, was still wary. Afraid of where all this affection from Rachel was leading too fast, and feeling unable to respond in kind, Jerry suggested they see each other only every other weekend. She thought such a formal restraint was silly, but he insisted.

Immediately, Rachel started going out with other people to fill in her weekends and immediately Jerry missed her. He found himself in a special relationship such as he had not had before, yet he was repeating a life-long pattern of withholding. He can remember relationship after relationship in which the girl became serious, and he could not commit himself. Once he went with a girl for a year and a half, and he never "let go," yet he was devastated when she finally found someone else. Now he wanted to find someone he could be secure with for the rest of his life, and he wanted to have children. Yet he was holding away the one person in his life at the time with whom he might enjoy such a relationship. He asked himself why.

Soon thereafter, Jerry had to have an operation—superficial surgery, he thought, no big deal. Rachel asked if he wanted her to be there. He said no. It was outpatient surgery; it was nothing. He'd be a little sore, he guessed, but he lived near the clinic; he would walk home by himself. Okay, she said. She'd call after a while.

After the surgery, he walked home and waited for Rachel's call. He waited and waited by the phone. The operation was suddenly becoming a really big deal and she didn't care.

"But she acted so affectionate, how could she leave me like this," he complained. "How can she turn her affection on and off like that?" He thought she was punishing him for having limited their relationship to every other weekend. He began to feel glad that he had not "let himself go." Her treatment of him was beginning to justify his reluctance.

When Rachel finally called, she was amazed by Jerry's anger. She explained that if he had asked her to be there by his side with pillows, juice, and cookies, she would have been there, but he had made a point of telling her it was no big deal.

Jerry recognized in her explanation the same truth that had been revealed to him in their dreams. When he didn't ask for attention, he didn't get it from her; and he hadn't asked. Still he felt hurt and angry that she had not had him more on her mind.

That night he had a dream:

1 I dreamed it was Sunday morning, and Rachel and I were waking up in a small building that belonged to her. The house was shaped like a hurdy-gurdy with antique carved wood painted brown and gold. There was a contraption like an old fortune-telling device that would tell you what to eat.

2 Rachel then turned on the light, and with the light there was a loud noise.

3 Rachel got dressed.

4 I asked her to tone down the light and the noise.

The next time Rachel and Jerry were together, he asked her to analyze the dream with him. She read out the elements and he free-associated as follows:

1 *Sunday morning*   when we have spent the night together and wake up and make love
   small building   cozy, lovers' cottage
   that belonged to her   she is in charge
   hurdy-gurdy   circus, fun
   antique carved wood   romantic
   brown and gold   antique
   contraption   quaint device
   fortune-telling device   knowing our future
   what to eat   what we need

2 *turned on the light*   her intellect, logic, reasonable explanations
   loud noise   her directness and objectivity is a bit much for me to handle

3 *Rachel dressed*   no more sex, intimacy; rejection

4 *I told her*   expressed my needs this time
   tone down   soften what I can't deal with

Rachel asked Jerry what the dream was about. "Fun, play, sex, in a romantic relationship in which you're in charge," he answered from the first scene. "We are seeking answers about what we need in the future from an old-fashioned model."

"What is the *problem?*" Rachel asked.

"I have trouble with your intellect and logic. Your directness is a threat," Jerry said.

"How does it *work out?*"

"You finish up with intimacy and go about your business. I feel rejected," said Jerry.

"So how are you going to *resolve* this problem?"

"I'm going to ask you to tone it down," he concluded.

"You want me to be less intelligent, less logical, and less direct?" she exclaimed. "I thought you admired those things."

"I do. I just can't understand how you can switch from being so loving to being businesslike and logical so quick. Like when you didn't call me for so long after my surgery, and you had some sort of logical explanation about concentrating on some project."

"You said you didn't need me," she reminded him.

"I know, but that's logic. If you really cared for me, how could you have waited so long to call me?"

"I have a lot of things to do. I have my job, my schoolwork, my son, the loose ends of the divorce, and you. The only way I can do it all is to compartmentalize my time and my mind. I have to concentrate on one thing and put the rest out of my mind. When I'm with you, I concentrate entirely on our relationship. When I'm not with you and you've told me you don't need me, I forget about you. How could I work if I were always mooning over you?"

The discussion that evolved out of the interpretation of Jerry's dream made it clearer to both him and Rachel what role each played in the other's life. Jerry saw how much Rachel was accomplishing in her multirole life and began to admire the concentration she used to accomplish it. Jerry realized that he was one of many things important in her life and not necessarily the most important. She loved him, but when he wouldn't commit himself to her, she was able to go on to other things and other people that satisfied her. He learned to consider that a strength. She, on the other hand, realized that he needed more frequent reassurance. She was willing to give him that, but even though the energy she invested in other things threatened him, she was not going to give up the other things.

They both agreed that they were not likely to change in what they gave to and required of a relationship. Still, they found the openness and excitement of their intellectual exchanges unique. Neither wanted to give the other up.

Both Jerry and Rachel could see that in both *his* dreams they were happy together in an old-fashioned setting. Both old-fashioned settings included, besides warmth and affection, the element of eating. In his first dream, they were trying to find a place in Old Town to eat and to be secure together. In his second dream, they had been happily loving in an antique hurdy-gurdy with a device that told them what to eat. For him, problems started when the setting became modern. In his first dream, a change to the well-lighted, modern setting marked a disturbance between them. In his second dream, an increase in light also marked the beginning of trouble for him.

In her first dream, by contrast, she was also finding a place to live, but in hers she was leaving the security of home and tradition to find a new place.

It was obvious that what he wanted was an old-fashioned relationship, in which the woman was his intellectual equal but not too assertive or direct and devoted herself above all to giving him attention. What she wanted was a modern life, in which she had a career and other interests and devoted her time and energy to intimacy only when she and her partner expressed a mutual need.

They agreed to call a halt to their sexual relationship but to continue to be good friends. They still see each other; they go to each other with their problems; they share their dreams. They feel comfortable together without any sexual demands. Though neither has yet found the permanent relationship they both want, they value the stability of their friendship. They feel strongly that they significantly deepened the possibilities of their friendship through a shared discovery of themselves in dreams.

So whether the stories end with friends helping one another, with lovers living happily ever after, or with lovers becoming friends, intimacy can be enhanced through dream interpretation.

THIRTEEN

Any Questions?

When I have finished a dream workshop, invariably participants ask good questions. Here are some of the questions I often field whose answers may not have been clarified in the text.

Q: Why do we forget dreams so easily?

A: The most important reason is that we're asleep. It's just hard to remember what's going on when we are sawing logs. The best way to remember a dream is to wake up completely at its end, but only a few dreams accompany us to a clearly waking state.

Another reason is that dreams consist of emotions primarily, which are expressed in often illogical manner as images. The images, except in psychic dreams, are not the dream; they are only the symbols of the dream. As such, they are not anything permanent; one set of symbols could have been used as well as another. In addition, dreams are not always organized in a logical way. As you may have found when you were trying to memorize a passage, if the piece is hard to understand, you will remember with difficulty which word goes where, but if it flows out in a coherent way, you can remember it better. Dreams are not always coherent. Also, when you are trying to memorize a poem, rhyme is a help. The form helps fix the words in your mind. In dreams, there frequently is no form.

Naturally, since dreams from which you awaken are remembered best, you are going to remember the kind of dream that would awaken you more than the kind that wouldn't. Bad dreams are therefore much more memorable than good dreams. From bad dreams you wake up frightened and shaking, and you wonder what it was that frightened you so. You are far less likely to ask yourself, "What was that dream that left me mildly comfortable?"

There does seem to be an additional factor that makes dreams particularly elusive. I myself have sometimes recorded a dream right after waking and then put the account away. Two or three days later, I pick up the account of my own dream and say, "What is this? I've never seen this before." It takes me quite a few paragraphs before I even recognize it as my own. Yet I believe I would never forget in such a short time someone else's dream recounted to me. We seem not only to forget but to resist remembering the messages from our sleep state that try to insert themselves into our conscious life.

Q: If you forget a dream, does that mean it wasn't important?

A: No.

In my research, dreamers told me of very important

dreams, which, after they told the dream to someone, they forgot. Later, after the dream came true, the person they told reminded them of the dream. On several occasions, the dream foretold a spouse's death, so the forgotten dream could hardly be called unimportant. An important dream that you do not heed may recur until you remember it and do something about it.

Q: How can I remember dreams better?

A: One of the tricks is, when you wake up, go over the dream in your mind and put it into *words*. Sometimes we think we are going over a dream well in our minds, but we are just repicturing it or refeeling it rather than translating it into the words that can serve as a handle for holding thoughts and feelings. Then, in the shower, we discover we can't remember what we were upset, excited, or puzzled about. The more completely you set a dream in words, the more clearly you will remember it. You will remember the words when the dream itself has fled, for you can't sink your teeth into a shadow.

The next most concrete way in which to set the dream is to say the words aloud. Hearing them will give you an auditory memory of the dream event.

The most concrete form of memory is a written or taped account. With such a record, you can respond later to the dream symbols, even if you do not remember them.

At bedtime, be sure to put the tools for recording where you can reach them in a hurry. If you put a pad of paper by your bed to write on in the middle of the night or first thing in the morning, don't forget your pen and your glasses. Be sure you can reach a light. Some dreamers I know use a pen with a built-in light for making nocturnal records without disturbing their sleeping partners. If you plan to use a tape recorder, be sure the tape is inserted, rewound, and ready to go. You may want to put paper or a recorder in the bathroom to record there. Don't be surprised if the record you make in the middle of the night sounds or looks as if the dreamer were drunk. Recording in an altered state is not as sober but more revealing than recording in a more alert state.

Q: How soon after the dream do you have to analyze it to achieve a benefit?

A: As soon as possible, for the most immediate benefit. For instance, if you analyze a dream over morning coffee, you may see a good way to respond at work that day. If you wait, you could miss an opportunity for the most positive response. However, most issues about which you dream are ongoing and can be dealt with to some degree sooner or later.

Q: Will the meaning of a dream be the same analyzed immediately as it would be if analyzed later?

A: Not necessarily. When an important issue pervades your whole life, a dream about it will be seen to represent that issue for a long time. Sometimes an immediate interpretation will be short-term and practical; a later interpretation, by comparison, may be more long range.

Josh, a man who lived in a rented apartment and at the same time owned rental property elsewhere, had this dream:

I dreamed I saw my landlord secretively hide a bag of marijuana inside a manhole cover. Later, as a trick, I opened the manhole, took out the marijuana, and hung it where my landlord would easily see it just so he would know I knew his secret. When he found it, he was very angry at my trick. But he didn't do anything to me.

Josh had analyzed the dream to his satisfaction when he woke up. He judged that the dream related to a court case he was involved in. He was suing a tenant for destroying some property. He wanted to tell the jury that the man had marijuana in the house to give the jury a convincing reason why the tenant may have been destructive. Josh was not personally opposed to the use of marijuana, but he thought marijuana possession might influence the jury. The judge, however, in a preliminary hearing had ruled that the marijuana was irrelevant and could not be introduced as evidence. Josh planned, therefore, to say in court, "The marijuana . . . ," and even though the judge would stop him, the word would have been introduced into the minds of the jury.

In the morning, Josh concluded, the landlord in the dream represented the judge, the one in charge of the chambers. The judge wanted to keep the marijuana hidden, but Josh could get it out in the open anyway. The judge would be angry, but, Josh concluded, he would get away with the trick.

"The dream gave me confidence in my plan," said Josh.

Several days later, however, Josh and I decided to analyze the dream again. This time, in word association, I asked Josh what *marijuana* meant to him. The first thing he thought of was the woman, a lover, to whom he had given his own marijuana to keep for a while. (He had thought that getting marijuana temporarily out of his own house would make him feel more confident when he brought it up in his case against his tenants.) His knowing the *secret hiding place* of the marijuana made him think of his own intuitive skill by which he thought he knew other people's thoughts and feelings. His word association with *manhole* was, in true Freudian form, a vagina. The *cover* made him think of beauty because some elaborately decorated manhole covers in Vienna had amazed him and his lover on a recent trip to Europe. The whole image of the manhole and cover confirmed the symbolism related to the beautiful woman with whom he was having a sexual relationship. His bringing the marijuana out of hiding reminded him of how he had pressed his lover with his intuitive knowledge of her thoughts and feelings. She had become angry over his bringing up things in a way she felt invaded her privacy. The problem had blown over this time, but Josh concluded that he came on too strong and that in the future he should keep his intuitions about the secret thoughts of other people to himself until such intimacy was invited.

Neither interpretation was the "right" interpretation or the "wrong" interpretation. Both were true and useful at different times.

Q: Why do I have the same dream over and over?

A: Recurrent dreams keep coming back to you because you have not resolved a bothersome matter. Many times psychic dreams are repeated several times, either exactly the same or with minor variations. Dreamers who wrote me that their recurrent dream finally came true added, "And after that, the dream never came back." Symbolic dreams often present an issue, a conflict, which works itself out in the dream to a climax. But if you wake up at the climax without a resolution, the dream may return. It is a sign that you are still troubled by the issue, and you must continue to seek a resolution.

An example is a young man who dreamed over and over that his mother, who had actually died years before, appeared vividly before him. Each time in the dream he reached out to her, and each time she said, "Don't touch me." He turned away, feeling rejected, and woke up. He dreamed this so often and felt so down afterward that he knew he had to answer the question of why she wouldn't let him touch her. Someone made the suggestion that the next time his mother appeared in a dream, he could ask her why he shouldn't touch her. Soon afterward, his mother appeared to him in a dream. As he reached out to touch her, she warned again, "Don't touch me." He then asked her, "Why can't I touch you?" She didn't answer, but she turned away from him as, in the past, he had done from her.

When the young man analyzed his dream, he realized that he had always been dependent on his mother's approval. When asked to associate with the image of *Mother*, he said, "To me, I guess she was the next thing to God." When she rejected him in the dream, he felt he must be unworthy of her approval, thus of God's approval, and ultimately of his own self-esteem. When he asserted himself, however, and questioned her, she backed down. He learned his mother was also human, vulnerable, and any disapproval or rejection she might have shown him in real life or in a dream was not necessarily something to carry around for a lifetime. After the dreamer had resolved the issue, the dream did not reoccur.

Recurrent dreams are important to resolve because the issues they represent are important enough to keep coming back in the same form.

Q: You suggest that, in case of a possibly psychic dream, the dreamer will benefit from telling someone. Is there ever a time when you should not tell someone your dreams?

A: I am inclined to think that it would always be appropriate to tell *someone.* It is also important not to tell just *anyone.* I certainly advise discretion. For example, I don't think it would serve any useful purpose to tell an old person you dreamed he was going to die. The thought has certainly occurred to most old people, but the message would probably only serve to upset the person.

I would not recommend recounting a dream to an untrustworthy person, a malicious person, or someone unsympathetic to you. If your boss has announced that he thinks anyone who believes in psychic phenomenon is a fool, I would not recommend telling him you expect your latest dream to come true.

Q: Is it true that creative people dream things like stories or works of art?

A: Yes, marvelously true. The plots to several of Robert Louis Stevenson's works and imagery in Robert Penn Warren's poetry are some of many contributions to literature said to have come to authors in dreams. Singer/songwriter Billy Joel has said that lines that came to him in dreams have been the initial inspiration for some of his songs. There are a hundred and thirty-one poems listed in Granger's

1986 *Index to Poetry* on the subject of dreams and forty-one titled "Dream." One dreamer wrote me a detailed description of a dream in which she wandered through a jungle of huge trees and low palms. When a lioness and cubs arrived on the dream scene, the dreamer ran joyfully to tell friends. On the way, she passed a huge mushroom striped in fuchsia and other brilliant colors. Several weeks later, the dreamer flew from her hometown of San Francisco to New York where she visited the Museum of Modern Art. Much to her astonishment she saw in a painting hanging on the museum's wall the very jungle scene she had dreamed. In the painting a woman, reclining on a sofa, is pointing to a lioness and cubs. The fuchsia and other color stripes were on the loincloth of a native in the background. Even greater was the dreamer's astonishment when she read the painting's title, *The Dream,* by Henri Rousseau. Apparently the famed turn-of-the-century French primitive artist had also been offered the scene in a dream, or, perhaps, he had imagined prophetically that a woman, lying down as if to sleep, would observe this lion family in that colorful jungle.

Many less famous creative people have had similar specific inspirations in dreams. A writer friend of mine says that, when he has difficulty conceiving of the structure for a nonfiction article that will encompass all his ideas and facts, he frequently dreams the entire outline and in the morning fleshes it out to a full feature story. A dress designer told me it is common for her and her colleagues to dream not only a single dress design but a whole fashion show, which they sketch out as soon as possible after waking. A February 1988 exhibition of Atlanta artist, Sandi Grow, at the Callanwolde Fine Arts Center was entitled, "Still Holding on to the Dream." It consisted entirely of what one critic called "sensual and reference laden" representations of dream imagery on canvas. Richard Hill, an Atlanta sculptor whose works have been exhibited nationally, was quoted in a recent issue of the Atlanta *Journal-Constitution* as saying that his deceased mother appeared to him in dreams detailing to him the concepts, materials, colors, and textures of sculptures he should execute. He has followed her instructions.

Q: Are artistic people like writers and painters, because they are intuitive, the only ones who have creative dreams?

A: No. A chemist, who regularly records all the dreams he remembers, told me, "Scientists are not immune to such dreams; they just aren't comfortable with them." Though he finds his colleagues somewhat skeptical, the chemist himself has been given solutions to research problems in dreams. Einstein is said to have got his idea for the theory of relativity from a dream. Another famous case of a scientific breakthrough is a discovery of nineteenth-century German chemist, Friedrich A. Kekulé, considered to be the father of the structure theory of organic chemistry. Kekulé was puzzling over the unknown molecular structure of the chemical substance, benzene. He fell asleep seeing the atoms slide about in his mind. At length, they turned into snakes, and when one snake turned and took hold of its own tail, Kekulé realized suddenly that the elusive structure for benzene was a ring.

Modern physicist Niels Bohr, likewise, in a dream conceived of a type of hydrogen atom subsequently named for him and in another dream foresaw the mushroom shape of an atomic bomb years before it was ever demonstrated. An engineer I met in Carrolton, Georgia, said that complex design problems that he has puzzled over at length are frequently resolved later in his dreams, and Kathryn Heath Gable, an Atlanta photographer recalled solving a difficult technical problem with her four-by-five camera after dreaming the solution.

Q: Are these creative or problem-solving dreams psychic?

A: It would be impossible to tell if such dreams were psychic or if they simply reassembled elements already existing in the dreamer's mind. Art is created out of elements that existed before, so these could be assembled in the dreaming mind without any psychic input. And the camera problem could have been figured out from information the photographer already had in her head, although Ms. Gable was not aware of having the necessary information. It doesn't really matter. A problem-solving dream may not be psychic but a product of the computerlike analysis of the mind. On the other hand, it may be psychic. As far as the response goes, it doesn't matter. Respond accordingly.

Q: If dreams are supposed to be analyzing information that is repressed, when a person associates with a word does he ever give an association that is wrong so that he is denying what he really feels and so the dream analysis doesn't "work"?

A: Yes. If you are defended against the emotion or thought coming up, you may not associate accurately. The idea behind analyzing your own dreams yourself in the privacy of your own home is that at least you can say what you think out loud, and no one will hear you. There is some safety in that.

Often, however, we are our own worst censors. The ones we're hiding the stuff from is ourselves. If you have a therapist and you inadvertently reveal something from deep inside, the therapist may note it and say, "Hey, what does this mean?" Sometimes an objective friend can hear something that you didn't know you said and help you bring it out in the open.

Q: What if you can't think of something to associate with a dream image?

A: Some people have a hard time with word association. At first, they can't think of anything to say about most of the dream images. They have to practice and try to loosen up. Usually a person is afraid what he says will sound silly, and he just needs to get used to the idea, to hear someone else do it first, to loosen up.

When a person is good with word association and responds well to a long list of images and then suddenly can't think of anything for one of them, it is called *blocking*. Some thought or feeling has been evoked by the word, which makes the dreamer feel uncomfortable. He may block the response so quickly that even he does not consciously know he is uncomfortable.

A dreamer named Bill was great at word association. He tossed off interesting but innocuous associations to everything in his dream, from loaded words like *naked* to dull words like *walk*. However, when I read back to him the phrase, "Ready or not," there was a long silence. I waited. Finally, he said, "Can I skip that one?" He did not even seem aware himself that his nonresponse was revealing. But, to my mind, it was a clear case of blocking, and the dream problem had to do with the dreamers fear that he was not ready for something that he was facing.

Another example is the dream about hiding some marijuana. The dreamer associated glibly with all his own dream phrases, until I said *manhole*. The dreamer could think of nothing. I finally suggested that Freud, with his one-track mind, would have said a manhole was a vagina. The dreamer replied, "That was the first thing I thought of, too, but I rejected it because it was just a standard Freudian symbol." The first thing you think of is the very thing you must say, but this man rejected that. I understood the man's argument against saying what Freud would have him say, but there was, after all, a reason why he thought of the Freudian symbol instead of something more literal like *water, pipes,* or *workman.*

The unwillingness to associate with an element when the dreamer begins to realize it has some scary meaning is not uncommon. There is nothing you can do about someone who refuses to examine a symbol, even when that someone is you. Try to accept yourself; try to accept your emotions because they just come; they aren't something you choose. Your feelings are there; they are going to come out in dreams. So get used to listening to them.

Q: Do dreams that present problems then resolutions change your life or do they just reflect changes that have already been made internally?

A: Sometimes solving a problem and realizing you have solved a problem internally are the same thing. Sometimes it seems the dream offers a solution that has not previously been thought of, or sometimes a line in a dream is like advice coming from some very wise force. It strikes you as true and you take it. In that case, the dream actually helps you solve the problem. Sometimes, however, the dream simply reflects the point you have come to in your life; it reflects growth rather than causes it. Such a reflection has the same value as solving the problem because it validates the decision you have made. The dream may show you the point you have consciously or unconsciously come to and may flood you with a wonderful feeling that, yes, the decision you have made is a good one, the change you have achieved is a good one.

CONCLUSION

An Echo of Connection

I've looked at scientific theory and noted its shortcomings. I have found there is no one theory that adequately explains where psychic material comes from or how it fits in with symbolic dreams. This does not mean there is no explanation. In time, I believe, it will be found. It is my hope that the patterns I have distinguished in hundreds of dream accounts and interviews will help illuminate the way.

There will always be those who say that, because explanations are not known, these phenomena do not exist. That is a mental hurdle the wary cannot yet leap. But you and I accept the existence of dreams out of time and space, dreams beyond life, literal and symbolic dreams that come true. You and I *know* because we have met the dreamers.

Whether we understand dreams as synapse and electron, as empathy and spirit, or as a concept that collapses time and space in a holistic model, we all hear the echo—we are part of the echo—of all the connections of the world.

As my colleague and I worked on this book together, word got around that we were investigating dream experiences. We were continually amazed at how many people came out of the woodwork telling us detailed dreams that had come true or symbolic dreams that had changed their lives. The first confirmed over and over my original findings that psychic dreams do exist, occurring more often than can be explained by chance. The second emphasized the desire and ability to find resolution, which each of us bears within us.

At the same time, we were amazed by those who shrugged off the meaningfulness of their dreams, those laden with psychic possibilities as well as those crying out with symbolic meaning. For the validation of dream wisdom is through positive response. Dreams, elusive or vivid, psychic or symbolic, come from a dimension we scarcely understand. Yet, pervasively, insistently, dreams draw us to look deep into ourselves to our hidden wisdom and, at the same time, to remind us constantly of our connectedness with others. As we learn to respond, we achieve an inner peace and a confidence in reaching out to the future, the distant, and the possible.

Finally, in a very real way, this work is unfinished. You, the reader, are invited to help in its completion. More accounts of psychic dreams are needed to convince my scientific colleagues and other skeptics whose resistance is healthy and challenging. Your accounts, particularly those psychic dreams accounts of which were documented prior to the actual event, will be most welcome. Please write to: David Ryback, Ph.D., 1534 N. Decatur Rd., Atlanta, Georgia 30307, USA.

Bibliography

Capra, F. *The Tao of Physics*. Boulder, Colo.: Shambhala, 1975.

Ferguson, M. "Karl Pribram's Changing Reality." In Wilber, K. (ed.), *The Holographic Paradigm and Other Paradoxes: Exploring the Leading Edge of Science*. Boulder, Colo.: Shambhala, 1982.

Ferguson, M. *The Brain Revolution: The Frontiers of Mind Research*. New York: Taplinger, 1973.

Orme, J. Cited in Ferguson, M., *The Brain Revolution: The Frontiers of Mind Research*. New York: Taplinger, 1973.

Pribram, K. H. "What the Fuss Is All About." In Wilber, K. (ed.), *The Holographic Paradigm and Other Paradoxes: Exploring the Leading Edge of Science*. Boulder, Colo.: Shambhala, 1982.

Rothman, T. *Discover*, February 1987, New York: Time, Inc.

Schmeidler, G., and McConnell, R. *ESP and Personality Patterns*. New Haven, Conn.: Yale University Press, 1958.